TASTES LIKE HOME

• • • • • • • • • •

MEDITERRANEAN COOKING IN ALASKA

BY

LAURIE HELEN CONSTANTINO

Published by
Holy Transfiguration Greek Orthodox Church

ISBN 978-0-9798019-2-1

All proceeds from the sale of this book go to the
Holy Transfiguration Greek Orthodox Church Building Fund

For book purchase contact:
Holy Transfiguration Greek Orthodox Church
2800 O'Malley Road
Anchorage, Alaska 99516
www.transfiguration.ak.goarch.org
Phone 907.344.0190
Fax 907.344.9909

Dedicated to

Nick Kollias

1928–2010

· TABLE OF CONTENTS ·

· ACKNOWLEDGEMENTS ·

I wrote this book to help bring to life Holy Transfiguration's dream of a new church building. Thank you to everyone who helped with the project. The book is only possible because so many people generously shared their lives, memories of food, and recipes, including: Salwa Abuamsha, Marianna Apetroeai, Aristotle Baskous, Maria Baskous, Spiro Bellas, Nawal Bekheet, Tina Chowaniec, George Chrimat, Helene Dennison, Antonia Fowler, John Galanopoulos, Sharon Galanopoulos, Andy Gialopsos, Carol Gialopsos, P.J. Gialopsos, Stephanie Joannides, Stathis Mataragas, Pamela Lloyd, Ankine Markossian, Aram Markossian, Marie Markossian, John Maroulis, Stathis Mataragas, Huda Peavy, Diane Primis, Maria Reilly, and Sonia Sarkissian.

If Sheila Toomey didn't exist, neither would the book. Her encouragement, nagging, good writing, and editing, helped me turn a messy stack of notes and recipes into a finished book. For that and many other acts of friendship, I'm forever in her debt.

Jim Lavrakas' photographs bring the pages to life, Amanda Saxton's cover and illustrations are gorgeous, and Harriet Drummond's book design makes the book easy to read and use. Toni Croft donated her time to the essential task of editing and proofreading the book. Thank you all.

My mother taught me the basic principles of cooking, my mother-in-law raised my husband to appreciate fine food, my father counseled "life is too short to drink bad wine," and my sister Marnie kept my spirits up when life was looking down. These acts of love, and many others, are the foundation on which this book is built.

Most of all, thank you to Steven, the love of my life, who ate every dish in the book, and whose suggestions, ideas, and palate are reflected on every page.

Finally, thank you to the Mediterranean people who, through the centuries, have bravely set off for foreign lands taking with them their languages, their music, their foods, their God, and their joy of life. I feel inspired and blessed by them all.

· INTRODUCTION ·

Wander the shore of a Greek island with the afternoon sun sparkling on blue Aegean waters, or jostle through teeming streets in an Egyptian metropolis at the edge of the ancient desert. Bargain for spices in a Moroccan market, or enjoy the shade of a cool glade in a Romanian forest.

Then, turn the world upside down.

Welcome to Alaska.

America is a land of uprooted people finding a new place to set down their roots. In most American cities, the new immigrant can easily find countrymen nearby to welcome and comfort them with the familiar sounds and tastes of home. Philoksenia—open-hearted hospitality—thrives wherever Greeks live.

Immigrant life can be difficult in Alaska, a sparsely populated land far from the large expatriate communities of New York, Chicago or San Francisco. Twenty years old, lonely for family back in Kastori, a Greek village near the site of ancient Sparta reputed to be the birthplace of Helen of Troy, Maria Baskous didn't know anyone when she and her husband, Alex, an American-born Greek, arrived in Anchorage in 1979. Maria soon was aching for the sounds and tastes of her homeland.

Where do people far from home find the language and food they crave? For many Greeks and their Orthodox Christian neighbors, the stand-in for life in the old villages, and with extended families, is the nearest Orthodox Church.

When Maria arrived in Anchorage, its Greek Orthodox Church had been closed for some time. As her first Easter in Alaska approached, she saw no sign of a communal celebration. There were no organized festival preparations, no Greek booth at the local college fair, no place to buy filo dough in an emergency. "I was feeling very homesick," Maria remembers. "You couldn't get anything Greek."

The situation called for action, but without a church, how could she and Tanya Clark, a new friend from Athens, identify and summon the local Greeks to a meeting? "We read the phone book," she said. "We started at "A" and picked out Greek names and wrote everyone a letter." Then they put an ad in the newspaper.

Thirty people showed up. The focus was on culture more than religion, Maria said, but everyone agreed the church must re-open.

In 1981, the group organized its first Greek dinner-dance and sold tickets for $20. Maria, whose family ran a sweet shop and café back home, was young and undaunted by the prospect of feeding a crowd. With generous contributions from several Greek businessmen, "we made tons of food," she said. "We brought a band from San Francisco. We painted a Parthenon for a background. We built columns. We practiced dancing in my garage."

Alaskans responded and "the line was going around the building," Maria said. Proceeds from the first dinner dance provided funds to reopen the church, and so were sown the seeds of an enduring Greek community in Anchorage.

A church without a priest is an empty shell. The Metropolitan (head of the Greek Orthodox Diocese) in San Francisco didn't get the message at first. Alaska was so far away and he was so busy. He promised to send a priest "once in a while." That was not good enough for Maria and Tanya.

"I'm a Spartan. I was blazing inside," Maria said. The women called the Metropolitan, and called him and called him and called him again. Years later, on a visit to Anchorage, the Metropolitan told the story with a laugh. He had been elevated to Metropolitan the very week that first call came in from Tanya, during which he had promised to look into Alaska's situation. Within days, another call came from Anchorage, and then the next, and the next. He said he soon realized he had met his match and assigned a priest to this little church at the edge of nowhere.

From the beginning, Holy Transfiguration Greek Orthodox Church has been multi-ethnic, a welcoming cultural hearth for Orthodox Christians from a dozen countries. To this day, each Sunday service includes the Lord's Prayer recited in eight or nine languages, starting with Greek and ending with English, so everyone may pray in their first language.

As more Orthodox families found their way to Alaska, the church services expanded. The Megali Evdomada (Holy Week) leading up to Easter is now a profound and inspirational week of renewed faith. In August, the annual Greek Festival in Anchorage is a major event for the whole city, attracting thousands of guests eager to gorge on wonderful Mediterranean food prepared by the church members whose recipes fill this book.

Food has supported the parish in spirit and body. The dinner-dances went on for more than 15 years and over the years there have been innumerable bake sales. Cooking together bonds the community and eases the incredibly long hours of work required to make all the food served at the Greek Festival. One year the volunteers made 8,000 pieces of baklava and 2,000 pieces of other pastry." We always sell out, no matter how much we make," Maria said.

Maria has been in Alaska for more than 25 years. She estimates there are now about 60 Greek families in the parish. "Every city in Southcentral Alaska has at least one family, and they're probably running a restaurant," she joked.

Like many expatriates, Maria visits her village, her family, and her friends in Greece every few years. She tells people about her church and parish in Alaska. "They stand with their mouths open," she said. "They can't believe there is Greek culture at the end of the world."

Mouth open—to enjoy the flavors of Greece and the Mediterranean—is a good way to approach this book.

· COOK'S NOTES ·

These recipes have roots in family kitchens throughout the Mediterranean basin. Many are adaptations of dishes learned from mothers and grandmothers who cooked by sight, smell, and feel; with a dash, a pinch, a bunch, a little handful, or a big piece. Any measuring was with the tools at hand: water and wine glasses, coffee cups and dessert spoons, whose sizes varied from household to household. Even the contributors to this book, many of whom are accomplished cooks, know their recipes so intimately they have never measured the ingredients.

My task was to grill the generous and patient contributors with relentless questions ("How big a handful? May I see your hand?"), and take what I learned back to my kitchen, where I duplicated their dishes with the benefit of measuring cups and spoons. The quantities specified here are those that worked when I tested the recipes.

Cooks cannot achieve the best results by slavishly following a recipe. Cooking is the art of combining flavors, smells, and textures, not just ingredients. To know your ingredients on any given day, you must taste. To appreciate how the flavors of those ingredients are combining in your pot, you must taste.

The tastes of vegetables, meats, and herbs change depending on when, where, and how they're grown. The best cooks taste and smell over and over again as each dish comes together, and make adjustments for the ingredients they have to work with that day. In other words, recipes are only a guide to the correct proportions of ingredients, rather than precise formulas.

SALT & SEASONING

A key to good cooking is mastering the art of seasoning. Seasoning well requires knowledge of ingredients, understanding flavor combinations in the finished dish and, as with all good art, timing and restraint.

The primary seasoning is salt. Salt has a unique ability to enhance and blend flavors. Salting during cooking deepens the flavors of other ingredients and brings them together in a way that salting only at the end cannot achieve. For this reason, the recipes in this book call for adding small amounts of salt at more than one stage of the cooking process.

The flavor an herb or spice imparts to the finished dish differs if added at the beginning of cooking or at the end. Heat tends to destroy or evaporate the volatile oils that impart bright flavors and aromas, while long cooking infuses deeper, rounder flavors into food. Whether an herb is dried or fresh also makes a difference. In general, dried herbs should be added earlier to ensure their flavors are fully released, while fresh herbs should be added near the last minute to preserve their flavor.

Seasoning well means using herbs, spices and flavorings to enhance and complement, but not overpower, the flavors of food. Correctly seasoning food depends not just on the dish you're preparing, but also on the palates you want to please.

People from the Mediterranean, and members of my family, love the flavors of olive oil, onions, garlic, herbs, and spices and use them generously. The quantities of seasonings called for in the following recipes reflect those loves. For your palate, the seasoning recommendations may be too overpowering or too bland. You must taste frequently while cooking and adjust the seasoning in each recipe to please your palate.

BLACK PEPPER

The recipes in this book call for freshly ground black pepper. Although pepper is available crushed or ground into powder, whole peppercorns, ground in a mill just before added to a dish, deliver the most flavor. Using whole peppercorns also protects against the adulterants that some manufacturers add to ground black pepper. I prefer to use Tellicherry or Sarawak black peppercorns and enjoy their rich and well-developed flavors.

· INGREDIENTS FRESH AND PRESERVED ·

Most foods begin losing flavor the moment we separate them from the earth. Compliment a Mediterranean cook on a particular dish and it won't be the cook's skill that is acknowledged, but the freshness and quality of ingredients. "Freskos" (freshness) is a mantra in Greek kitchens and in the best cooking everywhere.

In Alaska, abundant fish runs, game seasons, kitchen gardens, and farmer's markets yield truly fresh food during only a few precious months. For most of the year, northerners must rely on preserved and frozen foods, complemented by a few fresh ingredients. Unfortunately, what too often passes for "fresh" in Alaska stores would have been discarded long before it reached a Mediterranean table. Alaskans must shop carefully, choose wisely, and pay dearly, if necessary, for the freshest ingredients possible.

ALEPPO PEPPER

Aleppo Pepper is a moderately spicy red chili pepper sold in crushed flakes. Its sharp but fruity taste pairs well with Mediterranean food. Aleppo Pepper comes from Syria, near the city of Aleppo, but may be imported into the United States from Turkey. Supermarket crushed red pepper is a fine, but spicier and less flavorful, substitute for Aleppo pepper. One-half teaspoon of supermarket crushed red pepper should be used in lieu of one teaspoon Aleppo pepper. Aleppo Pepper is available from www.penzeys.com, www.thespicehouse.com, or www.worldspice.com.

BUTTER: HOW TO CLARIFY

Clarified butter is butter from which the milk solids have been removed. To clarify butter, melt it in saucepan or microwave and skim off and discard the white foam that rises to the top. Pour clear yellow butter into bowl, being careful to keep the milky liquid that sinks to the pan's bottom out of the clarified butter. This liquid should be discarded. If you don't clarify the butter used for separating layers of filo, the pastry won't cook correctly, and will be soggy, rather than crisp.

CAPERS

Capers are sold pickled or preserved in salt. Salt helps retain the subtle floral flavor of capers, which too often is overwhelmed by the vinegar used during pickling. For this reason, I recommend using the salt-cured variety when capers are an ingredient in a recipe. Local ethnic markets and specialty stores carry salted capers, and they're available from internet sellers. Salt-cured capers are not cheap, but because of their intense flavor, are worth buying.

To prepare salt-cured capers, place them in a small bowl and cover with cold water. Let the capers soak for 10 - 15 minutes to remove some of the salt, and rinse well. If you use pickled capers, be sure to rinse off as much brine as possible.

OLIVES

Canned, pitted, black or green California olives are tasteless compared to Mediterranean olives, and should not be used for the recipes in this book. Instead, use purple Kalamata olives, salt cured "dried black" olives, or Sicilian-style green olives, all of which can be found in local supermarkets.

PEPPERS: HOW TO ROAST

The traditional method of roasting peppers is over a hot wood fire, but you can also roast them on a gas grill, directly on a gas burner (without a pan), under the broiler, or by baking in a 450° oven for 30 minutes. Unless you're baking them in the oven, turn the peppers frequently as they roast to ensure the skins char evenly and the flesh beneath doesn't overcook. When the skin is blackened all over, place the peppers in a paper bag and close it up for 5 minutes. The hot flesh will release steam, loosening the charred skin, and make peeling easier.

Once the peppers are cool enough to handle, remove the burned skin from the softened flesh with your fingers or a paper towel, gently scraping away any stuck bits with a knife. Don't rinse the peppers in water, as doing so washes away too much flavor. If necessary, dip your fingers in bowl of water to release clinging charred pepper skins. Remove seeds and any white pulp from inside the pepper, reserving the liquid from inside the pepper to add to the recipe.

Roasted peppers can be stored for a week or more in the refrigerator covered with olive oil. They also freeze well sealed in portion-sized sandwich bags, for adding to recipes whenever you need them.

SQUID: HOW TO CLEAN

Squid is often sold frozen and cleaned, and is one of the rare foods whose flavor doesn't suffer from freezing. If you're able to find fresh squid, they're very easy to clean. Here's how:

1. Hold the body with one hand, and with the other, pull the head and tentacles away from the body.

2. Use your finger to clean out all contents from the squid's body, including the clear, plastic-like cartilage, and discard these contents.

3. Cut the head from the tentacles just below the eyes, and press the beak out from the center of the tentacles; discard the head and beak.

4. Pull off and discard the squid's purplish skin, and rinse out the inside of the body. The cleaned bodies and tentacles are now ready to use.

SUMAC

Sumac is a tart seasoning that is used throughout the Middle East. It comes from the dried red berry of the sumac tree and is sold ground, sometimes mixed with salt. In cooking, sumac serves the same souring purpose as lemon or vinegar, but also adds a pleasing, fruity flavor that makes it worth seeking out. Sumac is available from www.penzeys.com, www.thespice-house.com, or www.worldspice.com.

TOMATOES

Finding tasty tomatoes is a particular problem in Alaska. Supermarket tomatoes tend to be flavorless, and Alaskan-grown hothouse tomatoes all too often taste insipid and have bad texture. For tomatoes used fresh in salads, cherry tomatoes and those sold on the vine are the best choice. However, for cooking, canned tomato products are better. They're picked and packed when ripe and at the peak of their flavor, and add more true tomato flavor to food than do locally-available fresh tomatoes. I prefer using canned organic tomatoes and think those that are fire-roasted during processing are particularly suited for Greek and Mediterranean food.

· APPETIZERS ·

* New recipe this edition

John Maroulis was just old enough to work as a merchant seaman when he left his family on the island of Skopelos for a new life in America, but he was old enough to remember how his mother gathered food from the sea and garden and cooked over a wood fire.

Wonderful things grew on trees in Glossa, John's village. Skopelos is famous all over Greece for its plums and pears. John remembered, "We cut the pears before they were ripe and hung them in net bags from the exposed beams in our house…In the evenings, people would come over, tell stories and jokes and eat the pears. The whole house smelled of the fruit."

John's father was an olive farmer. The children's job was to gather the "hamades," ripe Amfissa olives that fell to the ground. Most were sold, of course. Whenever Greeks sit down to eat anywhere in the world, there are olives on the table—cured, dried, or marinated, by the handful, or with salad or bread.

Olives are rarely baked, but it's the taste of baked olives that evokes for John the most poignant memories of his father, of his island home built of stone, of hard wooden benches covered with rabbit fur, and of the aroma of bread baking in the "fourno," the wood-fired stone oven built in the yard by his grandfather.

One winter day when John was nine years old, he was pounding freshly-caught octopus against the rocks at the edge of the sea to tenderize it while his father built a fire in the orchard above from trimmed olive branches. "When I came back with the octopus, my father cooked it directly on the fire. With a little olive oil and vinegar, which we always had with us when we went to the fields, the octopus was incredibly delicious."

That day, John's father tossed a handful of "hamades," the ripe olives picked up off the ground, right into the fire. "When they were cooked through and kind of wrinkly, we brushed off the ash and put them on a plate with olive oil and vinegar."

Decades later, John shared his memory of fire-roasted olives with Stathis Mataragas, owner of Pizza Plaza Restaurant in Anchorage, bemoaning the long absence of this treat in his new life. Stathis tried to duplicate it by baking Kalamata olives in his pizza oven. The baked olives quickly became a favorite of local Greeks and Armenians.

ROASTED KALAMATA OLIVES *Elies sto Fourno*

Roasting deepens the flavor and softens the sharp brininess of Kalamata olives. It also firms olives' texture. Like the olives pulled from a Greek hillside fire that John Maroulis remembers, they're best served warm. Even when cold, baked olives are a special treat.

2 cups Kalamata olives
2 Tbsp. red wine vinegar

1/4 cup extra virgin olive oil
1 tsp. dried oregano, crushed

Preheat oven to 350° F. Drain and rinse brine from olives, place them in glass or stainless steel pan, and bake for 35 - 40 minutes. Olives are done when their flesh begins to shrink up and skins look wrinkled. Remove olives from oven, place in bowl, stir in vinegar, olive oil, and oregano, and serve.

MARINATED GREEN OLIVES
Elies Kyprou

Unlike other fruit, olives are never eaten raw. They're cured and dried, salted, or packed in brine. The goal of many olive recipes is to extract astringent bitter juice from olives, and replace it with another flavor. So it is with this recipe. The olives are infused with traditional Cypriot flavors of lemon and coriander. They're the perfect complement for freshly grilled fish and make a good addition to a mixed plate of appetizers.

1 cup green olives with pits
2 cloves garlic, very thinly sliced
1 Tbsp. coriander seeds, crushed

1 tsp. grated lemon peel
3 Tbsp. fresh lemon juice
1/2 cup extra virgin olive oil

Drain and rinse brine from olives. If they aren't already cracked, lightly crush olives to crack skin, or cut a slit in each olive with a knife, making sure not to crack the pit. Mix olives with garlic, coriander seeds, lemon peel, and lemon juice. Place in jar and pour in olive oil, adding more if needed to cover olives. Let olives sit at room temperature for at least 2 hours, then store them in refrigerator.

MARINATED KALAMATA OLIVES
Elies Marinates
GREEK FESTIVAL RECIPE

During the annual Greek Festival at Holy Transfiguration, marinated Kalamata olives are served on Greek salads and popped into mouths of hungry volunteers looking for a quick and tasty snack. The flavor improves with time, as the marinade sinks into the olive flesh.

1 2-pound jar Kalamata olives
1/2 cup fresh lemon juice
1/4 cup red wine vinegar

1 tsp. grated lemon rind
1 Tbsp. dried oregano, crushed
1 cup extra virgin olive oil

Drain and rinse brine from olives. Mix all ingredients, and place in jar, adding olive oil if needed to cover olives. Marinate for several hours or days.

ROASTED ALMONDS
Amigdala Psita

Throughout the Mediterranean, people love snacking on roasted seeds and nuts. On many busy Athens streets, nut sellers ply their trade from a push cart or tiny storefront, selling a wide variety of roasted seeds and nuts. Virginia Constantino, my mother-in-law, learned tricks for making perfect roast almonds from her mother, and prepared them regularly for my father-in-law, Constantine "Gus" Constantino, to snack on with his evening cocktail. Roasted almonds freeze well, so Virginia recommends making them in large quantities and keeping them on hand to serve drop-in guests. These are so good I serve them plain. Of course, they can be salted, herbed, peppered, or sweetened, if you desire more complex flavors.

Almonds, whole

Blanch Almonds: This is easiest to do in a microwave. Put almonds in bowl, cover them with water, and microwave on high for 3–4 minutes or until you can easily slip off almond skins. You can also blanch almonds by putting them in boiling water for 2–3 minutes. Remove skins from all almonds.

Dry Almonds: Thoroughly dry almonds with paper towels, and spread out on baking sheets to dry overnight. Don't leave almonds on paper towels to dry, as paper towels hold moisture around the nuts. The key to this recipe is making sure the almonds are perfectly dry before they're roasted; shake pan a couple times while almonds are drying to make sure all sides of the nuts are exposed to air.

Roast Almonds: Preheat oven to 350°F. Bake dried almonds for 15–25 minutes, or until they're golden brown. Check almonds regularly. They go from underdone to overdone very quickly. When almonds are done, immediately remove them from baking sheet (to stop the cooking) and set aside in bowl to cool completely (to firm them up).

Roasted nuts on display at the Athens Central Market

YOGURT AND CUCUMBER DIP
Tzatziki

Tzatziki is traditionally served as a sauce with gyros and souvlaki. It's equally good as a dip for raw vegetables, with meatballs (Keftedakia), or simply spread on bread. Although it isn't absolutely necessary to drain yogurt before mixing it with other ingredients, doing so results in a thicker and richer Tzatziki.

2 cups plain whole-milk yogurt
1 medium cucumber
2–3 cloves garlic
Salt

2 Tbsp. minced fresh dill
2 Tbsp. minced fresh mint
1 Tbsp. white wine vinegar
2 Tbsp. extra virgin olive oil

Line a colander with paper towels. Dump yogurt into lined colander and let liquid drain out of yogurt for 30–60 minutes.

Peel and grate cucumber. Squeeze as much water out of cucumber as possible by wringing grated cucumber in a clean dish towel. Puree garlic by mashing it into salt.

Mix drained yogurt, cucumber, mashed garlic and salt, dill, mint, vinegar, and olive oil. Taste and add garlic, salt, dill, mint, or vinegar, as needed. To serve, spread Tzatziki on a plate and drizzle it with olive oil.

EGGPLANT SPREAD
Melitzanosalata

The smoky flavor of eggplant grilled over an open fire makes the best Melitzanosalata. However, when grilling isn't possible, browning eggplant wedges in the oven is the best way to concentrate eggplant flavor. The amounts of lemon juice, olive oil, salt, and garlic depend on the eggplant's size and the compromises reached between cook and eaters: my husband prefers more lemon juice than I, and I prefer more garlic than most people. No matter how much lemon juice or garlic is used, Melitzanosalata is always gobbled up. Serve with rustic bread slices, olives and roasted red peppers for an appealing appetizer.

1 large globe eggplant, or 3 Japanese eggplant (about 1 pound)
2 tbsp. fresh lemon juice
1/4 cup extra virgin olive oil
1/2–1 tsp. salt
2–3 cloves garlic

Grill eggplant whole, with its skin, until it has softened and is slightly charred on all sides. Peel eggplant, cut into large chunks, and place in a colander to let excess juices drain off. After eggplant has cooled, use your hands to squeeze out any remaining liquid.

If grilling eggplant isn't possible, preheat oven to 400°F. Don't peel eggplant, and slice it lengthwise into six or eight wedges. Coat wedges with olive oil, lightly salt them, and place on oiled baking sheet. Bake for 40–50 minutes, turning wedges over halfway through cooking time. Eggplant is done when it's softened and browned on both sides. Let eggplant cool slightly and peel.

Place eggplant flesh on a cutting board and finely chop. Puree garlic by mashing it into salt. Mix all ingredients, taste and add garlic, lemon juice, olive oil, or salt, as needed. To serve, spread Melitzanosalata on a plate.

GARBANZO BEAN AND GARLIC DIP
Hummus

Garbanzo beans are a staple throughout the Balkans and Middle East. A version of hummus is a traditional appetizer wherever garbanzo beans are grown. Salwa Abuamsha learned to make hummus as a child in Beit-jala (a village near Bethlehem on the Jordan River's West Bank) in days when life there was more peaceful than it is today. This is her recipe. The flavor of hummus is brighter if canned beans are first drained and rinsed. If you want more bean flavor, use the canning liquid from the beans instead of water or oil to adjust the consistency of hummus.

2 cans garbanzo beans (chickpeas), drained and rinsed
4–6 cloves garlic, chopped
3 Tbsp. raw tahini (sesame paste)
1/4 cup fresh lemon juice
2 tsp. salt
1/4–1/2 cup water or extra virgin olive oil

Place garbanzo beans, chopped garlic, tahini, lemon juice and salt in the bowl of a food processor with 1/4 cup water or olive oil. Blend until ingredients have formed a soft creamy paste, adding water, olive oil, or canning liquid, as needed to achieve the right consistency. Taste and add garlic, lemon juice, or salt, as needed. To serve, spread on a plate, drizzle olive oil over hummus, and garnish with black olives.

GARLIC SPREAD
Skordalia

Skordalia is an intensely flavored garlic spread that is the perfect complement to fried fish or roasted beets. The flavor of Skordalia mellows over time and is best made at least a day ahead. It can also be served immediately after it's prepared. The amount of garlic used is based purely on personal taste, but Skordalia is delicious no matter how much garlic is used. Skordalia can be made with either a bread or potato base. Stathis Mataragas insists the best Skordalia is made with red potatoes and says if you make it that way once, you'll be hooked forever. If you do use potatoes, be sure to warn your guests. P.J. Gialopsos remembers being passed her first bowl of potato Skordalia and thinking it was mashed potatoes. Her dining companions laughed after P.J. took a nice big serving, and almost fell out of her chair when the garlic hit her taste buds.

1 cup soggy bread or mashed potatoes (see Note below)
3–5 cloves garlic
1/2 tsp. salt
2 Tbsp. white wine vinegar
1/3 cup extra virgin olive oil

Place soggy bread or mashed potatoes in bowl. Puree garlic by mashing it into 1/2 tsp. salt. Thoroughly mix pureed garlic, vinegar, and olive oil into bread or potatoes. You should end up with a puree that has the consistency of thick mayonnaise. If puree is too thick, mix in more olive oil. Taste and add garlic, vinegar, or salt, as needed. To serve, spread on a plate and drizzle a small amount of olive oil over Skordalia.

Note: To make soggy bread, remove crusts from stale bread (use artisan-style bread if possible), and immerse in water so bread is just covered. When bread has soaked up water and is soft all the way through, drain bread and use your hands to squeeze as much water out of bread as you can (you'll be left with a solid ball of bread). The bread is then ready to use in recipe.

FLAMING CHEESE SAGANAKI
Tyri Saganaki

Cheese Saganaki is the perfect companion to a glass of wine and a loaf of good bread. The lemon complements the rich flavor of melted, oozing cheese. Flaming cheese with cognac adds another layer of flavor, and makes a dramatic presentation. I don't recommend flaming Cheese Saganaki with ouzo as it's more difficult to light, although it makes a fine accompanying aperitif. The real trick with Cheese Saganaki is to stop from eating "just one more slice" while you're making it.

8 ounce piece of kefalotyri, halloumi, or kasseri cheese
1 Tbsp. olive oil
2 Tbsp. cognac (optional)
1/4 cup fresh lemon juice

Cut cheese into slices 3/8" thick. In a frying pan, heat oil until it's hot, but not smoking. Add slices of cheese to pan, and cook until cheese just starts to brown, then turn cheese over and cook other side. If using kasseri cheese, which melts more quickly than kefalotyri or halloumi, be sure to watch cheese carefully and turn it before it begins to completely lose its shape.

After cheese has cooked on both sides, add cognac to pan and light it on fire. Put fire out with lemon juice and serve immediately. If you're not using cognac, simply pour lemon juice over cheese as soon as it's done cooking. Serve hot with plenty of bread or toast.

SPICY FETA SPREAD
Tyrokafteri

Pureeing feta with spicy peppers lightens and enhances the flavors of both, with neither flavor dominating. The spiciness of dried red pepper intensifies the tang of the spread, which is particularly tasty served as a dip for fresh red, yellow, or green peppers. If possible, make Tyrokafteri several hours before serving to give flavors time to meld. Although the flavor is better when made with freshly roasted chilies, the version with canned chilies is still great and, better yet, can be made entirely with pantry staples.

8 ounces feta cheese, crumbled
2–3 Anaheim chilies, fresh or canned
1/3 1/2 cup extra virgin olive oil
1 Tbsp. fresh lemon juice
1 tsp. Aleppo pepper or 1/2 tsp. crushed red pepper
1 clove garlic, crushed
Freshly ground black pepper

If using fresh chilies, roast, skin and seed them as described in "Peppers: How to Roast" on page 14 in Cook's Notes. If using canned roasted chilies, drain well. Place cheese, chilies, 1/3 cup olive oil, lemon juice, Aleppo pepper, and black pepper in a food processor, and puree until smooth. If spread is too thick, add remaining olive oil, and puree well. Chill and serve.

ROASTED PEPPER AND FETA SPREAD
Piperies me Feta

Spiro Bellas learned this easy recipe from a friend and taught it to Sharon Galanopoulous, who makes it frequently—often by request. The flavors of salty feta and piquant pepper are particularly good served on toasted slices of baguette, lightly flavored with garlic. The peppers taste best if they're roasted over an open fire. Sharon varies the recipe by sometimes adding minced parsley or chopped Kalamata olives, or by using Piperies me Feta to top a green salad dressed with olive oil, oregano, salt, and pepper.

2 red peppers, roasted and peeled
   (see "Peppers: How to Roast"
   in Cook's Notes on page 14)
2 green onions, chopped
2–3 cloves garlic, minced finely

2 Tbsp. extra virgin olive oil
2 Tbsp. fresh lemon juice
2 tsp. dried oregano, crushed
Freshly ground black pepper
6 ounces crumbled feta cheese

Chop roasted peppers into 1/4" dice. Mix in all other ingredients, except feta cheese. Fold in crumbled feta. Taste and add salt, pepper, or olive oil as desired.

ROASTED RED PEPPERS
Florines

Florina is a town in northern Greece so famous for its red peppers that "florina" is now the commonly used Greek word for sweet red peppers. In Filakto, the village where Tina Karakatsanis Chowaniec grew up, healing hot springs are a big draw for Italian tourists. At the restaurant near the hot springs, roasted Florines, simply dressed with olive oil and lemon, are a favorite dish. Finely chopped fresh garlic sprinkled over peppers is glorious, but not necessary. Together with feta cheese and Kalamata olives, Florines make a tasty appetizer plate. Although they can be eaten immediately, the flavor is better if peppers are allowed to marinate for at least a day before serving.

3 red peppers
1 tsp. minced fresh garlic
2 Tbsp. fresh lemon juice

1/4 cup extra virgin olive oil
Salt
Freshly ground black pepper

Roast peppers and clean, reserving juices from inside peppers. See "Peppers: How to Roast" in Cook's Notes on page 14. Cut or tear roasted pepper flesh into 1" wide strips. Toss with garlic, lemon juice, olive oil, and any liquid from inside roasted peppers. Season to taste with salt and freshly ground black pepper.

BAKED FETA WITH PEPPERS AND TOMATOES
Feta me Piperies kai Domates sto Fourno

This recipe is very easy, very spicy, and very good. Maria Baskous discovered it when she was visiting Lily Koukourikou, a friend in Thessaloniki, Greece. Maria couldn't believe how good spicy baked feta tasted, and immediately asked for the recipe. Maria taught the recipe to her family, and she says it has now "spread like wildfire" through the Peloponnesus, where her family lives. Be careful—baked feta is addictive.

1/2 pound feta cheese
1/4 cup extra virgin olive oil
1 Tbsp. dried oregano, crushed
1 tsp. crushed red pepper
2 medium tomatoes, sliced, or 5 small tomatoes, sliced
2 jalapeños or 1–2 Anaheim chilies, cut into rounds
Crusty fresh or toasted bread

Preheat oven to 400°F. Cut feta into 1/2" slices, and cover bottom of baking dish with slices. Sprinkle feta with half the oregano, and the crushed red pepper. Drizzle with half the olive oil. Cover cheese with sliced tomatoes, and spread chilies over tomatoes. Sprinkle with remaining oregano, and drizzle with remaining olive oil. Cover and bake for 20 minutes, or until oil and cheese are bubbling. Serve immediately in baking dish. This can also be made in sealed aluminum foil packets that, when opened at table, infuse the air with aromas of cheese, tomatoes, and peppers. Serve with sliced bread or toast.

SWEET AND SOUR EGGPLANT WITH OLIVES AND CAPERS
Caponata

George Chrimat grew up in Taormina, Sicily, where half the population was Greek and, like George's family, attended one of Taormina's Greek Orthodox churches. He remembers the impressive ancient Greek theater in Taormina, a remnant of days when Sicily was a wealthy Greek colony. Caponata, an eggplant appetizer rich with aromatic vegetables in a sweet and sour tomato sauce, is a distinctive Sicilian specialty. It takes a while to make, but George says Caponata will last a month or more if you press plastic wrap down onto its surface, removing all air, every time you put it back in the refrigerator. Since my refrigerator is always full to overflowing, I cut George's restaurant recipe down to a more manageable quantity for home cooks. George uses only canola oil to prevent Caponata from turning cloudy when refrigerated. For this smaller recipe, which disappears quickly, I opted for the better flavor of olive oil. Serve Caponata with feta cheese and rounds of toasted bread.

1 large globe eggplant (about 1 pound)
Salt
4 ounces large green olives, preferably Sicilian
1/2 cup pine nuts
Olive or canola oil for frying
1 1/2 cups thinly sliced celery
2 cups diced yellow onions (3/4" dice)
3/4 cup diced red pepper (3/4" dice)
3/4 cup diced green pepper (3/4" dice)
Salt
Freshly ground black pepper
2 Tbsp. minced fresh garlic
2 cups crushed tomatoes
1/4 cup capers, rinsed
1/4 cup red wine vinegar
1/4 cup sugar

Preheat oven to 350°F.

Cut unpeeled eggplant into 2" x 2" cubes. Place eggplant cubes in colander, and toss with lots of salt. Cover with plastic wrap, place weight on top of eggplant (a pot full of water works well), and let eggplant sit for 1 hour.

Pit olives. Bring saucepan of water to a boil, and blanch olives for two minutes. Drain and, if olives are very large, cut them in halves or quarters. Set aside.

Toast pine nuts in preheated oven for 5–7 minutes until they're lightly toasted. Watch pine nuts closely because they burn very easily. Place pine nuts in bowl and set aside.

Rinse salt off eggplant and dry pieces well. Using a large pot (to help prevent oil from spattering), fry eggplant, lightly seasoned with salt and freshly ground black pepper, in olive oil until cubes are browned and cooked through, but not burnt. Fry eggplant in two batches to it from steaming rather than browning. Remove eggplant from oil, and place in colander to drain off excess oil (see Note below).

In same oil, sauté celery, lightly seasoned with salt and pepper, until it softens and begins to turn golden. Remove celery from oil and set aside. Adding oil if necessary, sauté onions and peppers, lightly seasoned with salt and freshly ground black pepper, until they soften. Stir in garlic and cook for 2 minutes. Stir in tomatoes, add olives, pine nuts, celery, and capers, and bring to a boil. Turn heat to low, stir in vinegar, and let simmer uncovered for 1 hour.

Stir in sugar and taste; the sauce should be both sweet and sour. Add vinegar or sugar as needed. Stir in cooked eggplant, and simmer for 15 minutes. Let cool, and refrigerate until ready to serve.

Note: Eggplant soaks up olive oil like a sponge during cooking. As it cools, it releases much of the oil. To reduce Caponata's oiliness, George drains eggplant for three hours, shaking colander from time to time, to remove as much oil as possible. I don't have patience to wait that long, plus I enjoy the taste of olive oil (which I use instead of canola), and only drain eggplant it's ready to go back in the pot; about 90 minutes.

GREEK MEATBALLS
Keftedakia

Makes approximately 24 meatballs

Keftedakia are a staple of the holiday table in Greece, where they're served on a communal platter and speared on forks of eager guests. Although many cooks add bread crumbs to the meat mixture to bind it, if meatballs are refrigerated for a short time before frying, bread binder is unnecessary. Grating onion, rather than chopping it, ensures onion flavor permeates evenly through the meatballs. To quickly shape meatballs, a 1 Tbsp. ice cream scoop is the ideal tool. For a main course, cook Keftedakia as described below, then pour tomato sauce seasoned with garlic, onions and oregano over meatballs in frying pan, and simmer for 20–30 minutes, or until flavors have blended.

1 lb. ground beef or lamb
1/4 cup grated yellow onion
1/4 cup minced green onion
2 cloves garlic, very finely minced
1/4 cup minced fresh Italian parsley
2 tsp. dried oregano, crushed
1 tsp. dried mint, crushed, or 2 Tbsp. fresh mint, minced
1/2 tsp. salt
1 tsp. Aleppo pepper or 1/2 tsp. crushed red pepper
Freshly ground black pepper
2 Tbsp. olive oil
2 Tbsp. red wine
1/2 cup freshly grated breadcrumbs (optional)
1 egg
2 Tbsp. olive oil (for frying meatballs)
Wedges of lemon

Place all ingredients (except olive oil for frying and lemon wedges) into bowl and knead, making sure they are well mixed. Heat a frying pan, and cook a thin test patty to make sure seasoning is correct; if not, add herbs, salt, or pepper to taste.

Cover baking sheet with waxed paper. Roll 1 Tbsp. of mix between your palms, shape into a meatball, and place on baking sheet. Repeat until mix is gone. Place baking sheet in refrigerator for at least 1/2 hour, allowing flavors to blend and meatballs to firm up. Fry meatballs in olive oil over medium heat until they're nicely browned on all sides. Serve with wedges of lemon.

SPINACH FRITTERS
Keftedakia me Spanaki

Makes approximately 24 fritters

Maria Baskous serves Keftedakia me Spanaki with fish and salad, for a mouth-watering spring meal. This recipe emphasizes the flavor of spinach, by using as little binding as possible. Frying spinach balls in oil adds to the bright vegetable flavor. Swiss chard can be used in place of spinach, and adding optional crushed red pepper intensifies the flavor of the finished dish.

1 pound cleaned spinach leaves, roughly chopped
2/3 cup red or green onion, minced
1/2 cup minced fresh dill
1/4 cup olive oil
2 eggs
6 Tbsp. all purpose flour
Salt
Freshly ground black pepper
1/2 tsp. crushed red pepper (optional)
1/4 cup olive oil for frying
Lemon wedges or Tzatziki (page 20)

Blanch spinach in boiling salted water for 1 minute. Drain and squeeze out as much water as possible from the spinach. Mix blanched spinach with minced onion, dill, 1/4 cup olive oil, eggs, and flour. The mix looks like thick cooked spinach. Heat remaining 1/4 cup olive oil in a frying pan over medium heat (if these are cooked too hot, the flavor of spinach suffers). Drop tablespoons of spinach mix into oil. Cook spinach fritters just until golden brown, turn over and cook until second side is also golden brown. Drain on paper towels and serve with lemon wedges or Tzatziki.

FALAFEL
Garbanzo Bean Fritters

Makes 25-30 small patties (serves 4 as a main course)

Falafel are crispy fried chickpea or bean fritters, seasoned with herbs, cumin, and coriander seeds. Salwa Abuamsha, who provided this recipe, serves hers with tahini sauce (1/2 cup tahini, 1/2 cup fresh lemon juice, 1 Tbsp. minced garlic, and 1/2–1 tsp. salt) and Tomato-Onion Salad. Falafel are delicious either on their own or in a pita sandwich. To make good falafel there are four important rules: 1. Don't use canned or cooked chickpeas. 2. Soak dried chickpeas for at least 24 hours. 3. Process chickpeas until they're very finely ground and easily hold together when formed into a ball. 4. Let dough rest before shaping it into patties. I like using a 1 Tbsp. scoop (size 60) to shape falafel, but some people prefer larger patties.

1/2 lb. dried garbanzo beans (chickpeas) (1 1/3 cups) or peeled, dried fava beans
1 cup chopped yellow onion
1 Tbsp. minced garlic
1/4 cup chopped fresh parsley
1/4 cup chopped fresh cilantro
1 tsp. freshly ground cumin
1 tsp. freshly ground coriander seeds
1/4 tsp. cayenne (ground red pepper)
1 tsp. salt
Freshly ground black pepper
1/2 tsp. baking soda
1/2 tsp. baking powder
Vegetable oil for deep frying

Soak chickpeas in water for at least 24 hours. Rinse and drain chickpeas; spread out on dish-towel to dry while you prepare remaining ingredients.

Put chickpeas, onion, garlic, parsley, cilantro, cumin, coriander, cayenne, salt, freshly ground black pepper, baking soda, and baking powder in food processor. Process until chickpeas are thoroughly puréed and ingredients form a very smooth dough; this can take up to 5 minutes of processing (remember to scrape down sides of bowl from time to time).

Let dough rest for 30–60 minutes. Scoop out tablespoons of dough; if using a 1 Tbsp. (size 60) scoop, fill scoop with dough, then level off. Form dough into balls and then flatten slightly to form small patties. Let rest for 30 minutes. (Falafel may be made ahead to this point.)

Heat oil to 350°F. Fry falafel in four batches, turning them over when half done, until they're golden brown (if you put too many in pan at one time, the oil's temperature will drop and falafel won't cook right). When done, place each batch on paper towels to drain; falafel cooks quickly so watch carefully to make sure they don't burn. Serve immediately.

GRAPE LEAVES WITH MEAT STUFFING
Dolmadakia
GREEK FESTIVAL RECIPE

Makes approximately 48 stuffed grape leaves

The Primis family has long been active in Holy Transfiguration Greek Orthodox Church. Until his death, Steve Primis was the church's chanter, and Diane Primis continues to teach traditional Greek dances to local children. This recipe for Grape Leaves with Meat Stuffing was used for years at the annual Festival and is based on one from Steve's mother Helen. Diane lightened Helen's original recipe by increasing the amount of rice in relation to meat, which Diane says "makes the dolmades lighter and tastier." I've further modernized the recipe by using fresh herbs and stock, and eliminating butter used in Helen's original. Meat-stuffed grape leaves should always be eaten hot and, when served in the home, are usually accompanied by egg-lemon sauce.

Filling:

1/2 cup grated yellow onion	2 Tbsp. dried oregano, crushed
3 Tbsp. olive oil	1/4 cup fresh Italian parsley, minced
1/3 cup water	1 tsp. freshly ground black pepper
1 lb. ground beef or lamb	2 tsp. salt
1 cup long-grain white rice, uncooked	8-ounce jar of grape leaves
2 Tbsp. fresh mint, minced, or 2 tsp. dried	2 cups beef stock

Sauté grated onion in olive oil until it softens slightly. Add water and cook until it is just heated. Put onion mixture, ground meat, rice, herbs and seasonings in bowl and knead them with your hands.

Rolling Grape Leaves: Rinse grape leaves in cold water, drain, and cut off stems flush with leaves. Spread out leaves on a flat surface, rough side up and shiny side down. Place a small amount of filling near stem end of each leaf (exact amount of filling varies depending on size of leaf   from 1 tsp. for small leaves to 1 Tbsp. or more for large leaves). Fold bottom of grape leaf up over filling, then fold in sides and roll leaf up so filling is fully encased. Don't use torn, tiny, or tough leaves for stuffing; use them to line bottom of pot in which stuffed leaves are cooked.

Cooking Grape Leaves: Line enameled Dutch oven or other large pot with unstuffed grape leaves. Closely layer stuffed leaves in grape-leaf-lined pot. When all stuffed leaves are in pot, cover them with a layer of unstuffed grape leaves.

Pour beef stock into pot. Top with upside-down plate to hold grape leaves in place while they cook. Cook over medium heat until liquid comes to a boil. Cover pot, lower heat, and simmer for 1 to 1 1/2 hours (after one hour, test one of stuffed grape leaves to see if it's done). Remove pot from heat; lift off plate and layer of unstuffed leaves. Reserve cooking liquid if you want to make egg-lemon sauce. Serve grape leaves with wedges of lemon or with the following egg-lemon sauce (page 33).

Place filling near the stem end of the grape leaf.

Fold in the sides and roll up the leaf so the filling is fully encased.

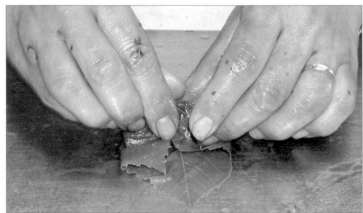

Finished stuffed grape leaves and closely-layered stuffed leaves in the pot, ready to cook.

EGG-LEMON SAUCE
Avgolemono

2 eggs
1/4 cup fresh lemon juice
1/2 cup reserved cooking liquid from grape leaves

Using electric mixer or whisk, beat eggs until they're very thick. Add lemon juice slowly while still beating eggs. Put egg-lemon mixture into a small pot, and slowly whisk in reserved cooking liquid. Cook over low heat until sauce thickens. Don't let sauce boil, or it will curdle. Place stuffed grape leaves on a serving plate and pour egg-lemon sauce over them.

GRAPE LEAVES WITH RICE STUFFING
Dolmas or Sarmas
GREEK FESTIVAL RECIPE

Makes approximately 72 stuffed grape leaves

Rice-stuffed grape leaves for the annual Greek Festival are made in such large quantities that it's difficult to get the seasoning correct. For this exacting task, we rely on the experienced taste buds of Marie Markossian, whose stuffed grape leaves are always flavorful and redolent of herbs and lemon. Although each Mediterranean culture and family has its own version of rice-stuffed grape leaves, it's Marie's Armenian recipe that is now used for the Festival. Vegetarian stuffed grape leaves are best served cold.

Filling:
1 cup short-grain white rice, uncooked
1 cup minced fresh Italian parsley
1/2 cup fresh lemon juice
2 cups minced yellow onions
1 cup minced tomatoes
1/2 cup olive oil
1 tsp. salt
1/2 tsp. ground white pepper
1 Tbsp. tomato paste

Leaves:
1 8-ounce jar grape leaves
3 cups water
3 Tbsp. tomato paste
1/3 cup fresh lemon juice
1/4 cup olive oil
1 tsp. salt

Mix all filling ingredients. Stuff grape leaves, line pot with unstuffed leaves, and layer with stuffed leaves, as described in preceding recipe for Meat-Stuffed Grape Leaves.

In saucepan, mix water, tomato paste, lemon juice, olive oil, and salt, and bring to a boil. Taste and add lemon or salt, as needed. Pour this liquid over layered stuffed leaves in pot. Top with upside-down plate to hold grape leaves in place while they cook. Cook over medium heat until liquid comes to a boil. Cover pot, lower heat, and simmer for 45–60 minutes (after 45 minutes, test one of stuffed grape leaves to see if it's done). Remove from heat and lift off plate. Let cool, chill, and serve.

ROASTED BEETS WITH GREENS AND GARLIC SPREAD
Pantzaria me Skordalia

Sweet beets and piquant garlic spread are one of those perfect food combinations in which each flavor improves and completes the other. Shortly after my marriage, I went to Greece for the first time and ate so much Pantzaria me Skordalia that I was forced to learn my first complete Greek sentence: "I'm sorry, I'm full, I can't eat anymore!"

1 bunch medium sized beets, preferably with fresh greens attached
Olive oil
Salt
Red wine vinegar
Skordalia (page 22)

Preheat oven to 350°F. Wash beets and any greens well. If beets have greens, cut them off, leaving 1" of stem attached to beets. Toss beets with a little olive oil, and place in aluminum foil packet, making sure seams of packet are sealed tightly enough to prevent beet juice from escaping. Put foil packet on baking pan, and bake for 60-90 minutes (depending on size) until tip of knife can pierce beets and they are cooked through. Remove beets from oven and let stand until they're cool enough to handle. Slip off beet skins and cut beets into wedges or 1/4" slices.

While beets are baking, if they have greens, bring pot of salted water to a rolling boil, and add washed beet greens and stems. If beet stems are young and tender, leave them attached to greens; with older beets, separate stems and start cooking them a few minutes before adding leaves. Cook greens just until they're tender; the length of time depends on beets' age. Drain greens well, and arrange on a serving plate with sliced, roasted beets.

Sprinkle beets and greens with salt and red wine vinegar, and drizzle with olive oil. Place Skordalia in a mound on same plate as beets and greens and serve. Urge your guests to eat beets and Skordalia in the same mouthful.

ROASTED OCTOPUS
Chtapodi sto Fourno

Octopus is a delicacy throughout the Mediterranean, where they average just over a foot long. Much larger octopus is abundant in Alaska's waters, growing to over eight feet in length. Octopus is not commonly used for food outside Alaska's immigrant communities. John Maroulis has a friend in Kodiak who sends him boxes of octopus with three-inch wide tentacles, a size unheard of in most of the world. John washes the octopus, cuts off the tentacles, and freezes each tentacle in a separate zip-lock bag. He roasts tentacles straight from the freezer. John says freezing octopus tenderizes it and is an effective technique to use with any size octopus. Roasted octopus is an unusual and flavorful appetizer, and is worth any effort it may take to locate octopus. I've bought octopus off the dock in Juneau where it was being sold for halibut bait, and can usually find it in one of Anchorage's Asian markets.

Frozen octopus tentacles, or whole frozen octopus
1 large yellow onion, sliced
5 bay leaves

Red wine vinegar
Olive oil
Dried oregano, crushed

Preheat oven to 400°F. Put frozen octopus in baking pan, along with onion and bay leaves and cover tightly with aluminum foil. Check octopus after one hour, and stir to make sure it isn't sticking to bottom of pan. Octopus releases abundant juice as it cooks and there should be liquid in the pan's bottom; if not, add some water or white wine. Cover and continue to bake for 1 hour, or until octopus juice has thickened and the flesh is tender. Let cool. Cut cooled octopus into 1/8" thin slices. Pour cooking juice over octopus, and sprinkle with red wine vinegar, olive oil, and oregano.

SPINACH TRIANGLES
Spanakopita
GREEK FESTIVAL RECIPE

Spanakopita is one of the most beloved foods served at the Anchorage's Greek Festival. Rich spinach filling contrasts perfectly with crisp, buttery layers of filo. For the Festival, Spanakopita is made weeks in advance and frozen uncooked; frozen Spanakopites are cooked right before they're served. Since freezing doesn't affect the flavor of Spanakopita, it's ideal for keeping in the freezer to treat unexpected guests. Spanakopita is best served hot, five minutes out of the oven.

1 pound fresh spinach leaves or 10 ounces thawed, frozen spinach	1 1/3 cup crumbled feta cheese
2 Tbsp. olive oil	2 eggs
1 cup minced yellow onion	1/2–1 tsp. salt
1/3 cup chopped green onion	Freshly ground black pepper
1/4 cup minced fresh Italian parsley	1 pound butter
1/4 cup minced fresh dill	1 pound package of filo
	1/3 cup sesame seeds

If using fresh spinach, bring a large pot of salted water to a boil, add spinach and cook just until spinach is wilted, approximately 30-60 seconds. Drain spinach, either fresh or thawed, and squeeze out all excess water using your hands or a clean dish towel. Roughly chop spinach.

Sauté yellow onion, lightly seasoned with salt and pepper, over medium heat until softened and beginning to turn golden. Mix spinach, cooked onions, green onions, parsley, feta and dill. Season spinach mix with 1/2 tsp. salt and freshly ground pepper, taste, and add salt as needed. Lightly beat eggs and stir into spinach mix, making sure eggs are thoroughly incorporated.

Preheat oven to 350°F.

Clarify butter, as described in Cook's Notes on page 13.

Remove filo from box and while it's still rolled in its plastic wrapping, cut into three 3" lengths. Cover filo you're not actively using with plastic wrap to prevent delicate dough from drying out.

Brush a rimmed baking sheet with melted clarified butter. Unroll one of the 3" lengths, and remove one strip of filo. Lay this strip of filo on a work surface, and brush it lightly with melted clarified butter. Top with a second strip of filo, and lightly butter second strip. Place approximately 1 Tbsp. of filling at bottom end of filo strip.

Fold one corner of stacked filo strips over filling to form a triangle, and continue to fold strip as if folding a flag. When done folding, you'll have a triangular packet with several layers of filo surrounding the stuffing. Place triangle, seam side down, on buttered baking sheet and lightly brush top of triangle with butter. Continue with remaining strips of filo until all filling is used. (The recipe can be made ahead to this point, and frozen for future use.)

Place buttered triangles in hot oven and bake for 20–30 minutes until they're golden brown. (It takes approximately 10 minutes longer to bake frozen Spanakopita.) Let cool for 5 minutes, and serve as an appetizer or snack.

Note: A fast way to make Spanakopita is to adopt an assembly-line approach. Use a work surface large enough to lay out 10–14 strips of filo at a time, butter all the strips, and top with and butter second layer of filo. Then put filling at end of each strip and finish as described above.

CHEESE TRIANGLES
Tyropita
GREEK FESTIVAL RECIPE

After forty days of Lenten fasting from meat, dairy, and oil, tyropita are a welcome part of Easter feasts in Greece. Soft fresh cheese is abundant during this season, as goats and sheep have recently given birth. It's this soft, creamy cheese, surrounded by flaky golden filo, that gives tyropita its rich delicate flavor. In Alaska, we approximate the flavor of fresh cheese used in Greece by mixing feta, ricotta, and cream cheese. Judging by the number of tyropita sold during the Greek Festival, this is a very successful substitution.

2 cups crumbled feta cheese	1/2 tsp. white pepper
1 cup fresh ricotta, preferably whole-milk	2 eggs
1/2 cup softened cream cheese	1 pound butter
1/4 tsp. ground nutmeg	1 pound package of filo

Mix feta, ricotta, and cream cheeses. Season with nutmeg and white pepper, taste, and add nutmeg or pepper, as needed. Lightly beat eggs and stir into cheese mixture, making sure eggs are thoroughly incorporated.

Clarify butter as described in Cook's Notes on page 13.

Preheat oven to 350°F.

Brush a rimmed baking sheet with melted butter and shape Tyropita following method set out above for Spanakopita.

Place buttered triangles in hot oven and bake for 20–30 minutes until they're golden brown. (It takes approximately 10 minutes longer to bake frozen Tyropita.) Let cool for 5 minutes, and serve.

· SALADS ·

* New recipe this edition

John Galanopoulos grew up poor in Kipseli, an area of downtown Athens. Times were hard, even before the war. The family of eight lived in the basement storage room of a three-story house and cooked on a one-burner propane stove. Life remained harsh when, shortly before World War II, John's family moved into a warehouse. They lived in curtained off living quarters and cooked in an outside oven built by the side of the road. When they could afford it, John's family brought breads, sweets, and savory dishes to the local baker, who finished them in his oven for a small fee.

When the war came, life in Athens became even worse. There was no food to be had because the occupying Germans confiscated it to feed its armies in Russia. "The winter of 1942 was the big starvation," John said. "Thousands of people in Athens died, many of them children. People dropped dead on the street…We ate lots of Horta (wild greens picked from fields). Sometimes we were so hungry we didn't have the energy to clean the Horta before we ate. We had no oil and no vinegar…we ate cabbage and cauliflower but we could only cook them with water." John felt lucky to have made it through the war alive.

After the war ended, John left Greece and wandered the globe, looking for work. He traveled from Brazil to Chile, Argentina, Uruguay, Peru, Japan, the east coast of the U.S., Chicago, back to Greece and, finally to Oregon and Alaska. He was often on his own, so John learned to cook, reveling in fresh produce he found during his wanderings. Even in the most exotic locales, the pleasure of eating fresh Horta from the fields, learned as a hungry child in Greece, stayed with John until the end of his life. John died in Anchorge in 2008 at age 76.

COOKED WILD GREENS *Horta*

Serves 4 to 6

Greeks enjoy eating a wide variety of wild greens (Horta) that Americans call weeds. Learning to recognize the best Horta is part of Greek culinary heritage passed on from ancient times. In Greece, it's common to see women doubled over in fields and along roadsides harvesting wild greens. (See page 41 for a list of Alaskan edible wild greens.} Wild greens are full of flavors not found in supermarket greens and are showcased best by a simple dressing of olive oil and fresh lemon juice. Each variety of Horta has its own unique taste. Using several varieties together makes for a more complex and authentic dish but, if you don't have time for elaborate foraging expeditions, this dish tastes great made only with dandelion greens. To gather wild greens, and make cleaning them easier, leave the root and cut the leaves off at the base. The hardest thing about using wild greens is cleaning them thoroughly, but the special flavor they bring to a meal is worth the extra effort. When you next see dandelions in your lawn, think of them as a delicious treat instead of a noxious weed.

2 pounds dandelion or mixed wild greens	2 lemons
1/2–3/4 cup extra virgin olive oil	Salt

Wash greens carefully. Discard tough or damaged stems, leaves, roots and any flower buds. Cook greens in boiling salted water for 3–5 minutes, or until they're just tender. Cooking time varies depending on type of greens; don't overcook. It's best to add tougher greens first, and tender greens only at the end of the cooking time.

Drain greens well. Dress with olive oil and salt to taste while greens are hot. Don't stint on salt as it enhances greens' flavor. Just before serving, drizzle fresh lemon juice over greens and mix in. Greens taste fresher if you add lemon juice at the last minute.

FRESH WILD GREENS
Freska Horta

Serves 4

Every year, I eagerly wait for snow to melt and the first spring dandelions to appear. Their leaves may be small, but these greens are the best of the season and help cure the desperate feeling that winter will never end. Once I brought this salad to a party and noticed raised eyebrows when I identified the greens as dandelions. The first helpings were tiny spoonfuls taken to be polite, but as word spread through the crowd, servings got larger and larger. The salad was gone quickly. Later, I overheard one teenager say to another, "Did you taste the dandelions? They were really good!" The best flavor in this salad comes from dandelions; the other ingredients are mostly window-dressing.

6 cups dandelion greens, or other tender wild greens
4 slices artisan-style bread
2–3 cloves garlic, peeled
2 Tbsp. red wine vinegar
1 1/2 tsp. Dijon mustard
1/3 cup extra virgin olive oil
8 anchovy fillets, finely minced
1 clove minced fresh garlic
Salt
Freshly ground black pepper
1/3 cup minced fresh Italian parsley

Wash greens carefully. Discard any tough or damaged leaves, stems, roots, and the tiny flower bud often found in the center of even young dandelions. Dry greens well and tear larger leaves into bite sized pieces.

Toast bread on both sides. As soon as toast is done, rub both sides with a peeled garlic clove. Cut bread into 1/2" cubes.

Whisk vinegar and mustard, and slowly whisk in olive oil. Whisk minced garlic and anchovies into dressing. Season dressing to taste with salt and freshly ground black pepper.

Right before serving salad, toss greens and parsley with half dressing. If needed, add remaining dressing and toss again. Top with cubes of garlic bread.

ALASKA WILD GREENS
Alaskana Horta

Alaska is rich in edible and tasty wild plants. In spring and early summer, I pick large quantities of my favorite greens (such as nettles and beach greens), blanch them in salted boiling water, and freeze them in zip-lock bags for winter use. I follow these rules for gathering wild plants:

1. Some plants can be confused with inedible or poisonous look-alikes. Be sure you know what you have harvested before eating any wild plant. There are many excellent field guides to edible plants; one or more should be consulted before going on foraging expeditions.

2. Even though a plant is edible, its flavor may not be worth the effort of harvesting or preparing it, particularly when there are so many other easily harvested plants around. Before gathering a large amount of a plant that is new to you, cook and taste a small amount to make sure it appeals to your palate.

3. Be careful about gathering wild plants in areas that have been sprayed with pesticides (or in areas where you don't know if spraying has occurred). I don't gather wild plants within 75 feet of a roadway, as pollution from exhaust fumes can contaminate plants. I also avoid gathering wild plants in areas where animal waste is likely to be found. No matter where I gather wild greens, I always meticulously wash them before using.

The wild greens most commonly found in Alaska that are good for Horta, Hortopita, or any other recipe calling for cooked greens include:

Beach Greens *(Honckenya Peploides)* Use leaves raw in salads, or cooked in soups, in mixed cooked greens, or in any dish that calls for cooking greens. Beach greens are also good pickled. Although beach greens taste best before flowers appear, they can also be eaten after. Beach Greens are also called Seabeach Sandwort, Sea Purslane, and Sea Chickweed.

Chickweed *(Stellaria sp.)* Use leaves raw in salads, or cooked in soups, in mixed cooked greens, or in any dish that calls for cooking greens. Chickweed takes a long time to clean well, so even though it's very tasty, it may not be worth the effort to prepare, especially since you need to gather a large quantity of chickweed to make a meal.

Dandelion *(Taraxacum)* Use leaves, which are best before flowers appear, raw in salads, or cooked in soups, in mixed cooked greens, or in any dish that calls for cooking greens. Dandelions are at their best in early spring, but in Alaska they reseed themselves more than once (at least in my yard), and new plants can be harvested throughout the summer, so long as leaves are small and flower buds are not present.

Devil's Club *(Echinopanax horridum)* Use emerging leaf buds cooked in soups, in mixed cooked greens, or in any dish that calls for cooking greens. They're particularly good sautéed in olive oil with onions and garlic. Devil's club can only be harvested when leaf buds first appear and are about an inch long. At this stage, spikes on the underside of leaves have not yet appeared.

Fiddlehead Fern *(Athyrium filix-femina, Dryopteris dilatata, and Matteuccia struthiopteris)* Use fiddleheads cooked in soups, in mixed cooked greens, or in any dish that calls for cooking greens. Gather fiddleheads when they first emerge in spring, and before they start to unwind.

Fireweed *(Epilobium angustifolium)* Cooked fireweed shoots are similar to wild asparagus and can be used in soups, mixed cooked greens, or any dish that calls for cooking greens. Fireweed shoots must be gathered when they first emerge; once leaves start spreading out, fireweed shoots are too bitter for most people. To remove some bitterness, boil shoots briefly, discard water and finish cooking in fresh water.

Goosetongue *(Plantago maritime)* Use young leaves raw in salads, or cooked in soups, in mixed cooked greens, or in any dish that calls for cooking greens. Goosetongue is best in spring and early summer, before flowers appear. Goosetongue can be confused with poisonous Arrowgrass, so careful identification is essential. Goosetongue is also called Seashore Plantain.

Lamb's Quarters *(Chenopodium album)* Use leaves raw in salads, or cooked in soups, in mixed cooked greens, or in any dish that calls for cooking greens. Lamb's Quarters are susceptible to leaf miners; be careful to harvest plants that are not infested. Although Lamb's Quarters are best before flowers appear, if fresh young tips are continuously harvested, lamb's quarters can be eaten all summer. Lamb's Quarters is also called Pigweed, Fat Hen, and Goosefoot.

Monkey Flower *(Mimulus guttatus)* Use leaves raw in salads, or cooked in soups, mixed cooked greens, or any dish that calls for cooking greens. Monkey Flower is best before flowers appear, although flowers are also edible and are good in salads or as a garnish.

Nettles *(Urtica sp.)* Use leaves cooked in soups, in mixed cooked greens, or in any dish that calls for cooked greens. Nettles are one of the best wild greens available in Alaska; they grow in big patches and are easy to gather. If the same patch is kept cut back, nettles can be harvested well into summer. Nettles should not be picked after flowering, and older leaves should not be used because they contain crystalline particles called cystoliths that are bad for the kidneys. Always use nettles cooked, and remember to wear gloves when harvesting to avoid being stung.

Spring Beauty *(Claytonia sp.)* Use leaves raw in salads, or cooked in soups, in mixed cooked greens, or in any dish that calls for cooking greens. There are many species of Claytonia, all of which are edible. The flowers are also edible and are good in salad or as a garnish. Spring Beauty is also called Miner's Lettuce and Rain Flower.

Shepherd's Purse *(Capsella sp.)* Use young leaves raw in salads, or cooked in soups, in mixed cooked greens, or in any dish that calls for cooking greens. Although leaves may be eaten throughout the summer, mature leaves have a peppery taste that doesn't appeal to all palates.

CURLY ENDIVE SALAD
Andithia Salata

Serves 4

Horta salads can be made with many different kinds of supermarket greens, including Swiss chard, spinach, and escarole. However, curly endive is Maria Baskous' favorite plant for Horta. "I must have it at least once a week," declared Maria. The flavor of cooked endive is slightly sweet, and very different from how it tastes raw. Because endive cooks fast, remove it quickly from the cooking water.

2 heads curly endive or other domesticated greens
1/2 cup extra virgin olive oil
2 lemons
Salt
Freshly ground black pepper

Wash endive, and chop it roughly. Blanch endive in boiling salted water for 1-2 minutes, or just until it wilts. (If you're using greens other than endive, the cooking time may vary.)

Drain endive well and, while it's still warm, dress with olive oil, salt, and freshly ground black pepper. Just before serving, drizzle fresh lemon juice over endive and mix in. Endive tastes fresher if the lemon juice is added at the last minute.

BEET GREENS WITH LEMON AND GARLIC
Pantzaria me Lemoni kai Skordo

Serves 4

Beet greens have a more robust and earthy flavor than most other supermarket greens, and benefit from a hint of garlic in the dressing. In summer, large bunches of beet greens can be found in farmer's markets, or pulled from the garden as part of thinning a beet crop (leave any tiny little beets attached). You need one large bunch of baby beet greens for every two people. Although baby beet greens are ideal for this salad, it can also be made with older greens, such as those found on supermarket beets. If you're using supermarket beet greens, you need greens from approximately one bunch of beets per person, with beets saved for another recipe. Beet Greens with Lemon and Garlic go well with simple grilled fish.

2 bunches of baby beet greens or 4 bunches of supermarket beets, greens only
   (beets reserved for other uses)
1/2–1 tsp. salt
2 cloves garlic
1/2 cup extra virgin olive oil
1/4–1/2 cup fresh lemon juice

Wash beet greens carefully, discarding any leathery or damaged leaves. If using supermarket beet greens, cut stems from leaves, and cut stems into 3" pieces.

Puree garlic by mashing it into 1/2 tsp. salt. Mix garlic and olive oil.

Bring salted water to a boil, and add stem pieces if you're using supermarket beet greens. After stems have cooked for 3 minutes, add beet leaves and cook until they're just tender. The cooking time varies depending on age and size of beet leaves. This could take as little as three minutes with young leaves, so watch carefully and remove leaves from water as soon as they're tender.

Drain beet greens well, and dress with garlic olive oil while still warm to allow flavors of greens and olive oil to meld. Taste and add salt as needed. Just before serving, drizzle fresh lemon juice over greens and mix in, starting with smaller amount and adding more as needed. Beet greens taste fresher if lemon juice is added at the last minute.

ROMAINE AND DILL SALAD
Maroulia Salata

Serves 4

Easter dinner in Greece isn't complete without Maroulia Salata to complement roast lamb and refresh the palate. Lettuce doesn't thrive in hot weather, so lettuce salad is a late winter and spring vegetable in most Mediterranean countries. In Alaska, this easy, flavorful and refreshing salad can be made year round. It goes well with fish and meats alike.

1 head romaine
6 green onions
1/4 cup finely minced fresh dill
2–3 Tbsp. fresh lemon juice
1/4–1/3 cup extra virgin olive oil
Salt
Freshly ground black pepper

Cut romaine into thin shreds and onions, green and white parts both, into thin slices. Mix romaine, onions, and dill. To keep salad fresh, dress just before serving. Toss salad with fresh lemon juice and olive oil, starting with the smaller amounts and adding lemon juice or oil, as needed. Sprinkle salt and freshly ground pepper over salad and toss it again.

GREEK SALAD
Elliniki Salata

Greek Salad is good for parties and festivals because it has a rich complex flavor, and includes a variety of vegetables in each serving. It's easy to make in bulk because everything but dressing the salad can be done in advance. Although this salad is an American invention, it's faithful to traditional Greek flavors. Although Greek Salad can be made using a single kind of lettuce, using romaine and iceberg helps salad retain its crunch. The amount of salad vegetables used depends on whether one or one hundred people are sharing your meal. The dressing recipe makes enought the dress salad for 20 or more. Keep a jar of dressing in your refrigerator to make quick dinnertime salads.

Dressing:
3/4 cup red wine vinegar
1/4 cup fresh lemon juice
2 cups extra virgin olive oil
1 Tbsp. dried oregano, crushed
3 cloves garlic, minced very fine
1-2 tsp. salt
Freshly ground black pepper

Salad:
Romaine lettuce, roughly chopped
Iceberg lettuce, roughly chopped
Tomatoes, sliced
Green onions, green and white parts, chopped
Cucumbers, sliced
Feta cheese, crumbled
Marinated Kalamata Olives (page 18)
Peperoncini, gold

Make Dressing: Place all ingredients in jar and shake vigorously, starting with 1 tsp. salt and adding more, as needed. Shake jar again just before dressing the salad.

Make Salad: Mix lettuces and place them in bowl. Top with tomatoes, onions, and cucumbers. Sprinkle crumbled feta over salad. To keep salad fresh, dress just before serving. Drizzle lightly with dressing, being careful not to overdress, and toss well. Taste and, if needed, add dressing and toss again. Garnish with marinated olives and peperoncini.

LETTUCE MIXED SALAD WITH OLIVE DRESSING
Maroulia Salata Anameikta me Saltsa apo Elies

Serves 4–6

Aristotle (Ari) Baskous was born and raised in Anchorage, the child of an immigrant Greek mother and third generation Greek-American father. From his earliest childhood, Ari has been an aficionado of well-seasoned and well-prepared food. He endeared himself to me when, at age 11, he enthusiastically dug into a bowl of Kalamata olive spread I'd brought to a potluck and heaped it on his bread. Ari immediately asked for the recipe, and when I didn't provide it fast enough to satisfy his craving, he was quick to call and ask again. Ari created this salad dressing when he was 13 and looking for ways to incorporate his favorite taste of olives into a salad. The dressing is full of strong flavors that complement each other and fresh vegetables. If you don't like anchovies, Ari says to leave them out and double the amount of olives.

Dressing:
4–5 crushed garlic cloves
3 anchovy fillets
6 Kalamata olives, pitted
2/3 cup extra virgin olive oil
1/4 cup red wine vinegar
1 teaspoon dried oregano, crushed
1/8 teaspoon sugar
2 tablespoons fresh lemon juice
Salt
Freshly ground black pepper

Salad:
1 head Romaine lettuce,
    torn into bite-size pieces
1 large tomato, cut in chunks
4 radishes, sliced
1/2 English cucumber, sliced
1/3 cup chopped fresh Italian parsley
1/2 cup chopped green onions
1/2 red onion, sliced

Place garlic, anchovies, and Kalamata olives in a food processor or blender, and finely mince. Mix with remaining dressing ingredients, taste and add salt or freshly ground black pepper, as needed.

Arrange salad ingredients in a large bowl. Just before serving, drizzle dressing over salad and toss.

LETTUCE AND RADISH SALAD WITH CHEESE
Salata de Ridichi cu Brînza

Serves 4–6

Marianna Apetroeai grew up in Botosani, a city of 150,000 in northern Romania, near the Ukrainian border. Her mother spent hours in the kitchen every day, preparing the family's food from scratch. In summer, when gardens and markets of Botosani are overflowing with fresh vegetables, Marianna's mother makes lettuce and radish salad with cheese. She recommends eating it with eggs, and said cheese can be crumbled into salad or eaten on the side. When made with garden-fresh vegetables, this salad is a delight.

Dressing:
 2 Tbsp. red or white wine vinegar
1/2 cup olive oil
Salt
Freshly ground black pepper
   4 ounces feta cheese

Salad:
1 head leaf or butter lettuce
8 radishes
1 cucumber, peeled
1 bunch green onions

Make Dressing: Place all ingredients in a jar and shake jar well. Shake jar again just before adding dressing to salad.

Make Salad: Tear lettuce into pieces and place in bowl. Slice radishes and cucumbers into bite-sized pieces (don't cut radishes paper-thin). Clean green onions and cut white and green parts into 1" pieces. Top lettuce with radishes, cucumbers, and green onions. Sprinkle feta over top. Just before serving, drizzle dressing over salad.

LAMB SALAD
Arni Salata

Serves 2

I'm always happy when there's leftover roast lamb because it means we can have lamb salad. Lamb has a robust flavor that contrasts well with the crisp freshness of greens and vegetables. The dressing for this salad has strong flavors to complement lamb. It's also light enough to not overwhelm vegetables, and preserves the contrast between savory lamb and fresh vegetable flavors that are the essence of this recipe. Lamb Salad is perfect for a light dinner when you want something fast and easy.

Dressing:
1/4 cup chopped yellow onions
1/4 cup chopped fresh Italian parsley
2 cloves garlic, chopped
3/4 cup extra virgin olive oil
1 Tbsp. Dijon mustard
1/4 cup red wine vinegar
Salt
Freshly ground black pepper

Salad:
1/2 pound roast lamb, cut into narrow strips
6 small tomatoes, cut into quarters
1 cup cucumber, cut into chunks
8 ounces baby salad greens
1/2 cup thinly sliced red onion
1/2 cup crumbled feta cheese
Kalamata olives

Make Dressing: Puree onions, parsley, garlic, olive oil, and mustard in a blender or food processor. Add red wine vinegar, salt, and freshly ground black pepper, and blend well. Taste and add salt or pepper, as needed.

Make Salad: Toss lamb with a small amount of dressing, and set aside. Lightly season tomatoes and cucumbers with salt. Put greens in bowl, lightly season with salt and pepper, add tomatoes, cucumber, red onion, and feta cheese. Toss with an appropriate amount of dressing; don't overdress (there may be dressing leftover to save for future salads). Arrange marinated lamb on top of salad, garnish with olives, and serve with fresh artisan-style bread.

SPINACH SALAD WITH BEETS AND MINT
Spanaki Salata me Pantzaria

Serves 4–6

Sharon Galanopoulous' late husband John loved beets, and one of Sharon's favorite salads combines beets with fresh spinach. Shredding spinach and cutting beets into matchsticks allows beet, spinach and mint flavors to be enjoyed in every bite. Sharon uses boiled beets in her salad, while I prefer roasting beets to concentrate their flavor; either cooking method works fine. This tasty recipe is a good way to use up leftover beets.

8 cups spinach, shredded
1 cup roasted beets, cut into matchsticks (see Note below)
1/2 cup thinly sliced red onion
1/4 cup crumbled feta cheese
1/4 cup shredded fresh mint
Salt
Freshly ground black pepper
2 Tbsp. red wine vinegar
1/4 cup extra virgin olive oil

Toss spinach, beets, onion, feta and mint. Season with salt and freshly ground black pepper and toss. Sprinkle red wine vinegar over salad and toss again. Drizzle salad with olive oil, and toss again. Taste and add salt, pepper, vinegar, or olive oil, as needed.

Note: To roast beets, preheat oven to 350°F. Wash beets well. If beets have greens, cut them off, leaving about 1" of stem attached. Toss beets with salt and a little olive oil, and place in an aluminum foil packet, making sure seams of packet are sealed tightly enough to prevent beet juice from escaping. Put foil packet on baking pan, and bake for 60-90 minutes (depending on size) until a knife tip can pierce beets and they're cooked through. Remove beets from oven and let stand until they're cool enough to handle. Slip off beet skins and cut beets into wedges or 1/4" slices.

SPINACH SALAD
Sbanakhi Aghtsan

Serves 4

In the Middle East, where many ethnic Armenians now live, a woman is known for the "table" she sets for her guests. A well-laid Armenian table never has only one or two dishes; it's a full array of beautifully presented and flavorful food. Salads are an important part of the meal, and cucumbers a popular ingredient. In this salad, parsley brings together spinach and cucumbers, with olives adding a complementary flavor. The dressing can be made ahead, but bright lemon flavor, an important component of the recipe, dulls if the dressing is refrigerated for more than a few hours.

Dressing:
1/4 cup fresh lemon juice
2/3 cup extra virgin olive oil
1/2–1 tsp. salt
Freshly ground black pepper

Salad:
9 ounces baby spinach leaves
2 cups peeled and diced cucumber
1/2 cup minced fresh Italian parsley
1 cup thinly sliced red onion
24 Kalamata olives, pitted and cut in half

Whisk together fresh lemon juice and olive oil. Whisk in 1/2 tsp. salt and freshly ground black pepper. Taste and add salt or pepper, as needed. Mix all remaining ingredients in bowl. Toss with appropriate amount of lemon dressing just before serving (don't overdress; there may be dressing left over).

CABBAGE SALAD
Gaghampi Aghtsan

Serves 4

Marie Markossian says cabbage in this Armenian salad should be shredded finely, "like hair." Shredding allows paprika, garlic, and lemon juice flavors to thoroughly permeate the cabbage. The salad goes well with grilled or fried meat.

5 cups finely shredded cabbage
1 cup diced tomato (1/4" dice)
1 tsp. paprika
2 garlic cloves

1/2–1 tsp. salt
6 Tbsp. extra virgin olive oil
1/4 cup fresh lemon juice

Toss cabbage, tomato, and paprika. Puree garlic by mashing it with 1/2 tsp. salt. Mix fresh lemon juice with garlic paste, and whisk in olive oil. Taste dressing and add salt, lemon juice, or garlic, as needed. Just before serving, toss salad with an appropriate amount of dressing (don't overdress; there may be dressing left over).

SALTED CABBAGE AND CARROT SALAD
Varză si Morcov Salată Varz

Serves 4

It isn't necessary to pickle your own tomatoes and sauerkraut to obtain the distinctive sour taste that Romanians love, says Marianna Apetroeai. Fresh cabbage, when salted and dressed with vinegar, makes an excellent sour salad to accompany savory meat dishes. Marianna particularly likes serving this salad with grilled pork steaks. Salting cabbage changes its texture and flavor, so it ends up halfway between cooked and raw. It still has the crunch of a raw vegetable, but the texture is softer and cabbage flavor more concentrated. Salted cabbage can be served on its own, but adding carrots and onions creates a more interesting and appetizing dish.

1 1/2 pounds cabbage, core
   removed and finely shredded
1 Tbsp. salt
1 1/2 cups thinly sliced red or
   yellow onions

1 1/2 cups shredded carrots
1/4 cup white vinegar
1/4 cup extra virgin olive oil
Freshly ground black pepper
Salt

Place cabbage in a colander and sprinkle it with 1 Tbsp. salt. Work salt into cabbage with your hands, squeezing cabbage as you do so. Let salted cabbage sit and drain for 30–60 minutes; rinse well with cold water. Squeeze as much water out of cabbage as possible with your hands, or by wringing it in a clean dish towel. Place cabbage in a large bowl, and mix in onion, carrots, vinegar, olive oil, and freshly ground black pepper. Taste and add vinegar, olive oil, pepper, or salt, as needed.

CYPRIOT SALAD WITH CILANTRO
Salata Kyprou

Serves 4

Stathis Mataragas invented this salad, using ingredients common in his native Cyprus, to serve with meat or fish. "I can never get enough cilantro," said Stathis, and he is always looking for ways to add it to his food. The salad's cilantro flavor is intense, but when eaten with meat, the combined tastes are dynamic. The salad dressing is also good served over lettuce.

Dressing:
4 small, or 2 medium, fresh whole tomatoes
1 1/2 Tbsp. white wine vinegar
1 1/2 Tbsp. fresh lemon juice
1/4 cup extra virgin olive oil
Salt
Freshly ground black pepper

Salad:
1 cup diced green peppers, 1/4" dice
1/2 cup diced yellow onion, 1/4" dice
1 cup diced tomatoes, 1/4" dice
1/2 cup diced celery, 1/4" dice
1 cup minced fresh cilantro
1 Tbsp. dried oregano, crushed

Make Dressing: Preheat oven to 500°F. Roast fresh whole tomatoes until they start to blacken, about 5–10 minutes. In a blender or food processor, puree roasted tomatoes with vinegar, fresh lemon juice, olive oil, salt, and freshly ground black pepper.

Make Salad: Place diced green peppers, tomatoes, celery, onion, cilantro, and oregano in bowl. Pour dressing over salad, and mix well. Spoon salad over meat or fish.

CUCUMBER SALAD
Angouri Salata

Serves 4

Greek cucumber salad is cool, juicy, and simple. It complements delicate dishes like fish, and refreshes the palate when paired with spicy foods. In March, when days are getting longer, but snow is still deep on the ground, I raise my spirits by making Spicy White Bean Soup and Cucumber Salad for dinner. It's essential to use fresh herbs in this salad. Splurging on fresh herbs and hothouse cucumbers in the middle of an Alaska winter may seem like an indulgence, but their vivid flavors remind you the snow will melt, and someday soon the garden will be green again.

2 cups diced peeled cucumber, 3/4" dice	2 Tbsp. minced fresh Italian parsley
1 cup diced red onion, 1/2" dice	1/4 cup fresh lemon juice
2/3 cup crumbled feta cheese	1/2 cup extra virgin olive oil
2 Tbsp. minced fresh dill	Salt
2 Tbsp. minced fresh mint	Freshly ground black pepper

Mix cucumber, red onion, feta, dill, mint, and parsley in bowl. Pour fresh lemon juice and olive oil over salad, season with salt and freshly ground black pepper, and toss well. Taste salad and add salt, pepper, or lemon juice, as needed.

GREEK VILLAGE SALAD
Horiatiki Salata

Serves 4

Horiatiki Salata is the "Greek salad" of Greece. Except during winter's depth, it's a staple at every Greek taverna (café) and table. Sitting in a seaside taverna, drinking cool white wine, and eating Horiatiki Salata is a happy memory many travelers bring home from a visit to Greece. Sweet ripe tomatoes bursting with flavor are this salad's centerpiece, so be sure to buy the best tomatoes you can find. In Alaska, this usually means Campari tomatoes sold on the vine or cherry tomatoes.

10 small tomatoes, or 2 large	2 tsp. dried oregano, crushed
1 cucumber, peeled	Salt
1 fresh Anaheim chili or	1/4 cup extra virgin olive oil
1/2 green bell pepper	Large slice of feta cheese
1/4 cup thinly sliced red or yellow onion	Kalamata olives

Quarter small tomatoes, or cut large tomatoes into 1" pieces. Cut cucumbers into pieces slightly smaller than tomatoes. Seed Anaheim chili, and cut into thin rings. Put vegetables in bowl and sprinkle with salt and crushed oregano. Toss well. Dress salad with olive oil and toss again. Top with large slice of feta cheese and garnish with Kalamata olives.

PALESTINIAN TOMATO AND ONION SALAD
Salatet Banadoura

Serves 4

Tomato and onion salad is a staple at Salwa Abuamsha's table. This juicy salad goes particularly well with Falafel (Fried Garbanzo Bean Patties) and Tahini Dipping Sauce (see Index for recipes). Eaten together, Salwa says the three dishes represent the taste of Palestine.

2 cups diced fresh tomatoes, 1/4" dice
2 cups diced peeled cucumbers, 1/4" dice
1 cup diced yellow onion, 1/4" dice
1/4 cup minced fresh mint

Salt
Freshly ground black pepper
2 Tbsp. fresh lemon juice
1/4 cup extra virgin olive oil

Mix tomatoes, cucumbers, onion, and mint. Sprinkle with salt and freshly ground black pepper, and stir salad. Drizzle fresh lemon juice and olive oil over salad, and mix well. Taste and add salt, lemon juice, or olive oil, as needed.

GREEK TOMATO AND ONION SALAD
Domatasalata me Kremmidia

Serves 4

This salad is simplicity itself. Fresh and unadorned, it's the salad I make most frequently; the flavor of tomatoes shines. Because tomatoes are the primary ingredient, it's important to use the best ones you can find. The amount of salt, oregano, and olive oil depends on personal taste. In my household, tomatoes are well salted and dressed richly with olive oil. This ensures that when the salad is gone, there's plenty of juice left at the bottom of the bowl: the perfect dipping sauce for crusty bread.

20 small or 10 medium tomatoes (preferably on the vine)
1/2 cup slivered red onions
Salt
Dried oregano, crushed
Extra virgin olive oil

Cut tomatoes into bite-sized chunks, and sprinkle with fine salt. Let salted tomatoes sit for 10 minutes so the salt dissolves and mingles with the tomato juices. Mix in onions and olive oil. Sprinkle with oregano and serve.

TOMATO SALAD FOR KEBAB
Domatasalata yia Kebab

Serves 4

This salad's fresh and spicy flavor makes it a terrific companion for grilled meat. Like a salsa, Tomato Salad for Kebab is served as an accompaniment to other foods. Because the tomatoes are diced, the salad is very juicy. I like serving it on the same plate as kebabs and feta cheese so the complementary flavors run together and season each other. My husband prefers the salad served in its own bowl. It's good either way.

2 cups diced fresh tomatoes, 1/4" dice
4 red or green jalapeños, minced
2/3 cup diced yellow onion, 1/4" dice
4 tsp. red wine vinegar, 1/4" dice

4 Tbsp. extra virgin olive oil
4 tsp. dried oregano, crushed
Salt
Freshly ground black pepper

Mix all ingredients. Taste and add salt, pepper, oregano, or vinegar, as needed.

MOROCCAN TOMATO AND PEPPER SALAD
Chakchuka

Serves 4–6

Helene Georgas Dennison grew up in a Greek household in Morocco. Helene described her favorite salad and showed me the recipe in her favorite Greek cookbook. The simple recipe was for peppers fried in olive oil. Helene said she adds tomato, cumin, garlic, and lemon to the recipe, additions she learned from her mother that turn the recipe into a classic Moroccan salad. Helene said when she makes this salad "it disappears too fast." We have the same problem at our house. Vegetable juices combine with spices and oil to make an incredibly good marinade for tomatoes and peppers. The salad should be made ahead and served cold.

3 large tomatoes, peeled and seeded
3 green bell peppers
4 cloves garlic, put through
   garlic press or pureed with salt
1 tsp. freshly ground cumin
1/4 tsp. paprika

1/8 tsp. cayenne
1 tsp. dried oregano, crushed
Salt
Freshly ground black pepper
1/4 cup fresh lemon juice
1/4 cup extra virgin olive oil

The easiest way to peel tomatoes is to drop them in boiling water for 1 minute, and immediately plunge them into bowl of cold water. The tomato skins then slip off easily. Cut skinned tomatoes in half and scrape out seeds.

Roast and clean peppers, reserving any liquid released in cleaning process. See "Peppers: How to Roast" on page 14 in Cook's Notes. Cut tomatoes and peppers in 1/2" dice, and mix them in bowl with remaining ingredients and liquid from peppers. Cover bowl and refrigerate overnight to let flavors marry. Before serving, taste and add salt, lemon juice, or olive oil, as needed.

TOMATO AND BREAD SALAD
Fattoush

Serves 4

After I first made Salwa Abuamsha's Palestinian Chicken and Onion recipe (page 134), I brought a piece of homemade pita bread to church for Salwa to taste for authenticity. She pronounced my effort successful, and told me to make Fattoush with the leftover bread. Fattoush is a complex Palestinian salad that is well-flavored with mint. When Salwa makes this salad, she adds an equal amount of bread and vegetables. Other people like different proportions, and the following recipe is heavy on vegetables. The better quality of bread used, the better Fattoush tastes. Homemade pita or artisan-style bread works best, and is an excellent way to use up slightly stale bread. Although many Fattoush recipes call for bread to soak in vegetable juices at least 30 minutes before serving, Salwa likes bread added at the last minute so it stays crunchy. Both versions are excellent and go well with roast chicken, meat, or fish.

2 Palestinian pita breads, or 8 slices
   artisan-style bread with crust
2 green Hungarian peppers or
   Anaheim chilies, or 1 green pepper
8 small, or 4 medium, tomatoes,
   preferably on the vine
6 green onions
1 medium cucumber, peeled
1/4 cup diced red onion, 1/4" dice

1/2 bunch minced fresh Italian parsley
1/2 cup minced fresh mint
10 leaves finely shredded romaine lettuce
Salt
Freshly ground black pepper
1/2 cup extra virgin olive oil
1/4 cup fresh lemon juice
2 cloves garlic, minced
2 Tbsp. sumac (see Cook's Notes p. 15)

Split pitas in half. Cut split pitas or sliced bread into 3/4"–1" pieces. Toast bread pieces under broiler until they're browned and crisped, but not burnt.

Cut peppers, tomatoes, green onions, and cucumber into 1/4" dice, and season with salt and freshly ground black pepper. Mix vegetables in bowl. Whisk olive oil into fresh lemon juice, and whisk in garlic and sumac. Toss vegetables, toasted bread, and salad dressing. Let salad sit for 30 minutes before serving or, if you prefer crunchy bread, serve immediately.

TOMATO, PARSLEY AND BULGUR SALAD
Tabbouleh

Serves 8–12

Tabbouleh is served across the Middle East and is a refreshing side dish for many main courses. Marie Markossian and Salwa Abuamsha agree the key to making Tabbouleh is using lots of parsley and cutting the vegetables very small. I like making enough Tabbouleh for leftovers; the taste of this salad improves when the flavors are given time to blend together and permeate the bulgur.

1 cup bulgur
2 cups very finely minced fresh tomatoes (10–12 small)
1 1/2 cups very finely minced green onions (1 bunch, using entire onion)
2 cups very finely minced cucumbers (1 large, peeled)
1/4 cup very finely minced yellow onion
4 cups very finely minced fresh Italian parsley (3 large bunches, stems removed)
1/2 cup very finely minced fresh mint (1 small bunch)
1 cup extra virgin olive oil
1 cup fresh lemon juice (approximately 4 lemons)
2–3 tsp. salt
Freshly ground black pepper

Mix bulgur and minced tomatoes. Let sit at room temperature until bulgur has softened, about 30–45 minutes. Add remaining ingredients to tomatoes and bulgur (starting with 2 tsp. salt), and mix well. Taste and add salt, pepper, mint or lemon juice, as needed. Refrigerate until salad is cold, and serve.

ROASTED EGGPLANT AND PEPPER SALAD
Vînita Salata

Serves 6

Romanians love eggplant, according to Marianna Apetroeai, and freeze summer's bounty to enjoy eggplant with winter meals. Women in Romania preserve eggplants by cooking them on the grill, peeling them, squeezing out excess liquid, and freezing the cooked eggplants in individual plastic bags. The women use a similar technique to preserve Romania's summer harvest of green peppers. Marianna said, "In Romania, freezers are always full in the fall." Although she now lives in Alaska, Marianna still freezes 30–40 green peppers and eggplants every summer, and uses them year-round to make a variety of flavorful salads. When making Vînita Salata, Marianna sometimes leaves out roasted peppers, and other times she substitutes mayonnaise for olive oil, or cooks onions before adding them. This version is my favorite. I've added jalapeño and garlic to Marianna's original recipe for extra bite. Serve this salad with any dish that needs a flavorful complement, or as part of an appetizer spread.

Marianna Apetroeai with Anna Maroulis at the annual Greek Festival

2 red or green peppers
1 large globe eggplant or 3 small Japanese eggplant (about 1 pound)
1/2 cup diced yellow onion, 1/8" dice
1/2 cup tomato sauce
3 Tbsp. fresh lemon juice
1/4 cup extra virgin olive oil
1 red or green jalapeño, minced (optional)
1 clove garlic (optional)
1/2-1 tsp. salt
Freshly ground black pepper

Roast and skin peppers. See "Peppers: How to Roast" on page 14 in Cook's Notes. Remove stems and seeds from peppers and cut into 1/4" dice. Grill or broil eggplant until it's soft and skin is charred all over. Let eggplant cool, remove skin, cut flesh into large chunks, and put in a strainer to drain off some liquid. Use your hands to squeeze any remaining liquid from eggplant and chop it into 1/2" pieces. Mix chopped eggplant, peppers, and onions with remaining ingredients, starting with 1/2 tsp. salt. Taste and add lemon juice, olive oil, or salt as needed.

POTATO SALAD WITH LEMON AND KALAMATA OLIVES
Patatosalata

Serves 6

Simple olive oil and lemon dressing on potato salad preserves the individual flavors of its ingredients. It's a nice alternative to heavy mayonnaise and mustard based potato salads often seen at summer barbeques. Slightly waxy red or yellow potatoes work best; their texture is better than baking potatoes which don't hold their shape well. Be careful not to overcook potatoes for the same reason. Because waxy potatoes are thin-skinned, they're easy to peel after cooking. Including Kalamata olives isn't traditional, but they add visual appeal and good flavor.

1 1/2–2 pounds red or yellow potatoes
1 cup diced yellow onions, 1/4" dice
1 cup diced celery, 1/4" dice
1/2 cup minced fresh Italian parsley
1/2 cup pitted and chopped Kalamata olives (optional)
1 tsp. salt
Freshly ground black pepper
1/4 cup fresh lemon juice
1/2 cup extra virgin olive oil

Boil potatoes until they can just be pierced with a fork. Remove skins and cut into 1/2" dice. In a large bowl, mix onions, celery, parsley, potatoes, olives (if using), salt, freshly ground black pepper, fresh lemon juice, and olive oil. Toss dressing with vegetables. Chill salad in refrigerator. Before serving, taste and add lemon juice, salt, or pepper, as needed. Serve garnished with Kalamata olives and parsley.

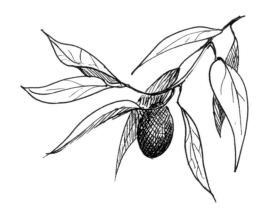

WHITE BEAN AND ONION SALAD
Fasolia Salata

Serves 8

In the northern Greek village of Filakto where Tina Karakatsanis Chowaniec was born, white beans frequently appear in soups and salads. Tina makes this salad using lemon juice. An equally good version substitutes vinegar for lemon. The salad is best made with dried beans (canned white beans are often too soft to hold up in salads), but when in a hurry, canned white beans will work. If using dried beans, start preparing the dish a day ahead. Adding salt to bean soaking water helps prevent the beans' skin from splitting and improves their flavor and texture. I like cutting half the onions in thin slices, and dicing the other half, in order to give the salad a variety of textures. Fasolia Salata goes well with spicy main courses like Grilled Halibut Chermoula or Pork and Garlic Stew (see Index for recipes).

2 cups dried navy, cannellini, or other small white beans
5 bay leaves
Salt
1/2 cup extra virgin olive oil
1/3 cup fresh lemon juice or red wine vinegar
1/3 cup minced fresh Italian parsley
1 1/2 cups thinly sliced or diced yellow onions
Freshly ground black pepper

Spread out dried beans and inspect carefully, removing any stones or debris. Put beans in large pot, cover with plenty of cold water mixed with 3 Tbsp. salt, and soak overnight. The next day, drain and rinse soaked beans.

Put soaked beans in large pot with bay leaves, salt and enough water to cover beans by 2 inches. Bring water to boil, turn down heat, and simmer for 30–45 minutes, or just until beans are tender. The exact length of time depends on size and age of beans. Drain beans and put in large bowl.

While beans are still hot, mix well with olive oil, fresh lemon juice or red wine vinegar, parsley, onions, salt and freshly ground black pepper. Taste and add lemon juice or vinegar, salt, or pepper, as needed.

CARROT-RADISH SALAD WITH CAPERS
Karoto-Rapanaki Salata me Kapari

Serves 4

Carrots and radishes are a natural flavor combination and in Alaska, if you plan ahead when you plant your garden, can be ready to pick at the same time. The idea for combining the two ingredients came from a British cookbook called **Let's Eat Greek At Home**, *but I've changed the balance of flavors in the original recipe. I've increased the amounts of the other ingredients in relation to carrots, and used the traditional Greek dressing of olive oil and fresh lemon juice. This crisp refreshing salad, with its hint of sweetness from carrots, goes nicely with grilled meats and fish, as well as generously spiced Moroccan food.*

4 tsp. capers (preferably preserved in salt)
2 cups grated carrots
1 1/4 cup sliced radishes, 1/8" thick
1/2 cup thinly sliced yellow onions
1/4 cup chopped fresh Italian parsley
1 tsp. dried oregano, crushed
Salt
Freshly ground black pepper
6 Tbsp. extra virgin olive oil
3 Tbsp. fresh lemon juice
Kalamata olives

If using salt-preserved capers, rinse off salt and let them soak in cold water for 10–15 minutes, and rinse them again. If using brined capers, rinse off brine. Dry capers and chop them if they're large.

Mix capers, carrots, radishes, onions, parsley, and oregano. Sprinkle vegetables with salt and freshly ground black pepper and stir well. Mix olive oil and fresh lemon juice into salad. Garnish with Kalamata olives and serve.

ORANGE AND ONION SALAD
Portokali kai Kremmidi Salata

Serves 4

Years ago, Pat Mowery, a parishioner at Holy Transfiguration, began writing a cookbook for the church. Unfortunately, she moved away before her book was finished. Many of Pat's recipes (including this one) were for Middle Eastern-influenced dishes characteristic of Greek communities that once thrived throughout western Turkey. When people in these communities were forcibly uprooted in the 1920s and shipped to Greece, they brought along their culinary traditions. Although onions and oranges might sound like an incongruous salad combination, each has its own kind of sweetness that blends well in this distinctive salad. Mint and cumin form a bridge between the two flavors. This unusual, but delightful and refreshing, salad goes well with roast chicken or grilled fish on a hot day when you're looking for a fresh and interesting side dish.

Salad:
3 medium oranges
1/3 cup thinly sliced and quartered red onion
3 Tbsp. minced fresh mint
1/3 cup minced Kalamata olives

Dressing:
1/4 cup fresh lemon juice
3/4 cup extra virgin olive oil
1 tsp. freshly ground cumin
1/2 tsp. salt

Cut a thin slice from top and bottom of each orange, stand on end, and cut away rind and white pith from sides (pith tastes bitter and must be entirely removed). Cut oranges in half from top to bottom, and remove any white pith from centers. Cut each half into three wedges, and cut each wedge crosswise in halves or thirds. Be sure to remove all orange seeds.

Toss orange pieces with onion, mint and olives. Whisk all dressing ingredients, taste, and add salt, cumin, or lemon juice, as needed. Pour dressing over salad, toss well, and serve.

ORANGE AND RADISH SALAD
Chalda Bartogal Wa Fijil

Serves 4

Orange trees outside Helene Georgas Dennison's home in Kasbah Tadla, Morocco, produced abundant sweet juicy fruit that Helene's mother frequently included in her family meals. Because Morocco is rich with citrus trees, oranges are often combined with vegetables in salads dressed with lemon juice and orange blossom water. Radishes go especially well with citrus flavors in this salad, and cinnamon adds a pleasing exotic taste. Traditionally, radishes are grated, and are absorbed and become part of the dressing. Thin slicing radishes, as I prefer, helps retain a fresher radish flavor that is complemented by the dressing. Bright flavors in this Moroccan fruit salad go well with Thanksgiving turkey. For a traditional Moroccan meal, serve it as an accompaniment for Chicken with Onions and Saffron, couscous, olives, and Moroccan Tomato and Pepper Salad (see Index for recipes).

3 medium oranges
2 cups grated or sliced radishes, 1/8" thick slices
6 Tbsp. fresh lemon juice
2 tsp. sugar
1 Tbsp. orange blossom water
1/2 tsp. salt
1/2 tsp. ground cinnamon

Cut a thin slice from top and bottom of each orange, stand on end, and cut away rind and white pith from sides (pith tastes bitter and must be entirely removed). Cut oranges in half from top to bottom, and remove any white pith from centers. Cut each half into three wedges, and cut each wedge crosswise in halves or thirds. Be sure to remove all orange seeds.

Toss orange pieces with radishes. In bowl whisk together lemon juice, sugar, orange blossom water, and salt. Taste and add salt or lemon juice, as needed. Pour dressing over salad and toss well. Dust lightly with ground cinnamon and serve.

WATERMELON, FETA AND ARUGULA SALAD
Salata me Karpouzi, Feta kai Roka

Cool and refreshing, sweet watermelon, salty cheese, and bitter greens come together in the perfect salad for a sunny day. We first ate this salad at Kuzina Restaurant on Adrianou Street in Athens, overlooking the Ancient Agora, and discovered it's simple to make. The keys are cutting watermelon thick enough to stand on edge, and finding firm feta that can be cut into large flat pieces. It's also important to use good quality traditional balsamic vinegar. If you can't find good balsamic, you can replicate its flavor by enhancing commercial balsamic with a little brown sugar. I use a ratio of 1 tsp. brown sugar per 5 tablespoons of commercial balsamic. If you don't care about a showy display, simply cut the watermelon and feta into chunks, place them on a bed of arugula, and drizzle with balsamic vinegar.

Watermelon
Feta cheese
Arugula
Best quality balsamic vinegar, or brown sugar-enhanced commercial vinegar

Cut watermelon into 1" slices. Cut off rind, and cut flesh into sharp triangles (use watermelon trimmings for another purpose). You may remove watermelon seeds for ease of eating, but it's not necessary to do so.

Cut feta into slices and then into the same shape triangles as watermelon, but slightly smaller. (Cut feta slices smaller than shown in picture for better balance of Ingredients.)

Wash, clean, and dry arugula.

Arrange watermelon and feta slices as shown in photograph, and fill center space with arugula. Drizzle balsamic vinegar over everything, and serve.

• SOUPS •

* New recipe this edition

"Kalos Orisate" (Welcome) is the greeting I hear each time I arrive in the Greek island village where my husband's grandmother, Fotine Psiroukis Constantino, was born more than a century ago. When we are on the island, we live in a little stone house that was part of Fotine's dowry.

"Kalos Orisate!" The greeting is repeated over and over as I pass through the narrow village streets, rising to a crescendo when I reach the sunny square. Although it always takes a few days before Greek fully returns to my mind, the warm welcome never fails to pull me into the village's rhythm.

"How are you? Good? Will you stay through the winter?" "How goes it in Alaska?" "You must have heard about your uncle, but did you hear about his son?" These are not just formulaic pleasantries, but part of a villager's lifelong quest to gather and impart news and gossip. Although I'm a "kseni" (foreigner), because of my husband's blood ties to the village, my efforts to speak Greek, attend church, cook meals, and bake sweets, and our regular trips to the island, we have become part of village life and the ever-evolving story it tells of itself.

After we renew our acquaintances, the bounty of the island begins pouring into our little house. Our one window abutting the street has a deep marble sill. When the shutters are open, I often find a bunch of ripe grapes, a pitcher of warm fresh sheep's milk, or a home-made cheese waiting for me on the windowsill. The milk and cheese are usually from Popi, the shepherd's wife across the street. The grapes could be from anyone.

Several times a week someone shouts out my name, opens our gate, and hands me a bag of eggplant, okra, beans, figs, or melons, a bunch of herbs, a basket of fresh eggs, or an old water bottle filled with last year's wine. Sometimes I receive delicacies: a brace of rabbits, a bag of snails, or a bottle of homemade ouzo. Every year, cousin Zafiris, one of our oldest and dearest friends, delivers a freshly slaughtered sheep or goat, to keep us in meat for our visit. "Kalos Orisate!"

Toward the end of summer, cousin Froso and our friend Kyria Fani make and dry a year's supply of noodles for their extended families. They make noodles in such large quantities that eggs from Froso and Zafiris' hens need to be stockpiled for weeks. Eggs are mixed with fresh sheep's milk and flour from wheat grown by Zafiris to make the flavorful noodles known on the island as Hilopites. Before we return to Alaska, Froso makes sure we have enough Hilopites in our baggage to last the winter.

The depth of flavors I achieve when using village ingredients reflects the depth of my feelings for our family and friends in the village. The warm satisfaction of sitting in my Alaska house, eating a big bowl of hearty soup made from an island recipe, sustains me until I'm once again able to return to the village and hear "Kalos Orisate."

LENTIL AND NOODLE SOUP
Fakes Me Hilopites

Serves 4–6

In Mediterranean countries, there are countless versions of lentil soup, all of them wonderful. On the northern Aegean islands, lentil soup is sometimes made with homemade dried egg noodles (Hilopites) and seasoned with fresh mint. The recipe works just as well when made with dried mint and purchased egg noodles or orzo. The resulting soup is rich and savory, with mint adding a bright fresh flavor. Village Salad (Horiatiki Salata) makes a sweet, slightly acidic, side dish that nicely complements hearty lentils.

Soup:
3 cups diced yellow onions (1/4" dice)
1 Tbsp. minced fresh garlic
1 tsp. Aleppo pepper or 1/2 tsp. crushed red pepper (optional)
1/4 cup olive oil
8–10 cups chicken stock or water
1 cup brown or green lentils
3 bay leaves
1/4 cup minced fresh mint or 2 Tbsp. dried mint, crushed
1–2 tsp. salt
Freshly ground black pepper
1 cup fine-cut egg noodles or orzo

Topping:
2 cups thinly sliced yellow onions
1/3 cup olive oil
1/4 cup minced fresh mint or 2 Tbsp. dried mint, crushed
Salt
Freshly ground black pepper

Extra virgin olive oil, best quality, for drizzling on top

Spread out lentils in pan and inspect carefully, removing any pebbles or debris. Rinse and drain lentils.

Heat olive oil in a large pot and sauté onions, lightly seasoned with salt and freshly ground black pepper, until they begin to turn golden. Stir in garlic and Aleppo pepper and cook for 1 minute. Stir in 8 cups chicken stock or water, lentils, bay leaves, 1/4 cup fresh or 2 Tbsp. dried mint, 1 tsp. salt and freshly ground black pepper. Bring soup to a boil, reduce heat to low, and simmer for 20–30 minutes or until lentils just start to soften, but are not completely done. Return soup to a medium boil, add noodles or orzo, and cook for 5–10 minutes until noodles are done. The exact cooking time depends on type of noodles used. If soup is too thick when noodles are done, add remaining stock or water, as needed. Taste and add salt or pepper, as needed.

While lentils cook, make topping. Sauté sliced onions, lightly seasoned with salt and freshly ground black pepper, in olive oil for 25–35 minutes, stirring regularly, until they soften and begin to caramelize. Stir in mint and cook for 1 minute.

Remove bay leaves and serve soup in individual bowls. Finish each bowl with a spoonful of topping and a drizzle of extra virgin olive oil.

LENTIL AND VEGETABLE SOUP
Faki

Serves 6

Faki is a traditional Greek fasting food that is delicious any time of year. Pamela Lloyd often makes her family's version of Faki, sometimes with tomatoes and sometimes without. Pamela grew up in Milwaukee, Wisconsin surrounded by her mother's large Greek family. Every Sunday after church, Pamela's family gathered at her Greek grandfather's house. The family laughed and told stories, but mostly they ate delicious food her grandfather cooked. The soup is very good made with a water base as in Pamela's original recipe, but using chicken stock gives greater depth to the flavor. Don't forget to drizzle the highest quality olive oil over each bowl of soup—oil's fruitiness helps bring out the vegetables' essence.

1 cup diced celery, 1/4" dice
1 cup diced carrots, 1/4" dice
3 cups diced yellow onion, 1/4" dice
1/4 cup olive oil
1 Tbsp. minced fresh garlic
1 cup green or brown lentils
8–10 cups water or chicken stock
3 bay leaves
1 Tbsp. dried oregano, crushed
1-2 tsp. salt
1 tsp. freshly ground black pepper
1 14.5-ounce can crushed tomatoes
1/4 cup minced fresh Italian parsley
Extra virgin olive oil, best quality
Red wine vinegar (optional)

Spread out lentils in pan and inspect carefully, removing any pebbles or debris. Rinse and drain lentils.

In a large pot, sauté celery, carrots, and onion, lightly seasoned with salt and freshly ground black pepper, in 1/4 cup olive oil over medium heat until onion softens and begins to turn golden. Stir in garlic and lentils. Add water or chicken stock, bay leaves, oregano, tomatoes, and remaining salt and freshly ground black pepper. Bring mixture to a boil, cover, turn heat down to low, and simmer for 30 minutes. Remove cover and simmer for an additional 15 minutes or until flavors have melded. Remove bay leaves, and stir in minced parsley. Taste and add salt or pepper, as needed. Serve soup drizzled with olive oil. Red wine vinegar is served on the table, to be stirred into soup as desired by each eater.

RED LENTIL SOUP
Vosbabour

Serves 4–6

Red Lentil Soup is hearty and filling. Marie Markossian advises the soup needs to be "a little thick." Finished soup should have the texture of rich split pea soup. Marie's son Aram likes his red lentil soup seasoned with curry powder. I prefer mine with cumin and it's also good plain with a drizzle of fruity olive oil on top. Red lentil soup is like a fresh canvas you can paint to please your family's individual palates. No matter how you season red lentil soup, it's complemented by a crisp lettuce or cabbage salad, simply dressed with olive oil and lemon.

1 cup red lentils
5–6 cups water
1/3 cup short-grain rice
1 1/2 cups minced yellow onion
1 Tbsp. curry powder or 1 tsp. freshly ground cumin (optional)
Salt
Freshly ground black pepper
1/2 cup olive oil

Spread out lentils in pan and inspect carefully, removing any pebbles or debris. Rinse red lentils, soak them for 30 minutes, and drain well.

In a large pot, mix soaked lentils with water, rice, 3/4 cup minced onions, curry powder or ground cumin (if using), salt and freshly ground black pepper. Cook soup over medium high heat until it comes to a boil, then cover, turn heat down to low, and simmer until lentils are soft (this takes about 1/2 hour). Sauté remaining 3/4 cup minced onion, lightly seasoned with salt and freshly ground black pepper, in olive oil until onions begin to turn golden. Mix onions and olive oil into soup. Taste and add salt or pepper, as needed.

SPICY WHITE BEAN SOUP
Kafteri Fasolatha

Serves 4–6

Tina Karakatsanis Chowaniec grew up in the village of Filakto in northern Greece, population 500, which is so close to the border you can see across into Turkey. In 1974, when Turkey invaded Cyprus, Greece and Turkey faced off, again, for war. Filakto was on the front line. This was a very frightening time; Tina and her family slept with their shoes on and individual pouches of food by their sides, ever ready to flee if war came. Soldiers from all over Greece poured into Filakto to protect the border, but provisions were slow to follow. The women of Filakto spent the summer baking and cooking for soldiers from their larders and storehouses. Small white beans grown and dried by Filakto farmers provided nutritious meals for hungry soldiers. The recipe Tina learned from her mother and grandmother for Fasolatha seasoned with paprika can easily be expanded to serve an army. Paprika and dried red peppers are common seasonings in northern Greece, but Tina points out that not everyone likes Fasolatha with red peppers and hot paprika. If you don't like spicy food, Fasolatha is excellent when seasoned only with sweet paprika. Adding salt to bean soaking water helps prevent the beans' skin from splitting and improves their flavor and texture. Serve with thin slices of hard cheese and a crisp green salad for a hearty winter meal.

2 cups dried navy beans (or other
   small white beans)
1/2 cup olive oil
3 cups diced yellow onions,
   1/4" dice
1 cup diced carrots, 1/4" dice
1 cup diced celery, 1/4" dice
1 Tbsp. minced fresh garlic

5 bay leaves
2 Tbsp. sweet or hot paprika
2 Tbsp. dried oregano, crushed
4 whole dried red chili peppers (optional)
Salt
Freshly ground black pepper
1 14.5-ounce can diced tomatoes

Spread out dried beans and inspect carefully, removing any stones or debris. Put beans in large pot, cover with plenty of cold water mixed with 3 Tbsp. salt, and soak overnight. The next day, drain and rinse soaked beans.

In large pot, sauté onion, carrots, and celery, lightly seasoned with salt and freshly ground black pepper, in olive oil until onion softens and begins to turn golden. Stir in garlic and cook 1 minute. Add drained beans, bay leaves, paprika, oregano, optional red chili peppers, and enough water to cover beans by 2 inches. Bring mixture to boil, cover, turn heat down to low, and simmer for 1 hour or until beans have softened, but are still slightly firm. The exact length of time depends on size and age of beans. Stir in tomatoes and season with salt and pepper. Cook for 30 minutes uncovered, or until beans are tender, but not falling apart, and soup is consistency you prefer. Remove bay leaves and optional red chili peppers. Taste and add salt or pepper, as needed.

MOROCCAN CHERMOULA AND CARROT SOUP

Serves 2 – 3

Well-spiced Carrot Soup is delicious on its own, but the addition of Chermoula, one of Morocco's classic sauces, turns it into something special. Fresh parsley and cilantro in the sauce set off the soup's deep richness. Mixed together, the components come together to form an entirely new, and wonderfully complex, single flavor. I make Chermoula while the soup is simmering, which means the entire recipe takes less than an hour from start to serving. It's hard to have too much Chermoula—I double or triple the recipe whenever I make it. I use extra Chermoula to top grilled salmon, halibut, or chicken, or to add flavor to salads. The easiest way to peel ginger is to scrape off the peel with the edge of a teaspoon. To mince peeled ginger, cut it across the grain into thin slices and whack each slice with a meat pounder. The slices break up into small pieces; if you prefer a finer mince, chop up the small pieces with a chef's knife.

Soup:
3 cups diced onion, 3/4" dice
1 cup diced leek, white and light green
   parts only, 3/4" dice
3 cups diced carrots, 3/4" dice (1 pound)
3 Tbsp. olive oil
Salt
Freshly ground black pepper
3 Tbsp. minced fresh ginger
1 Tbsp. minced fresh garlic
1 tsp. freshly ground cumin
1 tsp. freshly ground coriander seed
1 tsp. paprika
4–5 cups vegetable or chicken stock

Chermoula:
1/3 cup chopped fresh parsley
1/4 cup chopped fresh cilantro
1 Tbsp. chopped fresh garlic
1/2 tsp. freshly ground cumin
1/2 tsp. paprika
1/2 tsp. harissa or 1/8 tsp. cayenne
1/2 tsp. salt
3 Tbsp. olive oil
2 Tbsp. lemon juice

Make Soup: In a pot large enough to hold all the soup, sauté onion, leek, and carrots, lightly seasoned with salt and freshly ground black pepper, in olive oil until onions soften and start to turn golden. Stir in ginger, garlic, cumin, coriander, and paprika, and cook for 1 minute. Add 4 cups of stock, bring to a boil, turn down heat, and simmer for 30-40 minutes, or until carrots are tender. Puree soup until it's smooth in blender (or using immersion blender). Add stock as necessary until soup is the thickness you prefer. Taste and add salt, if needed.

Ladle soup into bowls and drizzle with Chermoula before serving. If there is extra Chermoula, serve it on the side so diners can add more, as desired.

Make Chermoula: Place all ingredients into blender and puree until very smooth. The sauce can be made ahead and stored in the refrigerator, but should be brought to room temperature before serving.

VEGETABLE SOUP
Hortosoupa

Serves 6

Sharon Galanopoulous' Hortosoupa is the essence of fresh vegetables in a bowl. With no meat or strong tomato flavors, the key to this soup's delicate taste is using the freshest vegetables possible. When I arrive home from the farmer's market carrying bags spilling over with glorious produce, I often make Sharon's vegetable soup. Although this recipe calls for fresh beans, Sharon says you can add or substitute any other vegetable. Leafy Greek celery (also called Chinese celery) adds the best flavor. If this isn't available, use as many leaves from regular celery as possible. Instead of potatoes, try fresh summer turnips for extra flavor. Fresh dill and grated cheese are not part of Sharon's original recipe, but add fresh highlights and body to the soup's vegetable flavors.

2 cups yellow onion, thinly sliced
1/4 cup olive oil
2 cups diced celery stalks and leaves, 1/4" dice
1 pound potatoes or turnips, peeled and diced, 1/4" dice
2 carrots, peeled and diced, 1/4" dice
1/2 small head of cabbage (1 1/2 pounds)
1/2 pound green beans, cut into 1" lengths
2 14.5-ounce cans diced tomatoes (small dice, if available)
1 cup roughly chopped parsley
1 Tbsp. minced fresh garlic
4 bay leaves
1–2 tsp. salt
Freshly ground black pepper
6 cups water
1/4 cup finely minced fresh dill (optional)
1 cup freshly grated kefalotyri or parmesan (optional)

Sauté onion, lightly seasoned with salt and freshly ground black pepper, in olive oil over medium heat. When onions begin to turn golden, stir in remaining ingredients, except optional dill and cheese. Bring soup to boil, cover, turn down heat, and simmer for 45–60 minutes. The soup is done when potatoes or turnips are fork-tender, and vegetable flavors have combined in the broth. Stir in fresh dill, and cook for five minutes. Taste and add salt or pepper, as needed. Serve with grated cheese on the side for sprinkling over soup.

EGG-LEMON SOUP
Avgolemono Soupa

Serves 6–8

When I first started talking about this cookbook, I asked Maria Baskous and Eugenia Primis what foods they most remembered from their childhoods. Each answered immediately: "Avgolemono soup." Eugenia said, "I never got enough of YiaYia's (grandmother's) Avgolemono." At Maria's family table in Greece, and at her husband Alex's family table in America, egg-lemon soup was always part of Sunday dinner. Today at their joint table in Anchorage, Maria continues the custom of making Avgolemono soup on Sundays. Eggs and lemon are natural flavor complements that make taste buds come alive. Traditionally, Avgolemono soup is made with a simple stock of chicken, water, and salt. I like the deeper flavor that results from including carrots, celery, and onion in the stock. Although not traditional, or to everyone's liking, I like eating this soup cold on hot days. Leftover chicken meat makes great chicken salad when mixed with onion, celery, mayonnaise, and lots of freshly ground pepper.

Chicken stock:
1 cut-up 4-pound chicken, or
   4 pounds chicken thighs
2 carrots, cut in chunks
2 celery stalks, cut in chunks
1 yellow onion, cut in chunks
2 bay leaves
Fresh Italian parsley stems
1 Tbsp. black peppercorns
1 tsp. salt
3 quarts water

Egg-lemon soup:
1 cup long-grain rice
10 cups chicken stock
2 cups cooked chicken, cut in
   bite-sized pieces
3–4 eggs, separated
3–5 lemons
1-2 tsp. salt

For Chicken Stock: Wash chicken and place it in a large pot. Add remaining stock ingredients and bring liquid to a boil over medium-high heat. Turn heat down, and simmer over low for 2 hours, or until chicken is very tender. Remove chicken from pot, strain stock into a large bowl, and discard cooked vegetables. Separate chicken from bones and skin, and discard them. Dice chicken and reserve. Let stock sit until fat rises to top and remove as much of fat as possible.

For Soup: Return 10 cups of chicken stock to pot, along with rice, diced chicken, and 1 tsp. salt. Cook soup until rice is tender. In the meantime, separate yolks and whites of 3 eggs, being careful not to get any yolk in with whites. Juice lemons; you need approximately one cup of lemon juice. Beat egg whites until they form stiff, but not dry, peaks. Whisk egg yolks into whites, and lemon juice into eggs. Temper eggs by whisking one cup of hot soup into egg-lemon mixture. Making sure soup isn't boiling and heat is turned down as low as possible, quickly stir tempered egg-lemon mixture into soup. Don't let soup boil, or eggs will curdle.

After adding eggs, let soup cook for a few minutes over low heat until it thickens slightly. If it isn't thick enough for your taste, stir in another egg, prepared as described above. Taste and add lemon or salt, as needed. Salt is essential; if this soup doesn't have enough salt, it tastes flat and uninteresting. Serve immediately.

ARTICHOKE AND LEEK EGG-LEMON SOUP
Anginares me Prassa Avgolemono Soupa

Serves 6–8

The vegetables in Maria Baskous' Artichoke and Leek Egg-Lemon Soup supply a counterpoint to the tart soup base. This variation of Avgolemono Soupa makes a filling main course. Rice adds body and substance to an intensely flavored dish, although the soup is lighter if you omit rice. It's important to chop dill finely so its distinctive and refreshing flavor spreads evenly through the soup. Maria's soup may be made with water rather than chicken stock, but using stock results in luxuriant complex flavors.

2 cups diced yellow onions, 1/4" dice
2 Tbsp. olive oil
2 Tbsp. butter
4 cups leeks, cleaned well and
　cut in 1/4" slices
4 cups chicken stock
4 cups water
1 pound frozen artichoke hearts, thawed

1/4 cup rice
3/4 cup fresh lemon juice
3 eggs
1/2 bunch dill, very finely minced
4 green onions, minced
Salt
Freshly ground black pepper

Heat olive oil and butter in a large pot, add diced onions lightly seasoned with salt and freshly ground black pepper, and sauté in combined oils until onions soften and begin to turn golden. Add leeks to onions and continue to sauté for 3 minutes. Stir chicken stock and water into pot. Cut thawed artichoke hearts in half or thirds, removing any tough leaves, and add to soup. Bring soup to a boil, turn down heat, and simmer on low for 15–20 minutes. Add rice and cook for an additional 20 minutes, or until rice is soft.

Separate yolks and whites of 3 eggs, being careful not to get any yolk in with whites. Beat egg whites until stiff, but not dry, then whisk egg yolks into whites. Whisk lemon juice into eggs. Temper eggs by whisking 1 cup of hot soup into egg lemon mixture. Make sure soup isn't boiling and heat is turned down as low as possible, and quickly stir tempered egg-lemon mixture into soup. Don't allow soup to boil, or eggs will curdle. Mix in dill and minced green onion. Serve immediately, with plenty of freshly ground black pepper.

EASTER LAMB SOUP
Mayeritsa

Serves 6–8

Greeks love grilled and roasted meats. Even so, for 48 days during Easter Lent, devout Orthodox Christians fast from all meat and dairy products. The season culminates with a liturgy late Saturday on the night before Easter. At precisely midnight, the priest disappears behind a screen of icons, and the church goes completely black. Long moments elapse in darkness. Young children wail and the congregation buzzes with anticipation. Then, a faint light flickers behind the screen, and everyone falls silent, focused on the light. The priest emerges with an ornate candle burning brightly and, holding the light at arm's length high above the congregation, he announces in a loud confident voice "Christos Anesti" (Christ Has Risen). Speaking these words, he lowers his candle and passes the flame to the crowd of wicks thrust towards him. The Light passes from one to another until the church is illuminated by candles like bright stars in the night. Cries of "Christos Anesti!" and "Alithos Anesti" (Truly He Has Risen) ring out. Fireworks explode, and Christ has risen again in the hearts of the congregation. It's now time to celebrate.

Mayeritsa is a rich meaty soup served late at night after the midnight Easter service to break the fast. It's traditionally made with organs of the lamb that will crown the Easter table. Maria Kakouratou Reilly's mother uses organ meat for her Mayeritsa, but when Maria prepares it for her husband Patrick and son Dimitris, she substitutes lamb meat for organs. The result is a warm and homey soup, full of strong individual flavors that blend into a comforting whole. Maria says the soup is very rich because everyone has been fasting for so long. Meat and stock can be cooked well in advance, so Mayeritsa is easy to assemble and serve at the last minute.

Stock:
2 pounds lamb shoulder steaks or chops
16 cups water
2 carrots, peeled and roughly chopped
2 celery stalks, roughly chopped
1 large yellow onion, roughly chopped
2 tsp. black peppercorns
1 tsp. salt

Soup:
10 cups lamb stock
4 cups cooked lamb, diced
1 cup chopped green onions
1 cup diced yellow onions (1/8" dice)
1 cup minced fresh dill
1-2 tsp. salt
Freshly ground black pepper
1/2 cup long-grain white rice
3–4 eggs
3/4–1 cup fresh lemon juice

Add all stock ingredients to a large pot, and bring to a boil. Reduce heat and simmer for 2–3 hours, until lamb meat is falling off bones. Strain stock into a large bowl through a fine-meshed strainer. Remove lamb from vegetables, and let cool. Discard vegetables. When lamb is cool enough to handle, separate meat from bones and fat, and discard them.

Dice lamb and reserve for soup. The recipe can be made ahead to this point, and stock and lamb refrigerated or frozen.

Let stock sit until fat rises to the top and remove as much of it as possible (this is easiest to do if stock is made ahead and refrigerated until fat solidifies).

Put defatted lamb stock in a large pot and bring to a boil. Add lamb, green onions, yellow onions, 3/4 cup minced dill, 1 tsp. salt, freshly ground black pepper, and rice. Reduce heat to low, and simmer soup until rice is tender.

Separate yolks and whites of 3 eggs, being careful not to get any yolk in with whites. Beat egg whites until stiff, but not dry, then whisk egg yolks into whites. Whisk 3/4 cup lemon juice into eggs. Temper eggs by whisking 1 cup of hot soup into egg lemon mixture. Make sure soup isn't boiling and is turned down as low as possible, and quickly stir tempered egg-lemon mixture into soup. Don't let soup boil, or eggs will curdle. Mix remaining dill into soup, and add lots of freshly ground black pepper. If soup isn't thick enough for your taste, whisk in another egg, prepared as described above. Taste and add salt, freshly ground black pepper, dill, or lemon juice, as needed. Serve immediately.

BEEF AND VEGETABLE SOUP WITH RHUBARB
Ciorba

Serves 12

Ciorba is a hearty meat and vegetable soup that is lightened on the palate by a tart rhubarb counterpoint. When tasters asked for thirds, I knew this recipe was a winner. Romanians love sour or tart soups, says Marianna Apetroeai, not only for the taste, but also because they're believed to be more nutritious. According to Marianna, acid in the souring agent helps release calcium from the bones into the soup, making it easier for the body to absorb calcium. In Romania, Marianna's mother made "bors" from fermented wheat bran to sour her Ciorba, but in Alaska, Marianna says rhubarb adds the perfect touch of tartness to her mother's recipe. Marianna freezes rhubarb every summer so she has some on hand during winter soup season. If rhubarb isn't available, lemon juice can be used instead. Marianna likes eating the meat and vegetables separately. First she sets her meat aside in a bowl, and eats only vegetables. Then she sprinkles minced fresh garlic over the meat and eats this as a second course. I prefer to serve the vegetables, meat, and garlic together for a hearty, satisfying meal.

4 pounds meaty oxtails or beef short ribs
1/4 cup olive oil
16 cups water
2 large yellow onions, cut in 1/8" dice
1 green pepper, cut in 1/8" dice
1 Tbsp. minced fresh garlic
3 carrots, peeled and cut in 1/8" dice
1 parsnip, peeled and cut in 1/8" dice
4 stalks celery, cut in 1/8" dice
1/2 celery root, peeled and cut in 1/8" dice
1 large bunch of fresh Italian parsley, leaves and stalks separately minced
1 Tbsp. salt
Freshly ground black pepper
1 tsp. Aleppo pepper or 1/2 tsp. crushed red pepper (optional)
1/2 pound fresh or frozen peas (optional)
1 cup rice or noodles or 2 cups diced potatoes, 1/8" dice (optional)
2–3 stalks rhubarb, cut in 1/8" dice or 1/4–1/2 cup fresh lemon juice
1–2 cloves of garlic per serving, minced
Sour cream

Wash and dry oxtails or short ribs. Salt and pepper meat and, using a large pot, brown all sides of meat in hot olive oil. Add water, and bring it to a boil, removing any scum that rises to surface. Cover pot, turn heat down to low, and simmer meat for 1 1/2–2 hours, or until meat is half done. Add onions, garlic, green pepper, carrots, parsnip, celery, celery root, minced parsley stalks (reserve parsley leaves for later), salt, lots of freshly ground black pepper, Aleppo pepper (if using), and continue to cook until meat is fully tender, approximately 1 1/2 hours (the time varies depending on the cut of meat used). The recipe can be made ahead to this point and chilled; doing so makes it easier to remove the thick layer of beef fat that renders from the meat as it cooks.

Remove as much fat as possible from soup's surface before continuing. If using peas or potatoes, add them 20 minutes before soup is done; if using noodles, cook them separately in salted boiling water and reserve for serving.

Three minutes before soup is ready to serve, add minced parsley leaves and diced rhubarb or 1/4 cup lemon juice. Taste and add salt, pepper, and rhubarb or lemon juice, as needed (soup is intended to be tart). Stir in noodles, if using.

To serve, fill bowls with vegetable soup, and stir a clove or two of minced garlic into each bowl (amount of garlic is based on personal taste). Add pieces of meat, top with a dollop of sour cream, and serve.

· PITES, BREAD, PASTA AND RICE ·

* New recipe this edition

A tiny grey-haired woman bent over a huge stainless steel bowl, her arms buried up to her elbows in Spanakopita filling. This is the picture Antonia Fiflis Fowler carries in her heart of her grandmother, Christine Karakitsios Fiflis.

Christine's life was filled with the stuff of family legend, starting with her birth in 1901 during a fierce storm in the mountains of Agios Vassilios, in the middle of the Peloponnesus. She was proud of her Spartan heritage, and liked to tell how one of her shepherd uncles waited for a lightning bolt to illuminate the cutting of her umbilical cord.

Christine's family emigrated to Dayton, Ohio in 1915 and built a successful restaurant named "The Philadelphia."

By Greek standards, Christine married late. She was already 26 years old and very picky about the men allowed to court her. Her parents promised she didn't have to marry a man she didn't want, and she wasn't interested in any man until James Fiflis showed up. She was immediately impressed by his "politeness and class," she said when telling the story. Christine withheld final judgment until James passed the "meatball test." At dinner, instead of shoving meatballs into his mouth whole, he cut the small rounds into halves. "The sign of a true gentleman," she declared.

Christine had seven children, marred by three miscarriages. After losing her third baby, she made a pact with God to dress her next child only in rags for five years if God let the new baby live. The new baby was Antonia's father, now a law professor in Colorado. He reports Christine, faithful to her pact, made his clothes out of coffee and sugar bags until he was old enough to go to school.

Over the years, Christine and James owned candy and ice cream parlors in Cicero and Berwyn, Illinois. The shops were always closed on Tuesdays. When customers questioned the closing, Antonia's uncle says they were told the store was closed because Tuesday is a bad luck day for Greeks. This is because the Turks conquered Constantinople on a Tuesday in 1453.

As the Fiflis family grew and prospered, so did Christine's legend. There's talk about prohibition and Al Capone who ran Cicero, where her uncle's restaurant was located down the street from a Capone gambling den. Christine worked as a cashier at the restaurant before her marriage, standing on a stool to stretch her 4-foot, 11-inch frame so she could reach the register. One day, as Christine stepped down from the stool to fetch a cigar, bullets crashed through the front window and into the wall behind where she had been standing. Just another day on the streets of Capone's Cicero.

When Antonia graduated from college, YiaYia (Grandma) Christine offered her any gift she wanted. Antonia's thoughts drifted back to the image of YiaYia in the kitchen, up to her elbows in Spanakopita. Knowing that YiaYia's special ingredient in everything she said and did was a healthy helping of love, Antonia decided essence of grandma was what she really wanted. So, without having to think twice, she asked for a batch of Spanakopita as her graduation present.

GRANDMA'S SPINACH PIE
YiaYia's Spanakopita

Serves 8–12

Lettuce in YiaYia Christine's Spanakopita makes her recipe unique and very good. One time Antonia's mother made the dish without lettuce, and never made that mistake again, as the sweetness of lettuce brings the other flavors together. The slight hint of cinnamon makes lettuce and spinach taste almost like wild greens. In Antonia's family, there is a debate over whether homemade filo should be rolled thick or thin. Christine always rolled filo tissue-thin, but her son (Antonia's dad) prefers a thicker crust. I tried the filo both ways. Because the filling is quite moist, I think a thicker crust is better suited to this version of Spanakopita. And, because it doesn't need to be rolled paper-thin, the filo is very easy to make. Using butter in filo isn't traditional, but helps the crust stand up to the filling. If you prefer making filo like YiaYia Christine, replace the butter with olive oil and roll out each half of the filo dough thin enough to cover a half-sheet pan. Spanakopita goes quickly, so I recommend doubling this recipe if you want leftovers—which, for me, are essential.

Filo:
2 1/2 cups all-purpose flour
1/4 tsp. salt
3 Tbsp. olive oil
2 Tbsp. butter, cold (or an additional 2 Tbsp. olive oil)
1/2 cup cold water

Filling:
1 1/2 lbs. cleaned spinach
1/2 head iceberg lettuce, roughly chopped
1/2 large bunch fresh Italian parsley, minced
1 bunch green onions, chopped
1/4 cup minced fresh mint
1 1/2 tsp. crushed fennel seeds
1/2 tsp. cinnamon
1 1/2 tsp. salt
1/4 tsp. freshly ground black pepper
1/4 cup long-grain rice
1/2 cup olive oil
1/4 pound fresh ricotta, preferably whole-milk
1/4 pound feta cheese, crumbled

Make filo: Mix flour and salt. Cut butter and olive oil into flour either in a food processor or with a fork. Add water and mix only until dough starts coming together. You may need to add 1–2 Tbsp. additional water. Divide dough in half, and form each half into a flat disk. Wrap each disk in plastic wrap, and set aside for at least one hour.

Make filling: In a very large bowl (I use a 16 quart stockpot when I make a double recipe) mix all filling ingredients. Mix filling with your hands to make sure spices, herbs, and rice are well distributed throughout filling. As you mix, liquid is released from spinach and lettuce, which later will be absorbed by rice.

Preheat oven to 375°F.

Roll out half the dough on a floured cloth until it's thin, round, and about 15" in diameter. Place rolled-out dough on a 14" diameter pizza pan (there should be at least one inch of dough overhanging edge of the pan), or if you want to make a free-form round, on baking sheet. Roll remaining dough to almost the same size. Spread filling over filo on the pan, leaving at least one inch of border, and cover with second sheet of rolled out filo. Seal edges of the two filo pieces by rolling edge of bottom piece over edge of top piece and crimping the two together. Cut cross in center of sealed Spanakopita, and brush filo with melted butter or olive oil. Bake at 350°F for 35–45 minutes, or until filo is crisp and golden. Cut into pieces and serve warm or at room temperature.

WILD GREENS PIE
Hortopita

8–12 servings

My favorite way to eat wild greens is in Hortopita. They have a stronger, richer flavor than supermarket greens and are magnificent when combined with cheese and herbs in a pie. Making Hortopita brings back happy memories of foraging for wild greens in Greek island vineyards, and sitting barefoot in the afternoon shade with my friends, cleaning our bounty while chatting about our lives and sharing village gossip. Although Hortopita can be made with store-bought filo, the more rustic and less delicate dough used in YiaYia's Spanakopita stands up better to wild greens and dramatically reduces the amount of butter used in the recipe. Dandelions and nettles are good in this recipe, as is a mixture of many different wild greens (see page 41). A combination of spinach, chard, and beet greens may be substituted for wild greens. Hortopita may be baked ahead, and when served with a Horiatiki Salata, crusty bread, and olives, is a vegetarian meal fit for the finest table.

Filo:
2 1/2 cups all-purpose flour
1/4 tsp. salt
3 Tbsp. olive oil
2 Tbsp. cold butter (or an additional 2 Tbsp. olive oil)
1/2 cup cold water

Filling:
2 pounds cleaned wild or other mixed greens
1/4 cup olive oil
3 cups diced yellow onions, 1/2" dice
Salt
Freshly ground black pepper
1 Tbsp. minced fresh garlic
1 cup minced fresh dill
2 cups chopped fresh Italian parsley
1 cup chopped green onions
1 pound fresh ricotta, preferably whole-milk
8 ounces crumbled feta cheese

Olive oil for brushing on crust

Make Filo: Mix flour and salt. Cut butter and olive oil into flour either in a food processor or with a fork. Add water and mix only until dough starts coming together. You may need to add 1–2 Tbsp. additional water. Divide dough in half, and form each half into a flat disk. Wrap each disk in plastic, and set aside for at least one hour.

Make Filling: Wash greens very carefully. Remove any tough or damaged stems, roots, flower buds, and leaves. Cook greens in boiling salted water for 2–4 minutes, or until they just wilt and start to become tender. The cooking time varies depending on type of green being used. If you're using a mixture of different greens, add tougher greens first, and tender greens only at the end of the cooking time. Drain greens well, squeeze out as much liquid as possible from them, and chop roughly.

Preheat oven to 400°F.

Sauté onions, lightly seasoned with salt and freshly ground black pepper, in olive oil until they begin to soften and turn golden. Add chopped greens and garlic to pan, and cook for an additional minute. Remove greens from heat, let cool slightly, and mix in dill, parsley, green onions, ricotta, and feta. Taste and add salt, pepper, or dill, as needed.

Assemble Pie: Roll out half the dough on a floured cloth until it's thin, round, and about 15" in diameter. Place rolled-out dough on a 14" diameter pizza pan (there should be at least one inch of dough overhanging edge of the pan), or if you want to make a free-form round, on baking sheet. Roll remaining dough to almost the same size. Spread filling over filo on pan, leaving at least one inch of border, and cover with second sheet of rolled out filo. Seal edges of two filo pieces by rolling edge of bottom piece over edge of top piece and crimping two together. Cut cross in center of sealed Hortopita, and brush filo with olive oil. Bake at 350°F for 35–45 minutes, or until filo is crisp and golden. Cut into pieces and serve warm or at room temperature.

ARMENIAN PIZZA
Lahmajoon

Makes 10–12 pizzas

Ankine Markossian grew up in an Armenian family living in pre-Gulf War Iraq. After the war, her mother and sisters moved to Lebanon. Despite living in Iraq, Ankine's family spoke Armenian at home (as she still does in Alaska), and her mother cooked mostly Armenian food. Lahmajoon is an Armenian specialty that Ankine ate as a child and now makes for her children, Taniel and Taline. Although Lahmajoon is traditionally made with fresh bread dough (and can be made using frozen bread or pizza dough), Ankine prefers making it with flour tortillas. Made this way, Lahmajoon is transformed into a delicious, but quick and easy, lunch or dinner. For even greater speed at mealtime, the meat mix can be made up to a day ahead. Red pepper is a traditional ingredient in Lahmajoon, and makes for a slightly more zesty pizza, although Ankine doesn't include it in her recipe. During Lent and other fasting periods, Ankine substitutes mushrooms for meat in her Lahmajoon.

1 pound ground beef
2 cups finely chopped tomatoes, liquid drained off in colander
1 cup minced yellow onions
1/2 cup minced green peppers
1 tsp. minced fresh garlic
2 Tbsp. tomato paste
1 tsp. salt
Freshly ground black pepper
1/2 tsp. allspice
1 tsp. Aleppo pepper or 1/2 tsp. crushed red pepper (optional)
1–2 tsp. dried mint
1 1/2 cups minced parsley
10–12 flour tortillas (8" size)

Preheat oven to 400°F. Place all ingredients except tortillas in bowl, and knead them with your hands. Spread 1/3 cup of meat mix thinly over each flour tortilla, and bake for 10 minutes. The tortilla should not get crispy. If meat isn't quite done after 10 minutes, put Lahmajoon under broiler for 1–2 minutes. To serve, fold tortilla in half and then into quarters.

Note: If you'd prefer to make your own crust, instead of using tortillas, use pizza dough or the preceding recipe for Palestinian Bread, and roll out dough very thinly. Place uncooked meat mix on top of uncooked bread dough. Then bake as set out above in the tortilla-based recipe.

OLIVE OIL FLATBREAD WITH TOMATO-ONION TOPPING
Ladenia

Serves 8–10 as an appetizer

Ladenia is a specialty of Kimolos, a tiny Greek island in the Aegean Sea; this recipe was adapted from Η Κουζίνα της Κιμώλου *(The Cuisine of Kimolos) by Filena Venardou. It's bread dough topped with fresh tomatoes, onions, and olive oil (from which it gets its name: "ladi" means "oil" in Greek), and baked until the edges are crunchy and the onions caramelized. Make with the best quality fresh tomatoes you can find. In Anchorage, Alaska, this means small, vine-ripened Campari tomatoes purchased at Costco and kept at room temperature until they're ripe, red, and juicy. If you like spicy food, sprinkle Aleppo or red pepper flakes over the tomatoes and onions before baking Ladenia. In order to prevent oil from running onto the oven floor, Ladenia must be baked in a pan with high sides, such as a round stainless steel baking pan with 1 1/2" sides or a bottom section of the 12" x 14" roaster/grill pan that comes with most American ovens.*

Dough:
1 cup warm water
2 1/4 tsp. dried yeast (1 packet)
1 tsp. salt
1/4 cup olive oil
2 3/4–3 1/4 cups all-purpose flour

Topping:
1 1/2 cups diced fresh tomatoes, 3/4" dice
1 1/2 cups thinly sliced onions
1/3 cup olive oil
1 tsp. salt
Freshly ground black pepper
2–3 tsp. dried oregano, crushed

Put warm water in large bowl and sprinkle with dried yeast. Let sit for 10 minutes while yeast begins working. Mix in salt and olive oil. Stir in smaller amount of flour, and add enough of remaining flour to form slightly sticky dough. Adding flour as necessary, knead dough until it is smooth, elastic, and no longer sticky. (Kneading dough in a stand mixer makes the task quick and easy.)

Spread 2 Tbsp. of olive oil over bottom of 15" round pan, or 12" x 14" roaster/grill pan. Make sure sides of pan are higher than dough will be after it rises and is covered by toppings.

Start stretching dough out with your hands, and then put it into pan. Press dough out until it fully covers pan's bottom. If some of olive oil oozes over dough, use it to lightly oil top of dough. Cover pan with dishcloth or plastic wrap and set it aside to rise in warm place until dough has doubled in size (about 1 hour).

Preheat oven to 400°F.

When dough has finished rising, use your fingertips to make little indentations all over it. Mix remaining olive oil, tomatoes, onions, salt, and freshly ground black pepper in bowl, and spread mix evenly over dough. Sprinkle with crushed oregano. Bake for 40–50 minutes, or until sides of Ladenia have browned and dough is cooked through.

Cut into pieces and serve warm, cold, or at room temperature.

GREEK VILLAGE BREAD
Psomi ap'to Horio

In the wheat-growing areas of Greece, farmers grind their crop at local mills to produce rustic, gold-colored flour. Bread made from this flour is slightly sweeter and has a grainier texture than bread made with America's gluten-rich flour. You can come close to replicating the taste of Greek village bread by mixing semolina and bread flours. Semolina provides flavor, and bread flour helps the bread rise and have good structure. This bread is wonderful fresh or toasted, and when it gets stale, works well as an ingredient in Fattoush or Skordalia.

2 3/4 cups warm water	2 Tbsp. olive oil
1 Tbsp. yeast	5 cups semolina flour
1 Tbsp. sugar	2–3 cups white bread flour
1 Tbsp. salt	

Place water in a large bowl. Sprinkle yeast over water, sprinkle sugar on top, and let sit for 10 minutes, or until yeast begins to foam. Using a standing mixer with paddle attachment (or by hand with a wooden spoon), mix in salt, olive oil, and semolina flour, and let sit for 10 minutes (this is necessary in order to properly hydrate the semolina). Start mixing in bread flour. When dough starts clumping together, switch to dough hook (or to kneading by hand), and keep adding bread flour until you have a moist, almost, but not quite, sticky dough. Flour a board or counter, and dump out dough, kneading in remaining flour as needed to make a smooth, soft dough that isn't sticky. Let dough rise for 1 hour, or until dough has doubled in size. Punch down dough, shape into 2 or 3 loaves (I like making 3 olive-shaped loaves or 2 long oval loaves), place on a parchment-paper lined baking sheet, and let rise until loaves have almost doubled.

Preheat oven to 475°F. Cut 3 diagonal slashes on each loaf with a razor blade or very sharp knife. Bake for 15 minutes. Without removing bread from oven, turn heat down to 275°F and bake for an additional 10–15 minutes, or until loaf sounds hollowed when tapped on bottom. Cool, cut, and serve.

GREEK EASTER BREAD, ALASKA STYLE
Tsoureki

Makes 2 loaves

Like classic Tsoureki, Alaska-Style Tsoureki is rich with butter and light with eggs. Mahlepi and mastiha, however, the flavors of classic Tsoureki, aren't available in Alaska. Instead, I've created a special spice mix to give wonderful flavor to Tsoureki in Alaska. When Alaska-style Tsoureki is in the oven, the entire house fills with the wonderful aroma of sweet spices. In Greece, Tsoureki is traditionally baked on Holy Thursday. It's not eaten until Easter because of the butter and eggs, which are prohibited during the pre-Easter fast.

Sponge:
1/2 cup warm water
2 packets dry yeast
1 Tbsp. sugar
1/2 cup all-purpose flour

Garnish:
2 Tbsp. milk
2 Tbsp. sesame seeds
Red eggs (optional)

Dough:
6 large eggs, room temperature
1 cup butter, softened
1 cup milk, warmed
1 tsp. salt
1 tsp. ground allspice
2 tsp. freshly ground coriander seeds
1 Tbsp. ground cinnamon
1 Tbsp. vanilla extract
1 Tbsp. vanilla extract
2 Tbsp. finely grated orange or lemon peel
6 1/2–7 cups all purpose flour

Make Sponge: Mix water, yeast, sugar, and flour. Let sit for 15 minutes, or until sponge begins to bubble.

Mix Dough: Mix sponge with eggs, butter, milk, salt, allspice, coriander, cinnamon, vanilla, and citrus peel just until sponge is incorporated into liquid. Don't try to smoothly mix in all the butter; there should be floating butter chunks when you're done mixing in the sponge. Stir in 6 cups of flour. Add remaining flour as necessary to form soft, slightly sticky dough. Put dough on floured surface and knead for 10 minutes, adding flour as necessary to prevent dough from sticking to your hands.

Place kneaded dough in lightly buttered bowl, cover tightly with plastic wrap, and then cover with dishtowel and let rise in a warm place for 1 1/2 hours or until doubled in size. Fold dough over on itself several times, cover, and again let rise for 1 1/2 hours or until doubled in size.

Shape and Bake Loaves: Preheat oven to 350°F.

Divide dough into 2 equal halves. Divide each half into thirds. To make long loaves: roll each third out into 18-inch ropes, braid the ropes, and tuck the ends under. To make ring-shaped loaves: roll each third out into 30 inch ropes, braid the ropes together, shape into a ring, and join the two ends together. Repeat with the remaining three ropes. Let loaves rise for 45 minutes, or until almost doubled in size.

Brush loaves with milk and sprinkle with sesame seeds. If using red eggs to decorate loaves, press eggs firmly into dough.

Bake for 30 to 35 minutes, until loaves are nicely browned and sound hollow when thumped on the bottom.

BAKED PASTA WITH MEAT SAUCE
Pastitsio
GREEK FESTIVAL RECIPE

Serves 12

At the Anchorage Greek Festival's dinner booth, many people don't bother trying to get their mouths around the name "Pastitsio," and ask instead for "that Greek lasagna stuff." No matter what you call it, Pastitsio is a mouth-watering treat. Subtle hints of cinnamon waft through meat-based tomato sauce, and rich, creamy béchamel topping contrasts nicely with hearty baked pasta. The pasta traditionally used for Pastitsio is spaghetti-length pasta tubes. If you can't find this special Pastitsio pasta, substitute small-sized penne or any other pasta with a hollow center. This dish is easy to make ahead and then bake just before serving.

Meat Sauce:
2 pounds ground beef or lamb
3 1/2–4 cups diced yellow onion, 1/4" dice
2 Tbsp. minced fresh garlic
1 5-ounce can tomato paste
1 1/2 cups red wine
1 tsp. salt
1 Tbsp. freshly ground black pepper
1 tsp. allspice
2 cinnamon sticks
1 Tbsp. dried, crushed oregano

Béchamel:
1/2 cup butter
1/2 cup all-purpose flour
5 cups whole milk
4 egg yolks
1/2 tsp. ground nutmeg
Salt
1 tsp. freshly ground white pepper

Pasta:
1 1/2 lbs. Pastitsio pasta, small penne, or other hollow pasta
2 cups grated kefalotyri, kasseri or parmesan cheese
1/4 tsp. ground cinnamon

Meat Sauce: Brown meat, lightly seasoned with salt and freshly ground black pepper, in a large pot. Add onions and continue browning. When onions have softened and begun to turn golden, add garlic and cook for 1 minute. Stir in tomato paste, wine, salt, pepper, cinnamon sticks, oregano, and allspice, and cook for one hour, until sauce is thick and rich. Taste and add salt, pepper, cinnamon, or oregano, as needed.

Béchamel: While meat sauce is cooking, make béchamel. Warm milk over low heat or in microwave; don't bring milk to a boil. Melt butter in a large saucepan, thoroughly mix in flour and cook for two minutes, stirring constantly. Slowly stir in warm milk and cook, stirring, until sauce is smooth and the thickness of heavy cream. Add nutmeg, salt and white pepper to taste. Quickly whisk one cup of hot milk sauce into egg yolks, and stir this mixture back into sauce. Cook over very low heat for two minutes, stirring constantly, and being careful not to let sauce get hotter than a low simmer. Remove sauce from heat and whisk in 1 cup grated cheese. Taste and add salt, pepper, or nutmeg, as needed. Cool.

Pasta: Bring a large pot of salted water to a boil, and cook pasta until it's al dente (the length of cooking time depends on size of pasta). Drain pasta in a colander. Mix pasta with one cup of béchamel.

Assemble Pastitsio: Preheat oven to 375°F. Place half pasta in bottom of a well oiled 9"x13" baking pan. Sprinkle pasta with 1/3 cup cheese and spread meat sauce evenly over cheese. Top with remaining pasta and 1/3 cup cheese. Spread remaining béchamel over pasta. Mix 1/3 cup cheese with cinnamon, and sprinkle over béchamel. Bake at 375°F for 20 minutes. Reduce heat to 350°F and cook for 40–45 minutes or until top of Pastitsio is golden and set. Let cool for at least 10–15 minutes before cutting into squares and serving. Don't try to cut Pastitsio immediately after removing it from the oven.

SPINACH AND RICE
Spanakorizo

Serves 4

In years past, during the Anchorage Greek Festival, Spiro Bellas slaved away in the kitchen, cooking an array of delicious dishes to serve at the dinner booth. Spiro was very particular about how he ran his kitchen, as am I, which resulted in a lot of friendly banter about the correct way to do things. A joke at Holy Transfiguration is that if there are three parishioners in a room, you're bound to hear five different opinions. So it is with Spanakorizo.

Spiro is the primary source of this recipe, but he makes it by first cooking onions, then putting spinach, rice and water on top, and using only mint for seasoning. He is adamant the dish should not be stirred until the rice is done. On the other hand, I prefer using a more traditional method of cooking pilaf that I steadfastly believe distributes flavors more evenly. I also like the flavor of dill and parsley in Spanakorizo, and think garlic greatly enhances the dish. Although this recipe uses my method and favored ingredients, spinach and rice combine beautifully, no matter the technique you follow.

1 pound cleaned spinach
1/4 cup olive oil
2 1/2 cups diced yellow onion, 1/4" dice
Freshly ground black pepper
1/2 cup long-grain rice
2 tsp. minced fresh garlic
1/2 cup minced dill
1/2 cup minced fresh Italian parsley
3 Tbsp. tomato paste
3/4 cup water
1/2 tsp. salt
Lemon wedges

Roughly chop spinach. Sauté onion, lightly seasoned with salt and freshly ground black pepper, in olive oil until it begins to turn golden. Stir in rice, and continue to sauté for 1 minute. Mix in garlic, 1/3 cup dill, 1/3 cup parsley, chopped spinach, tomato paste, water, 1/2 tsp. salt, and freshly ground black pepper. Cook, stirring, until spinach wilts. Cover, and turn heat down as low as possible. Cook for 15–20 minutes, or until rice is tender. Stir in remaining dill and parsley, and serve with lemon wedges for squeezing over Spanakorizo.

BOILED POLENTA
Mamaliga

Serves 4

Corn in Romania is different than in the United States, according to Marianna Apetroeai. She has never seen corn eaten as a vegetable there. Instead, Romanians dry corn, grind it into meal, and use it to make Mamaliga, which many call the national dish of Romania. Mamaliga is served countless different ways: boiled as a side dish, or as a snack, or grilled, or as a substitute for bread. Leftover Mamaliga can be warmed up in the microwave, or eaten with hot milk. Marianna insists Mamaliga is "light, not heavy on the stomach." One of Marianna's favorite ways to eat Mamaliga is in Tochitura, a traditional Romanian dish made by sprinkling feta cheese on a plate, spreading hot Mamaliga over the cheese, and topping with fried sausages, or small pieces of fried pork steak, and fried eggs. Marianna says it's essential to serve red wine with Tochitura. Even if you aren't ready for a plate of Tochitura, Mamaliga is a flavorful accompaniment to most meat dishes, served in lieu of potatoes.

4 cups water
2 tsp. salt
1 1/3 cups medium grind cornmeal

Bring water to a boil. Stir salt into boiling water. Turn heat down to medium and slowly pour cornmeal into water while stirring constantly. If you don't pour cornmeal slowly, lumps form in the Mamaliga. Adjust heat so Mamaliga is slowly bubbling, and cook for approximately 30 minutes, stirring the entire time so Mamaliga doesn't stick to the bottom of the pan. Serve immediately.

Note: Mamaliga is also good with crumbled feta cheese or grated parmesan cheese stirred in just before serving.

To grill, pour cooked Mamaliga into a bread pan and refrigerate. Once Mamaliga solidifies, remove it from pan and slice with a very sharp knife or with a taut piece dental floss. Brush with olive oil and grill.

· SEAFOOD ·

* New recipe this edition

Nawal Bekheet spent her early years in one of the biggest cities in the world—Cairo, population seven million, with another three million coming into the city to work during the day. She recalls concrete buildings 30 stories high, and rooftop apartments resembling magnificent villas with beautifully landscaped gardens.

Like so many Holy Transfiguration parishioners from faraway lands, Nawal's memories of childhood are scarred by war. In 1956, Great Britain, France, and Israel invaded Egypt in an attempt to depose President Gamal Abd al-Nasser and seize the Suez Canal. Nawal was 14, and planes came to bomb the town of Isma'iliya, where her family had moved. Nawal remembers being evacuated, "packed like bugs" on a train. The train in front of hers got bombed. The train behind hers got bombed. Nawal's got through.

After the United Nations intervened and imposed a ceasefire, life in Egypt returned to normal. Soon Nawal married and started a family with Kamal Bebawy, an engineer for the Egyptian Agriculture Ministry, who worked on big construction projects around the Middle East.

While the family was in Saudi Arabia for a project, Nawal's 18-year-old daughter, Huda, fell in love with an American pilot from Alabama, married him in 1989, and moved to America. Nawal and her husband, who had just retired, moved to Alabama with her daughter's new family, and later followed them to Alaska.

All these years later, still far from home, Nawal's food retains the exciting flavors of Egypt. She associates dishes with specific cities, like Cairo's Samaka Hara'aka (spicy fish), Alexandrian Kebdah Eskandaranie (liver and peppers), and the Dawood Pasha (meatballs and onions) of Asyut. Nawal's recipes, which she can recite in precise detail, are spiced perfectly and balanced with interesting flavors.

EGYPTIAN SPICY BAKED FISH
Samaka Hara'aka

Serves 4–6

Nawal Bekheet's Egyptian recipe for Samaka Hara'aka is one of my favorites in this book. The many individual ingredients come together to form a unique mouth-watering whole. When I eat this dish, all of my taste buds sing—citrus and peppers are wonderfully stimulating, while herbs and vegetables add a variety of bright flavors. To make Samaka Hara'aka in Alaska, Nawal recommends using white-fleshed fish, such as halibut, cod, or rockfish. Nawal prefers making the dish with fillets because they're easier to serve, while daughter Huda prefers whole fish so she can suck good flavor from the bones. The recipe calls for jalapeños, but Nawal says it can be made with any other fresh hot pepper, the hotter the better. Be sure to follow Nawal's recommendation and serve this with refreshing Egyptian Rice with Dill (page 99).

Topping/Filling:
3 cups diced yellow onion, 1/8" dice
1/4 cup olive oil
Salt
Freshly ground black pepper
2 Tbsp. minced fresh garlic
4 jalapenos, minced
1/2 cup diced green pepper, 1/8" dice
1 cup diced fresh tomato, 1/8" dice
12 stalks fresh cilantro, minced
12 stalks fresh Italian parsley, minced
12 stalks fresh dill, minced

Seasoning Mix:
2 tsp. ground cumin
1/2 tsp. ground allspice
1/2 tsp. ground nutmeg
2 tsp. salt

Fish:
2 1/2 lbs. skinless halibut or rockfish
   fillets or 4-lb. whole rockfish
Olive oil
5–6 cloves garlic, thinly sliced
2 small yellow onions, thinly sliced
3 limes, thinly sliced
4 medium tomatoes, sliced

Topping/Filling: Sauté onion, lightly seasoned with salt and freshly ground black pepper, in olive oil. When onion turns golden, stir in garlic and jalapeños. Sauté for 1 minute, add green pepper and tomatoes, and cook until juices from tomatoes start to evaporate. Remove from heat, add minced herbs, and season to taste with salt and pepper. Set aside to use as topping for fillets or filling for whole fish.

Seasoning Mix: Mix cumin, allspice, nutmeg, and 2 tsp. salt.

Preheat oven to 350°F.

If Using Fillets: Wash fish and dry it well. Rub seasoning mix into both sides of skinned fillets. Coat baking pan (large enough to hold fish in a single layer) with olive oil. Place seasoned fillets in pan, and drizzle with olive oil. Spread Topping/Filling evenly over fillets. Sprinkle with thinly sliced garlic, and top with onion slices, then lime slices, then tomato slices. Drizzle a little olive oil over tomatoes. Place fillets in oven for 10 minutes. Turn heat down to 250°F, cover pan with foil, and cook for 20 minutes. Turn heat back up to 350°F, remove foil, and cook an additional 5–10 minutes, or until fillets are done.

If Using Whole Fish: Clean, scale, and remove head. Enlarge belly opening so fish is slit all the way down to the tail. Cut 3/8" deep slashes every 1 1/2" on each side of fish. Rub seasoning mix all over fish, including in slashes and inside stomach opening. Coat baking pan (large enough to hold fish) with olive oil, place fish in pan, and drizzle it with olive oil. Place Topping/Filling inside opening and in slashes. Sprinkle with thinly sliced garlic, and top with onion slices, then lime slices, then tomato slices. Drizzle a little olive oil over tomatoes. Place fish in oven for 15 minutes. Turn heat down to 250°F, cover pan with foil, and cook 30 minutes. Turn heat back up to 350°F,, remove foil, and cook for an additional 15 minutes, or until fish is done.

Whether you're using fillets or whole fish, make sure not to undercook fish. Because heat is so low it takes longer to cook than you might think. When fish is done, remove it from pan to a serving dish, with all its toppings intact. Then pour liquid left in pan over fish. Serve immediately.

LEBANESE SPICY BAKED FISH
Samke Harrah

Serves 4

Aram Markossian remembers Sunday afternoons in Beirut, sitting in crowded restaurants specializing in Samke Harrah, eating the best fish in the world. His mother Marie recalls a cooking class in Beirut, where she learned to make this tasty dish. The recipe is a Lebanese version of Egyptian Spicy Baked Fish (see preceding recipe). Although they have many similarities, the two dishes are different enough to make it worth trying both. In Marie's original recipe, the fish and lemons were wrapped in aluminum foil and baked in a water bath to cook the fish at a low, even temperature. I modified Marie's recipe and accomplished the same result by baking the halibut in a tightly closed packet and very low oven. The result is moist and tender halibut enrobed with a flavorful, but not overwhelmingly spicy, sauce. Samke Harrah is good right out of the oven, or served cold, which makes it ideal for a buffet. It's also good with rockfish, either whole or in fillets.

Fish:
2 1/4 pounds skinless halibut fillets
Salt
Freshly ground black pepper
3 lemons
6 bay leaves
3/4 cup olive oil

Sauce:
1 1/2 cups diced yellow onion, 1/8" dice
1/3 cup olive oil
2 Tbsp. minced fresh garlic
1/3 cup minced jalapeños
2 cups diced fresh tomatoes, 1/8" dice
1/2 cup chopped cilantro
2 tsp. salt
2 tsp. cumin seeds, crushed
1/3 cup fresh lemon juice

Preheat oven to 250°F.

Wash fish and dry it well. Season it on both sides with salt and plenty of freshly ground black pepper. Slice lemon into 1/4" slices. Cut two pieces of aluminum foil, each 10" longer than fish. On baking sheet, place one piece of foil. Lay out a rectangle of lemon slices the same size as fish on the foil. Place seasoned fish on rectangle of lemons, and arrange bay leaves on top of fish. Cover fish with a layer of lemon slices. Fold up edges of foil, and drizzle olive oil over everything. Use remaining foil to cover fish, and seal edges of foil to make a tightly sealed packet. Bake for 50–70 minutes, depending on thickness of fillets, checking fish by opening packet after 50 minutes to see if it's done. If not, reseal and return to oven.

Sauté onions, lightly seasoned with salt and freshly ground black pepper, in olive oil. When onions turn golden, stir in garlic and jalapeños. Sauté for 1 minute, then add tomatoes, cilantro, salt, and cumin, and let sauce bubble for 15 minutes. Stir in lemon juice and set aside until fish is done.

If you're serving fish hot, remove bay leaves and lemon slices and put fish on a plate. Put warm sauce on top of fish, and use cooked lemons as a garnish around edges of plate. If you serve fish cold, refrigerate fish, lemon slices, and sauce separately, and arrange plate just before serving.

Note: Because fish cooks at such a low temperature, its flavor doesn't permeate the olive oil, which can be reused. I use a fat separator to divide fish juices from lemon-scented oil, and store the oil in the refrigerator. I also save the incredibly good fish juices to use as a replacement for water or stock in seafood recipes.

GRILLED HALIBUT CHERMOULA

Serves 4–6

Chermoula is one of the classic sauces of Morocco. Its complex, distinct and spicy flavors combine flawlessly with the mild smoky taste of grilled halibut, but Chermoula also goes well with grilled salmon or chicken. The fresh parsley and cilantro in Chermoula set off the deep richness of Moroccan spices. It's hard for me to get enough Chermoula—I try to make sure there is leftover Chermoula and halibut, so I can make a splendid halibut salad the next day. This is done by breaking the cooked halibut into pieces, and thoroughly mixing it with a little mayonnaise and as much leftover Chermoula as you like. Pair Halibut Chermoula with couscous and a fresh vegetable salad.

Chermoula:
2/3 cup chopped fresh parsley
1/3 cup chopped fresh cilantro
1 1/2 Tbsp. chopped fresh garlic
1 tsp. paprika
1 tsp. freshly ground cumin
1/4 tsp. cayenne
1/3 cup fresh lemon juice
1/3 cup olive oil
1 tsp. kosher salt or 1/2 tsp. table salt

Fish:
1 1/2–2 pounds skinless halibut or rockfish fillets
Salt
Freshly ground black pepper
2 Tbsp. olive oil

To make sauce: Place all ingredients into a food processor or blender and puree until very smooth. The sauce can be made ahead and stored in the refrigerator, but should be brought to room temperature before serving.

Wash and dry fish, and remove any bones from the fillets. Cut fish into 4–6 equal-sized pieces and season on both sides with salt and freshly ground black pepper. Just before placing fish on grill, rub both sides of each piece with olive oil to prevent them from sticking to grill. Using either an outside grill or a cast-iron grill pan on stove, grill fish on each side for 3–5 minutes, depending on thickness of fillets (don't overcook or fish will be dry). To serve, place a piece of grilled fish on each plate and pour sauce over or next to fish.

HALIBUT WITH ONIONS, PINE NUTS AND TAHINI SAUCE
Samaka Tarator

Serves 4–6

Salwa Abuamsha usually serves her tahini sauce with falafel, but it also goes perfectly with baked fish. The sauce is bright with the flavors of lemon and garlic, but these harmonize with the fish rather than overwhelming it. The rich taste of caramelized onions and the freshness of uncooked parsley add mouth-watering layers of flavor. Although the recipe works well with any white-fleshed fish, I prefer using halibut. You'll end up with more tahini sauce than is needed for the recipe, but the sauce keeps well in the refrigerator and makes an excellent dip for raw vegetables.

Tahini Sauce:
1 cup raw tahini (sesame seed paste)
1 cup fresh lemon juice
8 cloves garlic, minced
2 tsp. salt

2 pounds skinless halibut or rockfish fillets
3 cups thinly sliced yellow onions
1/2 cup olive oil
Salt
Freshly ground black pepper
1/4 cup pine nuts
1/4 cup minced fresh Italian parsley

Make Sauce: Whisk together tahini and lemon juice. Either use a garlic press for garlic, or puree it with salt in a mortar and pestle. The sauce should be the consistency of ranch-style salad dressing. If sauce is too thick, thin it with water or additional lemon juice.

Make Fish: Preheat oven to 450°F. Wash and dry fillets, and cut them into serving-sized pieces. Salt and pepper fish on both sides. Sauté onions, lightly seasoned with salt and pepper, in 6 Tbsp. of olive oil over medium heat for 25–35 minutes until they're soft and slightly caramelized. Add pine nuts, and cook for 2–3 minutes, being careful not to let pine nuts burn. Remove mixture from heat and set aside.

Heat 1 Tbsp. olive oil in ovenproof frying pan over medium-high heat, and add fish pieces in a single layer. Fry fish pieces for 2 minutes, turn over, spread a 1/4" layer of tahini sauce over each piece, and top with onion mixture. (If fish doesn't fit in frying pan in a single layer, brown it on both sides in batches, place pieces in oiled baking pan, and top with tahini sauce, onions, and pine nuts). Bake fish for 7–12 minutes, depending on thickness of fillets. When fish is done, put it on plates, and sprinkle with minced parsley.

HALIBUT AND POTATO STEW
Bianco

Serves 4–6

When Carol Gialopsos married her husband Andy, she had never eaten or cooked Greek food. Since Andy didn't cook, but still wanted to eat foods of his native Corfu, Carol became an adept Greek cook. Even while raising a family and running Romano's, their Anchorage restaurant, Carol and Andy took regular trips to Greece. Carol learned to cook Greek food by watching village women. She noticed that every woman cooked the same dishes, but in a slightly different way, each adding her own touch. Bianco is a classic fish dish Carol learned on Corfu and this is adapted from her recipe. Because Bianco's flavors are subtle and mild, fish must be of the highest quality. I made it with the first halibut of the season. The fish was moist and flavorful, and paired well with potatoes. The recipe includes a whole head of garlic, but the resulting dish has mild flavors because the garlic is braised in water. Bianco is a soupy dish, and is best served in a bowl, accompanied by chunks of crusty bread and a salad dressed simply with olive oil and lemon juice.

2 pounds skinless halibut fillets
1 head of garlic
2 pounds potatoes, white or Yukon gold
1/4 cup olive oil
Salt
Freshly ground black pepper
Lemon wedges

Wash halibut fillets and dry them well. Cut fillets into serving size chunks, and lightly season with salt and freshly ground black pepper.

Separate cloves of garlic, peel them, and cut into thin slices. Peel potatoes and cut them into 1 1/2" chunks. In a large pot, sauté potatoes, seasoned well with salt and freshly ground black pepper, in olive oil over medium-high heat until they're nicely browned on all sides. Turn heat down to medium and mix in sliced garlic. Add water to half cover potatoes. Bring liquid to a boil, cover, turn heat down to low, and simmer until liquid has thickened and potatoes are done.

Lay fish pieces on top of potatoes, and push pieces down into sauce to the extent you're able without breaking them. Put thinner pieces of fish on top. Don't stir fish. Cook covered about 5 minutes or until fish is done (be careful not to overcook fish). When done, heavily season with freshly ground black pepper and serve with plenty of lemon wedges to squeeze over Bianco.

FRIED COD WITH GARLIC SAUCE
Bakaliaros Tiganitos me Skordalia

Serves 4–6

Fried salt cod served with Skordalia is very popular in Greece, but the time it takes to make salted fish edible doesn't fit well with a busy life in Alaska. By substituting fresh cod, a complicated recipe turns into one that is quick and easy to prepare. Skordalia can be made days in advance, as its flavor improves over time. Although this recipe tastes great with any fresh white-fleshed fish, cod and rockfish are much better than halibut for frying because they retain their moisture better. Spices in the coating are subtle and don't overwhelm the delicate fish, and fresh lemon peel's bright taste brings out the flavor of cod. Garnish the finished dish with sprigs of fresh parsley and wedges of lemon.

Fish:
2 pounds fresh cod or rockfish fillets
1/2 cup semolina flour
2 tsp. allspice
1 tsp. cinnamon
3 Tbsp. freshly grated lemon peel
Salt
Freshly ground black pepper
Skordalia (page 22)
Oil for frying
Fresh Italian parsley sprigs
Lemon wedges

Wash and dry cod and cut into 2" square pieces. Mix semolina flour, allspice, cinnamon, lemon peel, salt, and freshly ground black pepper. Coat fish chunks in seasoned flour by shaking them together in a bag, and then shaking off any excess flour. Heat olive oil in a frying pan until it's hot, but not smoking. Fry fish in hot oil for 2–3 minutes on each side, until it's browned and crispy. Don't overcook. Remove fish to paper towels. Serve fried cod with a dollop of Skordalia on top of each piece of fish, or on the side.

SALMON IN GRAPE LEAVES WITH CAPER-LEMON SAUCE
Solomos se Ambelofilla me Kapari Latholemono

Serves 6

Just thinking about red mullet or sardines wrapped in grape leaves and grilled over a charcoal fire in a seaside Greek taverna makes my mouth water. Grilling improves and softens the flavor of grape leaves, and the smokiness of the grilled leaves marries well with any oily fish. In this recipe, salmon is cut into narrow strips to replicate the size of smaller Greek fish we can't get in Alaska. When cooked in grape leaves, salmon stays moist and tender. Be sure to eat grape leaves and salmon together, and don't stint on caper-lemon sauce. Sauce and salmon packets can be prepared early in the day, and grilled just before serving.

Sauce:
1/2 cup fresh lemon juice
1 cup olive oil
1/3 cup salted capers, or capers in brine
Salt
Freshly ground black pepper

Fish:
2 pounds skinless salmon fillets
Salt
Freshly ground black pepper
Olive oil
24 grape leaves

Sauce: Carefully rinse all salt or brine off capers, and chop them roughly. Whisk olive oil slowly into lemon juice, and whisk in capers. Season with salt and freshly ground black pepper to taste (be sure to taste for salt before adding if you used salted capers).

Fish: Wash salmon and dry it well. Using needle-nose pliers, remove as many pin-bones from salmon as possible. Cut fillets crosswise into 12 even strips, approximately 1 1/2" wide. Lightly season salmon on both sides with salt and freshly ground black pepper, and coat fish strips with olive oil.

Rinse grape leaves well, and cut off tough stems. Spread a grape leaf out flat, with shiny side down. Overlap this leaf with a second shiny-side-down grape leaf, with stem ends facing each other in center. Put a salmon strip on center of overlapping grape leaves. Fold sides of grape leaves towards center and over ends of fish strips, and then roll salmon up in grape leaves. Repeat until all strips have been rolled, and coat salmon-filled grape leaves with olive oil.

Grill salmon-filled grape leaves over a medium fire, or in a hot grill pan on top of stove, for 3–4 minutes on each side. Be careful not to overcook fish. Drizzle with sauce, and serve immediately.

GARLIC-CRUSTED SALMON WITH EGGPLANT SAUCE
Solomos me Skordalia kai Melitzanes

Serves 4–6

One day when there was nothing but leftover stewed eggplant and baked salmon in the refrigerator, I cooked the two together and discovered they have very compatible flavors. I couldn't quit thinking about the combination, and developed this dish to elaborate on the flavors of my serendipitous discovery. Walnut-based garlic sauce, typical of northern Greece, has more parsley than is normally found in such dishes, but the extra parsley is important to balance the richness of salmon. Feta cheese and olives go well with this dish.

Sauce:
2 cups diced yellow onions, 1/4" dice
1/2 cup olive oil
Salt
Freshly ground black pepper
2 cups diced eggplant, 1/2" dice
1 tsp. minced fresh garlic
1/2 tsp. Aleppo pepper or
   1/4 tsp. crushed red pepper
1 14.5-ounce can crushed tomatoes
1/4 cup minced fresh Italian parsley
2 Tbsp. minced fresh dill

Skordalia:
1 cup chopped walnuts
4–6 cloves garlic, chopped
1 cup chopped parsley
Salt
Freshly ground black pepper
1/2–2/3 cup olive oil
2 pounds skinless salmon fillets

Sauce: Sauté onions, lightly seasoned with salt and freshly ground black pepper, in 2 Tbsp. olive oil until they just start to brown. Remove onions from pan. Add remaining 2 Tbsp. olive oil, and sauté eggplant, lightly seasoned with salt and freshly ground black pepper, letting it char a little as it cooks, for 5–8 minutes or until eggplant is done. Stir cooked onions, garlic, Aleppo pepper, and tomatoes into eggplant, and cook until mixture forms a thick sauce. Stir in parsley and dill.

Skordalia: Puree walnuts, 4 cloves garlic, parsley, salt and freshly ground black pepper in a food processor. Add 1/2 cup olive oil, and puree Skordalia again. Taste and add remaining garlic, salt, or pepper, as needed, pureeing after each addition. Skordalia should be a thick, but spreadable paste. If it's too thick, add remaining olive oil.

Preheat oven to 350°F.

Fish: Wash salmon and dry it well. Using needle-nosed pliers, remove as many pin-bones from salmon as possible. Cut salmon into serving-sized pieces. Lightly season salmon on both sides with salt and freshly ground black pepper.

Spread eggplant sauce in bottom of oiled baking dish large enough to hold salmon in a single layer. Evenly pat Skordalia over salmon, and set salmon on top of eggplant sauce. Bake at 350 for 6–12 minutes (depending on thickness of salmon) until salmon is just done. Be careful not to overcook. Before serving, broil salmon briefly until Skordalia crust is bubbly. Serve immediately.

SALMON PASTITSIO SAUCE FOR PASTA
Makaronada me Saltsa Solomos Pastitsio

Serves 4

Harriet Anagnostis Drummond grew up in the Bronx, New York. Her paternal grandparents were immigrants from Limnos, a Greek island in the Northern Aegean Sea. In the United States, they farmed a 10-acre truck garden on Staten Island and sold vegetables in New York City. Harriet's father, Anthony, ran a neighborhood grocery store in Harlem. In 1951, he wed Harriet's mother Emilie, a young woman from Athens. Harriet grew up speaking Greek; she learned English only after she went to kindergarten. At home, her family ate traditional Greek food. When Harriet married and had children of her own, she also cooked Greek food, including Pastitsio, baked pasta with meat sauce, a dish Harriet had often enjoyed at her mother's table. After Harriet moved to Alaska, she was waiting in the supermarket line looking at a cookbook and saw a recipe for Salmon Pastitsio. She didn't think much of the recipe, but was inspired by the idea of using salmon in Pastitsio. After several consultations with her mother, Harriet developed a Salmon Pastitsio recipe that her family loves and insists she make regularly. Because the sauce, pasta, and topping are made separately, and then must be baked together, Salmon Pastitsio takes a couple hours to make. I wanted to capture the delicious

Anthony Anagnostis with employees in his 1950s Harlem grocery store. Canned goods include Icy Point Salmon, Del Monte Alaskan Sockeye Salmon, and Valley Stream Alaska Salmon.

flavors of Harriet's Salmon Pastitsio, but in a dish that could be put together quickly on a busy work night. Instead of baking the sauce and pasta together, this recipe pairs Harriet's rich, flavorful sauce, redolent with cinnamon and oregano, with pan-fried salmon, and uses them as a topping for pasta. It has all the flavor of Harriet's original dish with half the work. Leftover grilled or roast salmon may be substituted for pan-fried salmon. See Note below for details on turning Salmon Pastitsio Sauce into Harriet's Salmon Pastitsio.

Pan-fried Salmon:
8-ounce skinless salmon fillet
Salt
Freshly ground black pepper
1 Tbsp. olive oil

Sauce:

2 cups diced yellow onion, 1/4" dice
2 Tbsp. olive oil
1 Tbsp. minced garlic
1/2 tsp. Aleppo pepper or 1/4 tsp. crushed red pepper (optional)
1/2 cup dry white wine
1 15-ounce can crushed tomatoes, preferably fire-roasted
1/2 tsp. ground cinnamon
1 tsp. dried oregano, crushed

3/4–1 pound spaghetti or other dried pasta

Pan-fried Salmon: Wash salmon and dry it well. Using needle-nosed pliers, remove as many pin-bones from salmon as possible. Cut fillet into 4 even-sized pieces. Season salmon with salt and freshly ground black pepper. Heat olive oil in heavy skillet over medium-high heat until it's hot, but not smoking. Add salmon and cook for 2 minutes. Turn over and cook for 1-3 minutes, or until salmon is slightly underdone. The exact cooking time depends on the fillets' thickness. Let cool while sauce cooks, then cut into 3/4" pieces.

Sauce: Sauté onions, lightly seasoned with salt and freshly ground black pepper, in olive oil until they start to turn golden. Stir in garlic and Aleppo pepper and cook for 1 minute. Stir in wine, bring to a boil, and cook until reduced by half. Stir in crushed tomatoes, cinnamon, and oregano. Bring to a boil, turn heat down to low, and simmer for 10-15 minutes or until flavors have blended. Gently stir in salmon pieces and simmer for 5 minutes. Taste and add salt or pepper, as needed.

Pasta: While sauce is simmering, bring a large pot of salted water to a rolling boil. Cook until it's al dente. Drain pasta, reserving 1/2 cup of pasta cooking water. Gently combine pasta and sauce. If finished dish seems too dry, add reserved pasta cooking water, as needed.

NOTE: To make Salmon Pastitsio, preheat oven to 350°F. Oil 9"x13" pan and sprinkle bottom and sides with 2 Tbsp. breadcrumbs. Cook 3/4-pound penne pasta until it's al dente. Drain and rinse. Whisk together 3 eggs and 2 cups milk. Put half the pasta in prepared baking pan. Top with 1/2 cup grated Parmesan cheese. Top with remaining pasta. Pour egg-milk mixture over pasta, poking holes through pasta so egg-milk mixture permeates dish. Top with 1/2 cup grated Parmesan cheese. Bake for 45 minutes. Being a practical woman and grocer's child, Harriet makes Salmon Pastitsio with pantry staples—canned salmon and powdered milk— and swears by its flavor. To substitute canned salmon for the fresh used above, Harriet says to add one 14.75-ounce can, bones, skin, water and all.

GRILLED SALMON WITH GARLIC-LEMON SAUCE
Solomos me Skordo kai Lemoni

Serves 6–8

In the true spirit of Greek hospitality, when I went to John Maroulis' house to talk about cooking, the first thing he did was start pulling food out of the refrigerator for me to try. Among the dishes to emerge was Grilled Salmon with Garlic-Lemon Sauce that John had made the night before. It was so good the only comment I made in my notes was "YUM YUM" written in large letters. The garlic in the sauce isn't overwhelming, and is suffused with a deep lemon flavor that goes flawlessly with grilled salmon. And, as I discovered at John's house, the leftovers are great.

Fish:
3 pounds salmon fillets, skin on
2 tsp. dried oregano, crushed
Salt
Freshly ground black pepper
1/4 cup fresh lemon juice
1/4 cup olive oil

Sauce:
7 large cloves garlic, thinly sliced
6 Tbsp. water
6 Tbsp. fresh lemon juice
1/2 cup olive oil

Wash salmon and dry it well. Using needle-nosed pliers, remove as many pin-bones from salmon as possible. Cut fillets into 6–8 even-sized pieces. Season salmon with oregano, salt, and freshly ground black pepper.

Prepare grill. Just before putting fish on grill, drizzle with fresh lemon juice (if you add lemon juice earlier, it starts to "cook" the salmon flesh). Pour olive oil over salmon, and make sure it's well coated on both sides.

While you're waiting for grill to be ready, put thinly sliced garlic cloves, water, fresh lemon juice, and olive oil in a saucepan. Bring this mixture to a boil over medium-high heat, and let bubble until sauce has thickened and water has boiled off. Turn off heat.

Grill fish over a medium hot fire until done. Don't overcook salmon, which tastes much better slightly underdone than slightly overdone. Remove salmon skin before serving. Reheat lemon-garlic sauce, if necessary. Pour sauce over cooked salmon, making sure that each piece of salmon has some of garlic pieces. Serve immediately.

SALMON MARINATED IN LEMON AND PARSLEY
Solomos me Lemoni kai Maidano

Serves 4–6

Many lucky Alaskans end summer with a freezer full of salmon for winter use. After several months in the freezer, salmon's flavor becomes heavier and less pleasing. Maria Baskous noticed that when defrosted salmon is marinated overnight in lots of parsley, its flavor is fresh, clean-tasting, and lightly herb-scented. After initial success with four-month-old fish, I decided to try Maria's recipe with a packet of salmon that had been hiding in the freezer for two years. Even the ancient fish was shockingly good. Fresh lemon juice in the marinade partially "cooks" salmon, so the actual cooking time is extremely short. Serve with garlic potatoes (boiled potatoes tossed with olive oil and minced garlic) and a crisp green salad.

Fish:
2 pounds salmon fillets, skin on
1/3–1/2 cup fresh lemon juice
1 bunch fresh Italian parsley, finely minced
Salt
Freshly ground black pepper
Olive oil

Sauce:
1/2 cup fresh lemon juice
1 cup olive oil
2 Tbsp. dried oregano, crushed
Salt
Freshly ground black pepper

Prepare Salmon: The night before serving, wash salmon and dry it well. Using needle-nosed pliers, remove as many pin-bones from salmon as possible. Pour lemon juice over salmon so its surface is well covered, but fish isn't completely swimming in juice. Completely cover salmon with minced parsley. Do not salt salmon at this point.

Make Sauce: Whisk olive oil slowly into lemon juice, and whisk in oregano. Season with salt and freshly ground black pepper to taste.

Cook Salmon: When you're ready to cook salmon, start grill or preheat broiler. Remove and discard parsley, skin fillets, and cut them into serving-sized pieces. Season well with salt and freshly ground black pepper on both sides, and rub well with olive oil. If you're using grill, cook salmon on aluminum foil to prevent it from overcooking. If you're cooking fish under broiler, cook it for 2–3 minutes on each side (cooking time depends on thickness of salmon). Be very careful not to overcook fish. Serve immediately, with sauce on the side.

LEMON-MARINATED DUNGENESS CRAB
Kavouri me Latholemono

Serves 4–6

Spiro Bellas grew up in a Greek-speaking household where the men did all the cooking. His father died when Spiro was young, and the family moved from Seattle to San Francisco where his stepfather had a coffee business. When his stepfather left in the mornings, he gave Spiro's mother a list of the foods he wanted prepped and ready for him that evening. When he returned home after work, Spiro's stepfather would make dinner for the family. Spiro remembers going to Fisherman's Wharf in San Francisco and buying Dungeness crabs, which his stepfather dressed with lots of salt and pepper, olive oil and lemon juice, a recipe Spiro still makes. Although you can dress crab and serve it immediately, it tastes much better if it marinates long enough for the sauce to seep into the cracked crab. Serve with crisp white wine, fresh green salad, and crusty bread.

2 live Dungeness crab
1/2 cup fresh lemon juice
1/2 cup olive oil
4 cloves garlic, pressed (optional)

Salt
Freshly ground black pepper
1/3 cup minced fresh Italian parsley (optional)

Steam crab over boiling water, or boil crab in salted water, for 12 minutes. Remove crab from pot, and rinse with cold water. Let crab cool, then clean and crack them.

Whisk olive oil into lemon juice little by little so it forms an emulsion. Whisk in garlic (if using), salt, and freshly ground black pepper. Put crab in bowl or zip-lock bags, pour in marinade, and toss well. Refrigerate for at least one hour, or overnight. Toss crab with parsley and serve, marinade and all, with plenty of paper napkins.

SHRIMP IN TOMATO SAUCE WITH FETA
Garides Tourkolimano

Serves 4

In Piraeus, the port city near Athens, the waterfront is lined with seafood restaurants in an area that used to be called Tourkolimano. The best way to order in these restaurants is to go in the kitchen and look at the seafood to see what is freshest. When large fresh shrimp are available, Garides Tourkolimano is the ideal choice. Over the years I've made many versions of this dish, and Maria Baskous' may be the best ever. It has discrete vegetable flavors that highlight shrimp's sweetness. Feta cheese lightly toasts, but doesn't melt into the sauce, which complements, rather than dominates, the other ingredients. Large Alaska spot prawns or side stripe shrimp are particularly well-suited to this dish, because they're juicier and sweeter than shrimp from warmer waters. You may substitute clam nectar for shrimp stock, but stock takes such a short time to make and adds so much flavor, that it's worth the minimal extra effort. Maria serves Garides Tourkolimano for dinner parties, and says her guests are inevitably seduced by its superb flavors. It goes nicely with Egyptian Rice with Dill, a fresh spinach salad, and dry white wine.

Shrimp:
1 1/2 pounds shrimp, shelled (save heads
   and shells for shrimp stock)
1 lemon, juiced
2 Tbsp. olive oil
6 cloves thinly sliced garlic
1/2 pound crumbled feta cheese
Dried oregano, crushed
Dried oregano, crushed

Stock:
2 cups water
1 celery stalk, roughly chopped
5 black peppercorns
1/4 cup white wine
Salt

Sauce:
3 bunches green onions, chopped
   or 1 cup diced yellow onion, 1/4" dice
2/3 cups diced celery (1/8" dice)
1/4 cup olive oil
Salt
Freshly ground black pepper
1 14.5-ounce can diced tomatoes
1/2 cup white wine
1 Tbsp. dried oregano, crushed
1 cup shrimp stock or clam nectar

Shrimp: Clean and shell shrimp, squeeze lemon juice over them, and refrigerate.

Stock: Put shrimp shells in pot with water, celery, black peppercorns, white wine, and a little salt. Bring liquid to a boil, and simmer for 20–30 minutes. Strain out and discard solid ingredients.

Sauce: Sauté onions and celery, lightly seasoned with salt and freshly ground black pepper, in olive oil until vegetables are soft and partially cooked. Stir in diced tomatoes, white wine, oregano, and a little salt and pepper. Add 1 cup shrimp stock. Simmer vegetables for 30–40 minutes, until it has formed a nice thick sauce.

Preheat broiler. Make sure oven rack isn't too near broiler element, or feta will burn.

Remove shrimp from refrigerator. In another pan, briefly sauté shrimp with olive oil, garlic and salt, just until shrimp turns pink. Shrimp cook very quickly, especially when they have been marinated in lemon, so be careful not to overcook. Put half the sauce on bottom of baking dish, layer on shrimp, and cover with remaining sauce. Spread feta evenly over sauce, and sprinkle cheese with oregano. Turn on broiler, and broil just until cheese starts to brown. Serve immediately with rice.

ROASTED SHRIMP AND SPINACH
Garides me Spanaki

Serves 6

One sunny Greek September morning, the fish vendor drove through our village and announced over his loudspeaker he had fresh shrimp. The shrimp had been caught only hours before, and were so beautiful I bought too many. An hour later, I heard another announcement echoing through the streets. I couldn't quite hear what was for sale so went down to the square to investigate. A farmer was in town, and the back of his little pickup was entirely filled with just-harvested bunches of beautiful spinach. I couldn't resist the spinach either. Roasted Shrimp and Spinach was a natural way to use my lucky purchases. It combines the essences of earth and sea. Simple spinach, tart tomatoes, sweet shrimp, and creamy cheese, are harmonized and balanced by fresh lemon. We don't have itinerant fish vendors in Alaska, but our cold-water spot prawns and side stripe shrimp have the best flavor in the world and are often available fresh. Using cold-water Alaskan shrimp results in a sweeter, more delectable dish, so they're worth seeking out.

2 pounds large shrimp, peeled, washed, and dried
1/4 cup minced fresh garlic
1/2 cup minced fresh dill
2 cup diced fresh tomatoes, best quality, 1/2" dice
2 Tbsp. dried oregano, crushed
1/2 cup fresh lemon juice
1/2 cup olive oil
3 cups diced yellow onions, 1/4" dice
Salt
Freshly ground black pepper
1 tsp. Aleppo pepper or 1/2 tsp. crushed red pepper
1 pound cleaned spinach, drained but not dried
2 cups crumbled feta cheese

Preheat oven to 425°F.

Mix cleaned shrimp with 1/4 cup olive oil, one third of dill, one third of minced garlic, tomatoes, oregano, lemon juice, salt, and freshly ground pepper. Set aside.

Sauté onions, lightly seasoned with salt, freshly ground black pepper, and Aleppo pepper, in 1/4 cup olive oil until onions soften and begin to turn golden. Add remaining garlic and sauté for 1 minute. Add spinach in thirds, stirring after each addition, and stir in remaining dill. Continue cooking until all spinach has wilted. Season spinach to taste with salt and freshly ground black pepper.

Place spinach in bottom of a round glass or ceramic pie pan. If there is a lot of liquid in spinach, drain it off into a small saucepan. Boil this liquid until most of water has evaporated, and stir reduction into spinach. Spread shrimp mixture evenly on top of spinach. Bake for 5 minutes. Top with crumbled feta, and bake for an additional 5–7 minutes or until shrimp is just cooked through. If cheese isn't melted when shrimp is done, put dish under broiler for one minute. Grind plenty of black pepper over cheese, and serve with rice.

Note: If you use small or medium sized shrimp, reduce cooking time. Properly cooked shrimp are firm, but still moist and succulent.

GRILLED SHRIMP
Garides Psites sta Karvouna

Serves 6–8

Side stripe shrimp and spot prawns that grow in Alaska's cold waters are perfect for grilling. Although their meat is softer than that of farmed warm water shrimp that otherwise fill our markets, they're a lot sweeter and free from disagreeable chemicals. Cold water shrimp also have thinner shells that allow the flavors of marinade and smoke to permeate the flesh without overcooking tender shrimp. It's important to grill shrimp with their shells on so the meat stays juicy. An added bonus of leaving on shells is you get the smoky marinade on your fingers and on the shrimp meat as you peel and eat them. Rice pilaf and Horiatiki Salata round out the menu for a good summer barbecue.

3 pounds shrimp, in the shell (preferably head-on)
1/2 cup olive oil
Salt
Freshly ground black pepper
2 Tbsp. dried oregano, crushed
Lemon wedges

Wash and dry shrimp. Mix shrimp with olive oil, salt, freshly ground black pepper, and oregano, and let sit for at least 30 minutes. Cook on a medium hot fire for 3–4 minutes on each side, about 2 1/2–3" from fire, until shrimp are lightly charred here and there (don't char every one), and shrimp have just turned opaque. Cooking grilled shrimp is easiest if you use a grill basket. Be careful not to overcook. Serve with lemon wedges.

FRIED SQUID WITH LEMON AND GARLIC
Kalamaria me Lemoni kai Skordo

Serves 2 as a main course, or 4–6 as an appetizer

According to John Maroulis, the best way to make fried squid is to toss it in fresh garlic and lemon juice after it's fried. I was a little nervous about the raw garlic, but when I made John's squid I learned garlic, along with lemon and parsley, really cuts the oiliness and lightens the flavor of fried food. Squid is good when it's cooked for the briefest possible time, or when it's stewed for a long time. Anything in between makes squid tough and chewy, so remember that small squid cooks in mere minutes. I love making a meal out of hot fried squid and a salad, but also never hesitate to serve Kalamaria in the center of the table for my guests to spear as an appetizer.

1 pound cleaned squid tubes and tentacles	Canola oil for frying
1/2 cup all-purpose flour	2–4 Tbsp. fresh lemon juice
Salt	2 cloves of garlic, minced very small
Freshly ground black pepper	1/4 cup minced parsley

Clean squid (see page 14 in Cook's Notes) and dry them completely. If squid are large, cut tubes into strips and tentacles into pieces. If squid is small, cut bodies into rings and leave tentacles whole. Put flour, seasoned with salt and freshly ground pepper, in a bag. Add squid pieces, and shake to coat. Remove squid from flour, shaking off any excess. Heat 1/2" of oil in a large pan until it's hot, but not smoking. Add half floured squid, and cook for 2–4 minutes, depending on size of squid, and turning squid over halfway through cooking process. Drain on paper towels. Repeat with remaining squid. This is cooked in two batches so oil stays hot. If oil isn't hot, the coating won't get crispy or stay on. Place squid in bowl, salt lightly, and toss with garlic, parsley, and lemon juice to taste.

SQUID IN GARLICKY TOMATO SAUCE
Kalamaria se Domata Saltsa

Serves 6–8

Alex Baskous loves squid stewed in a spicy tomato sauce, so his wife Maria cooks it regularly. Thick, peppery sauce is balanced by plenty of parsley and the mild taste of tender squid. Fresh squid is only occasionally available in Alaska, so in this recipe Maria uses frozen squid that have already been cleaned. If tomato sauce is made ahead and frozen, this can be a quick and reliably good meal for those days when speed is important. Serve with steamed rice, the better to enjoy each drop of tasty sauce.

1 cup olive oil
5 cups diced yellow onion (1/2" dice)
2 14.5-ounce cans diced tomatoes
2 bunches fresh Italian parsley, minced
2 Tbsp. minced fresh garlic
1 tsp. Aleppo pepper or 1/2 tsp. crushed red pepper (optional)
Salt
Freshly ground black pepper
3 pounds cleaned squid

Sauté onion, lightly seasoned with salt and freshly ground black pepper, in olive oil, until it softens and starts to turn golden. Add tomatoes, parsley, garlic, Aleppo pepper, salt, and freshly ground black pepper, and stir well. Bring to a boil, turn down heat to medium low, and cook for 30–45 minutes, or until vegetables have formed a sauce, and oil is starting to separate. For a thinner sauce, cover pan as sauce cooks.

While sauce is cooking, clean squid (see page 14 in Cook's Notes) and dry them completely. Separate tentacles, and cut tubes into large rings. Just before serving, stir squid into tomato sauce. Cook for about 3 minutes or until squid is just done, being careful not to overcook. Grind lots of black pepper over squid when you serve it.

Fresh squid and octopus at the Central Market in Athens.

· CHICKEN ·

* New recipe this edition

The Second Intifada was well underway and making ordinary life difficult when Salwa and Ramzi Abuamsha married in Beit-jala, a small village just outside Bethlehem on the Jordan River's West Bank. Even though their celebration was held in a private house because of the fighting, the new couple managed a traditional Palestinian wedding feast.

The feast's centerpiece was Mansaf—lamb layered on rice with yogurt sauce, garnished with roasted pine nuts and almonds. Mansaf was served on a huge communal platter. Guests gathered round the platter and used nimble fingers to serve themselves bite-sized morsels of rice and lamb.

In Beit-jala, everyone has olive trees growing in their yards, Salwa said. Each family takes its olives to a local mill to be pressed into oil. Fresh olive oil's vivid, slightly bitter, taste enhances Palestinian food's flavor.

By junior high school, Salwa was responsible for preparing dinner on Fridays, and often cooked lentils and rice. She remembers that shopping for food could be a challenge in the mostly Arab Christian, but multi-cultural, community. Muslim stores were closed on Fridays, Jewish stores on Saturday, and Christian stores on Sunday.

When they married, Ramzi already lived in Alaska. He emigrated to the U.S. for freedom and opportunity. He tried being a steel worker in Detroit, but the city was too big and lonely for someone from a tiny village, so he moved back to Beit-jala. Ramzi discovered fighting in his region had worsened while he was gone, so he soon returned to America to join a cousin who fished in Chignik. He and Salwa married a month after they met on one of Ramzi's visits home, and immediately left for the United States, eventually making their way to Alaska.

Now an Alaskan for many years, Salwa works as an accountant but still cooks the Palestinian food of her youth for her husband and twin sons Anton and Admon.

PALESTINIAN CHICKEN AND ONIONS
Masakhan

Serves 4–6

Masakhan, a dish common in her village of Beit-jala, is one of Salwa Abuamsha's specialties. Tender chicken, sweet onions, and tangy sumac combine to form a richly flavorful dish. Sumac is an unusual spice in American kitchens, and can be purchased from local and internet spice merchants. The pita bread base is very effective in soaking up rich juices. Salwa says if pita is crisp when added to broth, it soaks up more juice and adds texture and flavor to Masakhan. This is a good recipe to make on cold winter Sunday afternoons, when smells of slow-cooked chicken and onions help warm the house. Chicken, broth, onions and pita may all be cooked ahead, and assembled quickly for a last-minute meal. As a bonus, this recipe leaves you with a large pot of savory chicken broth, perfect for soup (see page 78 for Palestinian Chicken Soup recipe) or in rice dishes instead of water.

3 1/2–4 pound whole chicken
12 cups water
1 tsp. allspice
1/2 tsp. ground nutmeg
Salt
Freshly ground black pepper

3 1/2–4 pounds yellow onions
1/2 cup olive oil
2 Tbsp., plus 1–2 tsp., sumac
  (see page 15 in Cook's Notes)
4 Palestinian pita breads
  (see page 89)

Wash chicken, and put it in a large pot with water, spices, salt and freshly ground black pepper. Bring to a boil, turn down heat, and simmer for 1 1/2 hours or until chicken is tender.

While chicken is simmering, cut onions into thin half-moon slices. Sauté onions, lightly seasoned with salt and freshly ground black pepper, in olive oil until onions are well coated with oil and begin to soften. Sprinkle onions with 2 Tbsp. sumac, cover, reduce heat to low, and cook for 45–60 minutes, or until onions are very soft and slightly caramelized. Stir from time to time so the onions don't stick to the bottom of the pan.

Preheat the oven to 350°F.

When the chicken is done, remove it from the broth and cut into quarters or sixths. Soak the pita in broth until it's saturated and limp. Keep the remaining broth for another use. Line baking pan with the pita, and top with the chicken pieces. Cover with the cooked onions, and sprinkle with the remaining 1–2 tsp. sumac. Bake for 20–30 minutes.

Note: If you use Greek-style pita bread from the supermarket, which is moister than Palestinian pita, put it in the oven to crisp a little before soaking it in the juice.

BAKED CHICKEN AND ORZO IN TOMATO SAUCE
Kotopoulo me Manestra

Serves 4–6

Stephanie and Alex Joannides' father came to the United States as a baby. His parents had jobs writing for a Greek newspaper in New York. Their mother was born in America, the child of an arranged marriage between a Greek-American businessman and a young woman he brought over from Greece. After Stephanie and Alex's father became a lawyer, he was hired by the U.S. government, and stationed in Greece, where Stephanie and Alex spent most of their childhood. Their maternal grandmother Angeliki lived with the family much of the time, and passed her love of cooking on to Stephanie. One of Angeliki's specialties that Alex remembers fondly is chicken and baked orzo. Cooking orzo and well-seasoned chicken together permeates orzo with flavor, and when paired with a green salad and feta cheese, makes a tasty family meal.

Stephanie Joannides and her nephew Alex, her brother Alex's son

3 lbs chicken thighs or 1 3–4 lb. chicken, cut up
Salt
Freshly ground black pepper
2 Tbsp. olive oil
2 cups diced yellow onions, 1/2" dice
1 14.5-ounce can tomato sauce

1 1/2 cups red wine
1 Tbsp. minced fresh garlic
1 tsp. Aleppo pepper or 1/2 tsp. crushed red pepper
1 Tbsp. dried oregano, crushed
5 bay leaves
1 1/2 cups water
1 cup orzo

Wash and dry chicken, and season it on both sides with salt and freshly ground black pepper. Heat olive oil in a large pot until it's very hot, but not smoking (if oil is hot, chicken won't stick to pan and skin will stay on chicken). Put chicken pieces in pan, skin side down. Don't crowd chicken pieces together, or they steam instead of brown—you may need to brown chicken in batches. Cook chicken until it's well browned on both sides. Remove chicken from pan, and pour off most of oil.

Preheat oven to 350°F.

Sauté onions, lightly seasoned with salt and freshly ground black pepper, in remaining chicken oil and cook until they soften and begin to turn golden. Stir in tomato sauce, wine, garlic, Aleppo pepper, oregano, bay leaves, salt and pepper. Return chicken and any accumulated chicken juices to pot. Bring mixture to a boil, cover, reduce heat to low, and simmer for 30 minutes. Remove chicken from pot, and stir water and orzo into tomato sauce. Pour tomato sauce and orzo into a 9" x 13" baking pan. Place chicken on top of orzo, cover pan with foil, and bake for 20–30 minutes until orzo is done. If orzo is too dry, stir in a little water. If orzo is too juicy, remove foil and return pan to oven for a few minutes to dry out. When chicken is done, put pan under broiler for a few minutes until chicken skin is nicely browned. Serve immediately.

NAHKLA'S GRILLED GARLIC CHICKEN
Djaj Mashwi Bl'towm

Serves 4–6

In Beit-jala, a village on the Jordan River's West Bank, Salwa Abuamsha's Uncle Nahkla Qabar owns a restaurant that is well-known for its grilled garlic chicken. People come from all over the country to Nahkla's restaurant, says Salwa, without regard to religion – Christians, Jews, and Muslims gather to gorge on her uncle's chicken. Nahkla always butterflies and flattens chicken before grilling for better flavor and a shorter cooking time. The garlic sauce used in this recipe is "everyone's favorite," according to Salwa, who says it's used "with everything" and makes an especially good dip for bread or vegetables. You might be skeptical about using so much raw garlic, but its fire is tempered by lemon juice and harmonizes with the smoky taste of well-grilled chicken. Garlic sauce keeps in the refrigerator, and chicken tastes best if you rub it with garlic sauce several hours before cooking. Serve chicken with Orange and Onion Salad and slices of feta cheese.

Sauce:
10 cloves garlic
1 tsp. salt
1/2 cup fresh lemon juice
1/2 cup olive oil

3–4 pound whole chicken
Salt
Freshly ground black pepper

Sauce: Pound garlic and salt in a mortar and pestle to form a paste. Add lemon juice, and incorporate it into garlic paste. Slowly add oil, a little at a time, to form a thick sauce. The sauce can also be made in a blender or food processor by pureeing garlic and salt, mixing in lemon juice, and slowly adding olive oil (see Note below).

Chicken: Place chicken on a cutting board, breast side down. Using poultry shears, kitchen scissors, or a sharp knife, cut through ribs on either side of backbone, and remove it. Turn chicken over, and flatten it by pressing down on breastbone until you hear a snap. Wash chicken well and dry it thoroughly.

Rub half the garlic sauce onto all sides of chicken. If possible, marinate garlic-rubbed chicken for at least two hours before cooking.

To grill chicken: When grill is hot, coat hot rack with a thin coating of olive oil, using wadded-up paper towels to spread oil. Season chicken with salt and freshly ground black pepper, and cook over a medium hot fire with grill cover on, turning chicken frequently. Chicken is done when a thermometer stuck deep in thigh (but not touching bone) registers 170°F or when juices from a cut near thigh joint run clear; about 30 minutes total cooking time.

Remove chicken from grill, let sit for 5 minutes, and cut into serving-sized pieces. Serve with remaining garlic sauce on the side or, for garlic lovers, pour sauce over grilled chicken, coating it on all sides.

Note: Although it takes slightly more effort, I like making half the sauce in a blender to use for marinade, and making the rest of the sauce (used for serving with chicken) in a mortar and pestle. Because blender-made sauce is smoother, garlic in it is less likely to burn while chicken is on the grill. On the other hand, sauce made in a mortar and pestle tastes better, so I prefer it for dressing cooked chicken.

STATHIS' GARLIC CHICKEN
Kotopoulo me Skordo tou Stathi

Serves 4

One day after church I was trying to think of something fast and easy to cook for dinner. Stathis Mataragas suggested his garlic chicken which cooks quickly because it's made with boneless breasts and a simple garlic sauce. Fresh garlic adds a rustic touch, and its powerful taste is tempered by chicken and oregano. Serve with feta cheese, Kalamata olives, and any kind of salad.

Sauce:
6 cloves garlic
1–2 Tbsp. fresh lemon juice
1/2 tsp. salt
1/2 cup extra virgin olive oil
2 tsp. dried oregano, crushed

Chicken:
4 boneless, skinless chicken breast halves
Olive oil
Salt
Freshly ground black pepper

Sauce: Pound garlic and salt in a mortar and pestle until it forms a paste. Mix in lemon juice. Add olive oil slowly, a few drops at a time, until it forms a nice smooth paste. Taste and add lemon juice, salt, or olive oil, as needed.

Chicken: Wash and dry chicken. Place each boneless chicken breast between sheets of waxed paper or plastic wrap, and lightly pound to an even thickness. Season chicken with salt and freshly ground black pepper on both sides, and rub with olive oil.

Cook chicken over a medium hot grill, turning frequently, or on very high heat in a grill pan on top of stove. Chicken breasts take about 8–10 minutes to cook. When chicken is done, Stathis says to get out the garlic sauce and "spread it on the chicken like butter."

CHICKEN WITH SPICED TOMATO SAUCE
Kotopoulo Kapama

Serves 4–6

Pamela Lloyd learned how to make Chicken Kapama from her mother, Yiannula Demos Johnson. When Yiannula makes Kapama, she serves chicken on the bone as called for in this recipe, with sauce and pasta on the side. Daughter Pamela skins and debones chicken for Kapama, and then cuts it into bite-sized pieces which she mixes in sauce to serve over pasta. Cinnamon and tomatoes have a natural affinity and give Kapama an exotic flavor. Serve Kapama with pasta and grated myzithra cheese, and lots of feta cheese on the side.

Chicken:
1 4-pound whole chicken, cut up,
   or 4 pounds chicken thighs
1 lemon
Salt
Freshly ground black pepper
Ground cinnamon
1/3 cup olive oil
   1 cinnamon stick
   5 bay leaves

Sauce:
3 cups diced yellow onion, 1/2" dice
1 14.5-ounce can crushed tomatoes
   or tomato sauce
1 5-ounce can tomato paste
2 14.5-ounce cans full of water
1 Tbsp. minced fresh garlic
1 Tbsp. sugar

Wash chicken pieces and dry them well. Squeeze juice from lemon over chicken, and rub it into all sides. Sprinkle both sides of chicken with salt, freshly ground black pepper, and cinnamon (give it a good dusting of cinnamon, but not so much that chicken is brown all over).

Heat olive oil in a large pot until it's very hot, but not smoking (if oil is very hot, chicken skin is less likely to stick to pan). Place chicken in pan, skin side down, and let cook until it's well browned. Turn over and brown other side of chicken. You need to brown chicken in two batches—don't try to crowd all chicken into pan at one time or chicken will steam, rather than brown.

Remove chicken from pan, and pour off most of oil, leaving only enough in pan to sauté onions. If debris at bottom of pan is burnt black (browned bits are fine), clean pan with water, and return a little of chicken cooking oil to pan.

Cook onions until they have softened and begin to turn golden, scraping up any browned bits on bottom of pan. Add crushed tomatoes (or tomato sauce) and tomato paste, mixing well. Add water, garlic, sugar, cinnamon stick, and bay leaves and mix well. Return chicken to pan, submerging chicken in sauce to greatest extent possible. Bring sauce to a boil, then reduce heat to low, and simmer for 45–60 minutes or until chicken is tender and sauce has thickened. Remove cinnamon stick and bay leaves, and serve.

CHICKEN WITH ONIONS AND SAFFRON
Djaj Bisla Zafron

Serves 4

Morocco is a country of high mountains and searing deserts, and has welcomed traders from across the Mediterranean for thousands of years. Spices brought by traders were used by skilled Moroccan cooks to develop sophisticated recipes, like this one for Chicken with Onions and Saffron. Tender chicken, braised with Moroccan spices and honey, warms the body on even the coldest Alaska night. Even though flavors in this recipe are complex, it's easy to make because it doesn't need any attention after the chicken and onions are browned. Chicken with Onions and Saffron keeps well, so this is a good meal to make ahead. Serve with couscous and a fresh salad.

8 chicken thighs	2 14.5-ounce cans diced tomatoes
Salt	2 Tbsp. honey
Freshly ground black pepper	1 1/2 tsp. ground ginger
1/4 cup olive oil	1/2 tsp. cinnamon
6 cups thinly sliced yellow onions	1/2 tsp. saffron
1 Tbsp. minced fresh garlic	1/2 cup blanched slivered almonds

Wash chicken thighs and dry well. Season on both sides with salt and freshly ground black pepper. Heat olive oil in a large pot until it's very hot, but not smoking (if oil is very hot, chicken skin is less likely to stick to pan). Place chicken in pan skin side down, and cook until skin is well browned. Turn and brown underside of chicken. You need to brown chicken in two batches – don't try to crowd all chicken into pan at one time, or chicken will steam rather than brown.

Remove chicken from pan, and drain off all but 1/3 cup oil. In same pot, sauté onions, lightly seasoned with salt and freshly ground black pepper, scraping up any browned bits on bottom of pan. Cook until onions start to turn golden brown. Mix in tomatoes, garlic, honey, ginger, cinnamon, and saffron. Cook for 15 minutes, taste and add salt, pepper, or honey, as needed. Mix in chicken. Cover and simmer for 1 1/4 hours, or until chicken is falling off bone.

While chicken is simmering, preheat oven to 350°F. Place blanched slivered almonds on baking sheet, and roast for 5–10 minutes or until almonds are lightly toasted.

When chicken is done, serve it on a plate with couscous, and sprinkle roasted almonds over everything.

CHICKEN AND OKRA
Kotopoulo me Bamies

Serves 6

Rooster stewed with okra is a special summer food of Greeks on the island of Limnos, according to Ourania Vayiakou in her book Sintages Limniakis Kouzinas (Recipes from Limnos). Roosters are fat from feeding on freshly threshed grain just when the okra crop is ready to be picked, she explains. Ourania tosses fresh okra with salt and vinegar, and dries it in the sun for an hour before cooking to improve its texture. In Alaska, cooking with okra is a challenge because it's rarely available fresh and our sun doesn't have the heat necessary to effectively dry okra. In this recipe, which is adapted from Ourania's, frozen okra is dried in the oven for a short time before it's stewed. The result is okra with good texture and a taste that marries well with braised chicken. A big benefit of using frozen okra is it allows this hearty dish to be made year-round.

Chicken:
1 3 1/2–4 lb. chicken, cut up, or 4 lbs. chicken thighs
Salt
Freshly ground black pepper
1/3 cup olive oil
3 cups diced yellow onions (1/2" dice)
2 Tbsp. minced fresh garlic
1 14.5-ounce can diced tomatoes
1 14.5-ounce can crushed tomatoes
1 cup red wine
2 cups chicken stock
3 bay leaves
1 tsp. Aleppo pepper or 1/2 tsp. crushed red pepper (optional)

Okra:
20 oz bag frozen whole okra, thawed
1/4 cup red wine vinegar
Salt
1/2 cup chopped parsley

Preheat oven to 300°F.

Wash chicken pieces and dry them well. Season chicken on sides with salt and freshly ground black pepper. Heat olive oil in a large pot until it's very hot, but not smoking (if oil is very hot, chicken skin is less likely to stick to pan). Place chicken in pan skin side down, and cook until skin is well browned. Turn over and brown underside of chicken. You need to brown chicken in two batches—don't try to crowd all chicken into pan at one time, or chicken will steam rather than brown.

Remove chicken from pot, and drain off all but 1/4 cup oil. In same pot, sauté onions, lightly seasoned with salt and freshly ground black pepper, scraping up any browned bits on bottom of pan. Cook until onions soften and begin to turn golden. Return chicken to pan, along with garlic, two kinds of tomatoes, wine, chicken stock, bay leaves, Aleppo pepper, and freshly ground black pepper. Bring liquid in pot to a boil, reduce heat to low and simmer for 45 minutes, or until chicken is almost done.

While chicken is cooking, place thawed okra on a rimmed baking sheet, and sprinkle with red wine vinegar and salt. Gently mix okra, vinegar, and salt, and spread okra out in a single layer on baking sheet. Bake seasoned okra for 20 minutes.

After chicken has simmered for 45 minutes, carefully add roasted okra to pot and stir gently. It's important not to break up okra, or its texture will be damaged. Cover and cook without stirring for 40 minutes. If sauce is too thin, remove cover during last 15 minutes of cooking. Gently stir in chopped parsley and serve.

CHICKEN WITH SAUERKRAUT TOURSI AND CINNAMON-SCENTED RICE PILAF
Kotopoulo me Toursi kai Pilafi

Serves 6

After World War I ended, active conflicts between Greece and Turkey continued until 1923, when each country adopted the Treaty of Lausanne. One of the Treaty's provisions required a population exchange: Turkey expelled most of its citizens who were Greek Orthodox, as Greece did its Muslim citizens. Two million people were instantly turned into refugees, forced from countries where their families had lived for generations. Regional stability was realized, but individual Greeks and Turks involuntarily paid the price to achieve it. In 1905, half the population of Kirk-Killisseh (Saranda Ecclessias in Greek), a Turkish town in Eastern Thrace, was Greek Orthodox. Because of the Treaty, Greeks residents of Saranda Ecclessias were banished from their ancestral homes. Some came to the United States, bringing with them their religion, their culture, and their cuisine.

On holidays and other special occasions, most of us want the familiar foods of our childhoods. So it was with Greeks who were forcibly evicted from Saranda Ecclessias in the 1920s. On Thanksgiving, the most American of holidays, these Greeks combined turkey with Toursi and Cinnamon-Scented Rice Pilaf, a dish redolent with the smells and flavors of their former homes in Eastern Thrace. Evanthia Valassiades described the dish in A Festival of Recipes: A Collection of Recipes from the Annunciation Greek Orthodox Church in Dayton, Ohio: "This combination may sound unusual but it is really wonderful. Families from Saranda Ecclessias enjoy this meal at Thanksgiving. The stuffing and sauerkraut portions would be doubled for turkey. We don't stuff the turkey, but bake the rice accompaniment separately."

For a rich and hearty winter meal, sweetened sauerkraut and flavorful chicken, served with Cinnamon-Scented Rice Pilaf, is an exotic, and uniquely compelling, flavor combination. Sugar renders the sauerkraut sweet and sour. I modified the original recipe by significantly reducing the sugar (from 1 cup to 1/4 cup), and by adding onion and thyme to round out the flavors. I once made this dish using only olive oil and it tasted fine, but it tastes better when the onions and sauerkraut are cooked in butter. Evanthia roasts the chicken whole, which makes a more attractive holiday presentation. By cutting the chicken up, as I've done here, its flavors infuse and richen the sauerkraut. The dish can easily be made ahead; its flavor improves over time.

1 quart sauerkraut (2 pounds), preferably from the market's refrigerator section
3 1/2–4 pound chicken cut into pieces, or 8–10 chicken thighs
1/4 cup olive oil
1/4 cup butter, plus 2 Tbsp. for baking sauerkraut
3 cups thinly sliced onions
Salt
Freshly ground black pepper
1 tbsp. dried thyme, crushed
1/4 cup sugar
2 cups chicken stock
3 bay leaves

Drain sauerkraut into strainer and rinse it very well. Leave sauerkraut in strainer to drain while you cook chicken.

Wash chicken pieces and dry them well. Season pieces on both sides with salt and freshly ground black pepper.

Heat olive oil in large pot until it's very hot, but not smoking (if oil is very hot, chicken skin is less likely to stick to pan). Place chicken in pan, skin side down, and cook until it's well browned, about five minutes. Turn pieces over and brown other side. Brown chicken in two frying pans or in two batches – don't try to crowd all chicken into pan at one time or chicken will steam, rather than brown. Place browned chicken on paper towels to drain.

Melt butter in pan large enough to hold onions and sauerkraut. Cook onions in butter, lightly seasoned with salt and freshly ground black pepper, until they soften and begin to turn golden. Add thyme and rinsed sauerkraut, and sauté until sauerkraut begins to caramelize. Add sugar and cook, stirring constantly, for 5 minutes. Stir in browned chicken, stock, and bay leaves. Place in buttered baking dish, dot with 2 Tbsp. butter, and bake uncovered for 45 minutes.

CINNAMON-SCENTED RICE PILAF

Serves 4-6

Cinnamon-Scented Rice Pilaf is a good accompaniment to any chicken or lamb dish. Pine nuts and currants turn it into special occasion fare. If your chicken comes with giblets, chop them up and add them to the pilaf with the rice and celery.

3 cups diced yellow onion (1/4" dice)	2 Tbsp. tomato paste
1 cup diced celery (1/4" dice)	1/2 cup pine nuts, lightly toasted
1/4 cup butter	1/2 cup currants
1 cup rice	1/2 tsp. cinnamon
1/2 cup minced fresh parsley	Salt
2 cups chicken stock	Freshly ground black pepper

Preheat oven to 350°F.

Sauté onions and celery, lightly seasoned with salt and freshly ground black pepper, in butter. When onions have softened, add rice and cook, stirring, until rice begins to turn golden around the edges. Add parsley, chicken stock, tomato paste, pine nuts, currants, cinnamon, salt, and freshly ground black pepper.

Pour rice mixture into buttered baking dish, cover, and bake for 1 hour.

NOTE: To toast pine nuts, bake in 350°F oven for 5 – 8 minutes. Watch them carefully; pine nuts burn very easily.

· MEAT ·

* New recipe this edition

In the 1940s, there was no Greek Orthodox Church in the village of Kasbah Tadla. Greeks living there, near a military post in French Morocco, traveled 120 miles each spring to celebrate Holy Week in Casablanca with Orthodox families from all over Morocco.

Helene Georgas Dennison was born in Casablanca to a father from the Greek island of Rhodes and a mother from Constantinople. She remembers Easter trips as a week of church followed by days of spectacular food. On Easter afternoon in Casablanca, her family shared an "agapi" (love) meal with friends and family before returning to Kasbah Tadla. Back in the village, Kasbah Tadla's Greek community celebrated with an outdoor picnic in unfailingly sunny weather. Each family spread its picnic tablecloth with mountains of food, which was shared by all.

Kasbah Tadla sits along the Oumerbia River, one of only two rivers in Morocco with water year-round. Villagers brag about their two bridges, one dating from the 15th century, and both contributing to the village's prosperity. Along with her brother, sister, and cousins, Helene fished in the river and played in an olive and mimosa grove. Lemons and oranges grew in her back yard.

Helene's family spoke Greek at home. Her parents ran a grocery store that serviced the military post. They had a servant and a mountain cabin where they stayed during the two hottest months. Helene went to boarding school, where she was a national volleyball champion and on the national swimming team. For a child it was an idyllic existence.

In 1953, all that changed when Moroccans rebelled against their French and Spanish rulers. The civil war that followed produced horrible acts of violence by both sides, with non-combatants, especially many foreigners—Italians, Spaniards, Greeks, Jews—caught in the middle.

Despite the dangers, the Georgas family stayed in Morocco. In 1956, the country won its freedom, and life returned to a semblance of normalcy. Helene was able to leave Morocco for a trip to Rhodes, where she visited her father's family, traveling on donkey back to the island's traditional villages. When she returned to Morocco, Helene met Gary Dennison, an American soldier from West Virginia, and married him. Luckily, Gary enjoyed Greek food, so Helene kept cooking delicious dishes she learned in Morocco from her Greek family.

ROAST LAMB WITH TOMATO SAUCE AND POTATOES
Arni Psito me Domata Saltsa kai Patates

Serves 8–10

Every year since her marriage, Helene Georgas Dennison has made roast lamb with tomato sauce and pota-toes for her husband, children, and now, grandchildren. The lamb in Helene's recipe turns out savory and well roasted, with enough garlic and oregano to complement, but not dominate, the meat. The potatoes are lovely, with a meat and tomato flavored crust and soft, sweet-tasting insides. Salad, feta cheese, and olives round out the table, for a good company meal any time of year. Use leftovers to make Lamb Salad, Moroccan Lamb and Onion Stew, or Baked Orzo with Lamb (see Index for recipes).

1 4–5 pound leg of lamb
4 cloves garlic
Salt
Freshly ground black pepper
Olive oil
1/4 cup fresh lemon juice
3 pounds Russet (baking) potatoes
1 Tbsp. dried oregano, crushed
1 cup tomato sauce
2 cups boiling water

Preheat oven to 450°F.

Wash lamb, and dry it well. Cut garlic into thin slivers. Cut slits all over lamb leg, and push a piece of garlic into each slit. Rub salt and freshly ground black pepper all over lamb, including into slits, and rub seasoned lamb with olive oil and lemon juice. Place lamb in a large roasting pan, fat side up, and cook in preheated oven for 15 minutes.

While lamb is in oven, peel potatoes and cut them into 6 lengthwise wedges. Season potato wedges with salt, pepper, and oregano, and mix them with tomato sauce.

After lamb has cooked for 15 minutes, reduce heat to 350°F. Arrange potatoes around lamb, pour tomato sauce over potatoes, and add boiling water. Bake until potatoes are tender and temperature of lamb is 145°F, about 45–75 minutes, depending on shape of lamb leg and whether or not it's boneless. Baste potatoes and lamb with tomato sauce from time to time. When lamb is done, place it on a cutting board and let it rest 5–10 minutes before carving. While lamb is resting, place potatoes under broiler until they're nicely browned. Serve lamb on a platter, surrounded by potatoes and sauce.

GRILLED LAMB SAUSAGES
Kebab

Serves 4

In Athens' Monastiraki district, the smell of grilled meat permeates the air and pulls passers-by into kebab houses lining the streets. My favorite place to eat in Monastiraki is called O Thanasis—their kebabs are well-spiced, nicely browned on the outside, and juicy on the inside. This recipe is my attempt to recreate O Thanasis' kebabs. They're best when cooked outside on the grill, but can also be made on a stovetop grill pan. I prefer making 16 small 3" kebabs, but you may also use larger skewers and divide meat into 8 pieces instead of 16. Serve with Tomato Salad for Kebab, Tzatziki, feta cheese, Kalamata olives, and warm pita bread (see Index for recipes).

1 pound ground lamb
3 cloves garlic, finely minced
1/3 cup grated yellow onion
1 tsp. ground allspice
1/2 tsp. ground coriander seeds
1 Tbsp. dried oregano, crushed
1/2 tsp. salt
1/2 tsp. freshly ground black pepper
2 Tbsp. red wine
Bamboo skewers

Place all ingredients in bowl, and knead everything together with your hands. Divide seasoned meat into sixteen equal pieces. Roll each piece of meat around a small skewer into three inch logs. Refrigerate until you're ready to cook kebabs (recipe may be made ahead to this point).

Grill kebabs over a charcoal fire, being careful not to overcook. To cook on the stove, heat a grill pan until it's very hot, cook kebabs until they're well-browned on one side, turn them over, immediately turn down heat, and cook an additional minute on the other side. Serve immediately.

LAMB AND EGGPLANT KEBAB
Sempoog Kebab

Serves 4

One day, Ankine Markossian asked my plans for dinner. When I described Greek lamb kebab, Ankine said she made a similar Armenian kebab that was her kids' favorite, and grilled it with chunks of eggplant. The image of beautifully browned meat and pretty purple eggplants was so vivid, I went home and made it that night. Meat and eggplant absorb flavor from the smoky fire and, when bites of eggplant and meat are eaten together, soft, sweet eggplant acts almost as a sauce for the meat. Ankine doesn't use garlic or red pepper flakes in her meat mix, but other Armenian cooks do; they're included here because they add appealing flavors and complexity.

3–5 thin Chinese eggplants
1 pound ground lamb or beef
1/2 cup grated yellow onion
1/4 cup minced fresh Italian parsley
2 tsp. minced fresh garlic
1/2 tsp. Aleppo pepper or 1/4 tsp.
   crushed red pepper (optional)

1 tsp. allspice
1/2 tsp. salt
Freshly ground black pepper
Olive oil

Cut unpeeled eggplant into 20 chunks, approximately 1 1/2" square (don't peel eggplant). Knead ground meat, onion, parsley, garlic, Aleppo pepper, allspice, and salt with your hands. Shape meat into 12 round meatballs.

Using flat or double pronged metal skewers, alternate eggplant chunks and meatballs on skewer. (Rounded skewers are harder to use because the kebab may twirl around the skewer when you turn it.) Start and end skewers with eggplant chunk, so that each skewer has 3 meatballs and 5 eggplant chunks. Reshape meatballs on skewer to make circumference of each meatball smaller than circumference of eggplant chunks. This helps prevent kebab from sticking to grill as it cooks. Brush eggplant pieces with olive oil.

Grill kebabs over medium hot fire, turning frequently and carefully, until eggplant chunks are soft and meatballs are cooked through. Serve immediately.

MOROCCAN LAMB AND ONION STEW
Mrouzia Tajine

Serves 6–8

As a child growing up in Morocco, Helene Georgas Dennison ate a mix of Greek, French, and Moroccan food, with lamb being the main meat in all cuisines. Helene remembers enjoying Moroccan tajines cooked with lots of onions and lamb, and eaten with couscous. This recipe is for the type of tajine Helene ate. The flavors are complex, with peppery and mild spices blended to form an astonishingly good sauce. Adding optional raisins makes the dish more traditional, but they're unnecessary to its success. This stew can be made with either fresh or leftover roast lamb. Because it's quite rich, the stew should be served with a neutral side dish, like couscous, accompanied by big, succulent, green olives.

3 pounds lamb shoulder steaks, bone-in, or leftover roast lamb
3 cups very finely minced or grated yellow onion
2 Tbsp. minced fresh garlic
4 cups water
1 Tbsp. ras al hanout spice blend (see Note below)
2 tsp. ginger
1/2 tsp. crushed saffron
1-2 tsp. salt
Freshly ground black pepper
1 1/2 tsp. cinnamon
2 Tbsp. sugar or honey
1 cup seedless raisins (optional)
1/2 cup blanched whole or slivered almonds

Cut lamb off bone into 2" chunks. Put lamb and all bones in large pan. Add onions, garlic, water, ras al hanout, ginger, saffron, 1 tsp. salt, freshly ground black pepper, 1 tsp. cinnamon, and 1 tbsp. sugar or honey and mix well. Bring to a boil, cover, turn heat to low and simmer meat until very tender, approximately 2 hours for raw lamb and 1 hour for leftover lamb. When meat is almost done, add remaining 1/2 tsp. cinnamon, 1 tbsp. sugar and raisins (if using)

While lamb is simmering, preheat oven to 350°F. Place blanched almonds on baking sheet, and roast them for 5–10 minutes until they're lightly toasted.

After lamb is fully cooked, remove cover, turn up heat, and boil sauce until it's thickened and reduced, stirring frequently to make sure it doesn't burn. Before serving, taste and add sugar or honey, cinnamon, salt, or pepper, as needed. Arrange meat on a platter and cover with sauce, sprinkle with roasted almonds and serve with couscous.

Note: "Ras al hanout" is a blend of 12 to 100 different spices. Each merchant sells a different blend. I order mine from Internet spice sellers. Simple recipes for ras al hanout can be found on the internet and in many Middle Eastern cookbooks. Quick recipe for ras al hanout: Mix 2 Tbsp. freshly ground black pepper, 1 Tbsp. ground cumin, 1 Tbsp. ground cardamom, 1 Tbsp. ground cinnamon, 1 Tbsp. ground nutmeg, 1 Tbsp. ground allspice, 4 tsp. ground coriander, 2 tsp. ground ginger, 1 tsp. cayenne pepper, 1 tsp. ground cloves, 1 Tbsp. dried thyme, and 1 Tbsp. crushed fennel seeds.

LAMB BRAISED WITH LEMON AND ONION
Arni me Lemoni kai Kremmidia

Serves 4

Meat next to the bone has the most flavor, and this Greek recipe capitalizes on that property. Rendering bones, marrow and cartilage results in a sauce that is tart, sweet, and succulent all at once. This one-pot meal is easy to make, and can be finished well in advance and reheated. Be sure to serve it with lots of napkins because the only way to get every bit of meat and flavor from bones is to eat them with your fingers.

2 1/2 pounds lamb neck bones, or 2 pounds bone-in lamb steaks
1/4 cup olive oil
Salt
Freshly ground black pepper
3 cups diced yellow onion, 1/8" dice
2 cups white wine
1/2 cup fresh lemon juice
1 Tbsp. minced fresh garlic
1/2 cup minced fresh Italian parsley

Wash and dry meat and bones. If using lamb steaks, cut meat off bones into 1" cubes and reserve bones. Season lamb and bones with salt and freshly ground pepper and, in a large pot, brown on all sides in olive oil. Stir in onions, lightly season again with salt and freshly ground black pepper, and sauté until onions begin to turn golden. Add wine, lemon juice and garlic, bring to a boil, cover, turn down heat as low as possible, and simmer for 2 hours, or until lamb is very tender and onions have melted into sauce. Stir sauce from time to time and, if it starts sticking, add some wine. When lamb is done, stir in parsley, taste, and add salt, pepper, or lemon juice, as needed. Serve immediately.

BAKED ORZO WITH LAMB
Arni Yiouvetsi

Serves 2–4

Under the direction of Diane Primis, boys and girls in Holy Transfiguration's dance troupe, Asteria tou Vorra (Stars of the North), entertain the crowds during Anchorage's annual Greek Festival. Kids really work up an appetite after dancing so energetically. When each performance is over, they rush out of their costumes and line up for food. At the dinner booth, most dancers ask for big mounds of Yiouvetsi, a traditionally Greek dish using leftover roast lamb. When you taste John Maroulis' Yiouvetsi, you'll understand why. John says the recipe can be made with just water, but he adds red wine, as is done here, when he wants a fuller-flavored dish. Yiouvetsi is terrific with Cooked Wild Greens (page 39).

Leftover lamb bones with meat attached or 2 bone-in lamb steaks
2 Tbsp. olive oil
1 cup minced yellow onion
Salt
Freshly ground black pepper
1 14.5-ounce can crushed tomatoes
1 14.5-ounce can full of red wine
1 14.5-ounce can full of water
3 bay leaves
1–2 tsp. cinnamon
1/4–1/2 tsp. ground cloves
1 cup orzo
Grated kefalotyri or parmesan cheese

Using either fresh or leftover lamb, cut some of the meat into very small pieces, and leave the rest on the bone. Season well with salt and freshly ground black pepper.

In a large pot, sauté onions, lightly seasoned with salt and freshly ground black pepper, in olive oil until they soften and begin to turn golden. If using fresh lamb, brown it in olive oil. If using leftover lamb, just add it to pot. Add tomatoes, wine, water, bay leaves, cinnamon, and cloves, mix well, and bring to a boil. Cover, reduce heat to low, and simmer for 1 1/2 hours, or until lamb is tender and falling off bone. After 1 hour of simmering, taste and add salt, pepper, cinnamon, or cloves, as needed. Check meat from time to time as it cooks, and add water if necessary—you want a lot of juice because you need it to cook orzo. Remove bay leaves.

Preheat oven to 350°F.

Put orzo in baking pan with 3 cups of cooking liquid from meat. Cover pan with foil and put in preheated oven. After 30 minutes, check and see if it needs any additional liquid, and add meat juice or water if orzo is too dry (I usually add a cup of water at this point). Remove foil, and cook uncovered for 10 to 15 minutes. Reheat lamb in a covered pot on stove. Stir lamb into orzo and serve sprinkled with grated cheese.

LAMB PACKETS WITH ONIONS, TOMATOES AND FETA
Kleftiko

Serves 4

During the Greek War of Independence against Ottoman Turks, Klefts were irregular guerilla fighters who harassed and fought Ottomans whenever they could. Klefts were famous for stealing sheep and roasting them slowly over fires buried in sand to prevent alerting Ottomans to their presence with the smell of cooking meat. Kleftiko now refers to a method of cooking lamb, named after Klefts, in which meat is wrapped tightly in foil or parchment paper, and cooked slowly with vegetables. The meat ends up succulent, having captured a medley of slow-roasted flavors while sealed inside the packet. I make this in foil packets as that is easiest, but individual parchment paper packets make a more attractive presentation for serving. The packets take only a short time to put together, but must roast for 2 hours, so plan ahead when you make this tasty dish.

5 cups diced yellow onion, 1/2" dice
1/3 cup olive oil
Salt
Freshly ground black pepper
3 cups diced fresh or drained, canned tomatoes, 1/2" dice
2 Tbsp. plus 1 tsp. dried oregano, crushed
1 tsp. Aleppo pepper or 1/2 tsp. crushed red pepper
2 Tbsp. minced fresh garlic
2 pounds lamb shoulder steaks (4 steaks)
8 ounces feta cheese

Preheat oven to 350°F.

Sauté onions, lightly seasoned with salt and freshly ground black pepper, in olive oil until they soften and begin to turn golden. Add tomatoes, 2 Tbsp. oregano, Aleppo pepper, and garlic, and cook just until liquid released from tomatoes begins to evaporate. Don't cook into a sauce.

Wash meat and dry it well. Season on both sides with salt and freshly ground black pepper. Cut off four pieces of aluminum foil or parchment paper big enough to wrap a lamb steak and some vegetables, and lightly oil inside of wrappers. Put one piece of lamb in middle of each wrapper, and spoon equal amounts of vegetables over each piece of lamb. Cover vegetables with slices of feta, sprinkle with 1 tsp. oregano, and tightly seal packets.

Bake for 2 hours, or until meat is very tender. Serve one packet to each person, with potatoes or rice on the side. Packets can either be opened at the table by each diner, or in the kitchen and plated before serving.

BEEF BRAISED WITH TOMATOES AND GARLIC
Pastitsada

Serves 4–6

When I interviewed Andy and Carol Gialopsos about foods of Corfu, I discovered Carol did all the cooking but, like most Greek men, Andy had definite opinions about how each of Carol's recipes should be prepared. Carol's recipe for Corfiot Pastitsada benefits from her cooking skills, as well as Andy's strong opinions about seasoning, and produces a rich beef stew with a flavorful sauce. Serve it over pasta with grated cheese. This easy recipe can be made several days ahead, with stew reheated and pasta cooked just before serving.

2 1/4 pounds beef stew meat or steak cut into 1" chunks
Salt
Freshly ground black pepper
1/4 cup olive oil
4 cups diced yellow onions, 1/2" dice
2 Tbsp. minced fresh garlic
1 tsp. Aleppo pepper or 1/2 tsp. crushed red pepper (optional)
10 whole cloves
2 cups water
14.5-ounce can crushed tomatoes
1/4 tsp. ground cloves
Bucatoni or small penne pasta
Grated kefalotyri or parmesan cheese

Wash and dry beef, and season it with salt and freshly ground black pepper. In a large pot, heat olive oil, and brown meat on all sides in two batches. When meat is done, remove it from pan with a slotted spoon, leaving oil in pan. Sauté onions, lightly seasoned with salt and freshly ground black pepper, until they're translucent, using moisture from onions to help scrape up any browned bits on bottom of pan.

Return meat to pan, and stir in garlic, Aleppo pepper, whole cloves, water and tomatoes. Bring to a boil, cover pan, turn down heat, and simmer until meat is very tender, about 2 hours. Stir in ground cloves.

Cook bucatoni or small penne pasta in boiling, salted water, drain, and mix pasta with some of the sauce. Serve meat on top of pasta, with grated cheese available to sprinkle on top.

ROSEMARY BEEF STEW WITH PEARL ONIONS
Stifado

Serves 4–6

Savory Stifado, with onions, vinegar, rosemary, and cinnamon, is surprisingly rich, featuring meat slowly in-fused with the flavors of its complex sauce. The recipe uses two kinds of onions – long-cooked yellow onions that melt into the sauce, and perfectly caramelized pearl onions that add sweetness to balance the intensely flavored sauce. When it's done, Stifado should have a distinct taste of cinnamon. If it doesn't, add a little powdered cinnamon near the end of the cooking time. The flavor of Stifado deepens and concentrates over time, so it can easily be made ahead and reheated. Because it has a lot of terrific sauce, Stifado goes well with pasta or boiled potatoes.

2 1/4 pounds beef stew meat or steak cut into 1" chunks	3 cups beef stock
Salt	1/2 tsp. ground cloves
Freshly ground black pepper	1 tsp. ground nutmeg
1/4 cup olive oil	1 tsp. freshly ground cumin
3 cups diced yellow onions, 1/2" dice	1 cinnamon stick
1 Tbsp. minced fresh garlic	2 Tbsp. minced rosemary
2 cups red wine	5 bay leaves
1/4 cup red wine vinegar	20 ounces fresh pearl onions
1 14.5-ounce can crushed tomatoes	2 Tbsp. butter
	2 Tbsp. olive oil
	3/4 cup minced fresh Italian parsley

Wash and dry the beef, and season it with salt and freshly ground black pepper. In a large pot, heat olive oil, and brown meat on all sides in two batches. Cooking in small batches ensures the pot stays hot enough to brown meat, rather than steam it. When meat is done, remove it from pan with a slotted spoon, leaving oil in pan. Add onions to oil, and sauté them, lightly seasoned with salt and freshly ground black pepper, until they're translucent, using moisture from onions to help scrape up any browned bits on bottom of pan.

Return meat to pan, and stir in garlic, red wine, red wine vinegar, tomatoes, beef stock, cloves, nutmeg, cumin, cinnamon stick, minced rosemary, and bay leaves. Bring liquid to a boil, cover pan, turn down heat to low, and simmer until meat is very tender, about 2 hours. Remove cover, and cook until sauce is thick and flavors have thoroughly blended, about 1 hour.

While beef is cooking, peel pearl onions and cut X in root end to help hold onion layers to-gether. An easy way to peel onions is to drop them in boiling water for one minute. Remove onions from water and slip off peels. Sauté peeled pearl onions, lightly seasoned with salt and pepper, in 2 Tbsp. butter and 2 Tbsp. olive oil until onions are well browned on all sides and cooked through.

Five minutes before stew is fully cooked, stir in browned pearl onions and minced parsley. Taste and add salt, pepper, or ground cinnamon, as needed. When stew is done, remove bay leaves and serve immediately.

SERBIAN BEEF STEW WITH ONIONS AND PEPPERS
Manga

Serves 4

Fran Conlan is a mainstay at Holy Transfiguration and always goes out of her way to help anyone and everyone with whatever needs doing. When I began this cookbook project, Fran was the first to search her files for traditional recipes. Fran learned to cook Manga from her in-laws after she married Herb, her Serbian-American husband. Fran modestly told me this recipe was good, but that was an understatement. The first time I made it, my husband had seconds and I had thirds. Dried herbs work better than fresh in this recipe. Their flavor is released by long cooking that tenderizes meat and concentrates wonderful flavors. When I make Manga, I intentionally make enough for leftovers, because its flavors continue to develop and improve as it sits. For the same reason, Manga is a good dish to make ahead and reheat at the last minute. Serve with potatoes or pasta.

2 lbs. beef round or chuck steak
2 Tbsp. olive oil
Salt
Freshly ground black pepper
2 cups diced yellow onions, 1/4" dice
1 cup diced red or green bell
   pepper, 1/4" dice
1 14.5-ounce can tomato sauce
   or crushed tomatoes

1 14.5-ounce can full of water
1 Tbsp. minced fresh garlic
1 Tbsp. dried oregano, crushed
1 Tbsp. dried thyme, crushed
1 tsp. dried sage, crushed
1/2 tsp. celery seeds, crushed
1 tsp. Aleppo pepper or 1/2 tsp.
   crushed red pepper (optional)

Wash and dry beef. Trim off any fat, and cut it into medium chunks. Season meat with salt and freshly ground black pepper. Heat olive oil in a large pot and brown meat on all sides. Add onions and bell pepper, stir well, and cook for two minutes. Stir in tomato sauce, water, garlic, oregano, thyme, sage, celery seeds, and Aleppo pepper. Bring to a boil, cover, turn heat down, and simmer for 45-60 minutes, or until meat is tender. Taste and add salt or pepper, as needed. Remove cover, and continue to simmer for an additional 30 minutes. Serve immediately.

SMYRNA SAUSAGES IN TOMATO-WINE SAUCE
Soutzoukakia

Makes 20 large sausages or 40-50 small sausages

On holidays in Greece, when the table is laden with special treats of all kinds, I'm happiest when seated near a plate of garlicky meatballs, which diners spear off the serving dish with their forks. Sometimes the meatballs are round and fried (Keftedakia, page 28), and occasionally they're shaped into oblong sausages, seasoned with cumin, and served in winy tomato sauce. These sausages are called Soutzoukakia, and are one of my favorite dishes. Greeks settled Smyrna (now the Turkish city of Izmir) in the 11th century BCE. Smyrna remained important to Greece for over 3000 years, even though Greeks, Persians, Romans, Byzantines, and Ottomans controlled its government at various points. From its settlement until 1923, Smyrna was largely Greek. Following the 1923 Treaty of Lausanne, the entire Greek population was ejected from Smyrna and forced to seek refuge in new countries. Most went to Greece. The displaced Smyrna residents brought their customs and cuisine with them to their new homes. Soutzoukakia is one of the dishes that originated in Smyrna, and remains a popular menu item in Greek homes and tavernas today. I use a combination of beef and pork for Soutzoukakia, which results in juicy, flavorful sausages; they can also be made just with beef. I don't use breadcrumbs, as is called for in many recipes, because I prefer Soutzoukakia's texture without it. The sausages are robustly spiced; the tomato sauce is not. The contrast is pleasing.

Sausages:
1 pound ground beef
1 pound ground pork
2 cups minced yellow onion
2 eggs
2 Tbsp. red wine vinegar
1 Tbsp. olive oil
1 cup minced fresh parsley
1 Tbsp. minced garlic
4 tsp. cumin, ground
2 tsp. Aleppo pepper or
   1 tsp. crushed red pepper
Salt
Freshly ground black pepper

Sauce:
2 cups diced yellow onion, 1/4" dice
2 Tbsp. olive oil
Salt
Freshly ground black pepper
28-ounce can or 3 cups crushed tomatoes
1 cup dry red wine
1 Tbsp. honey
1 tsp Aleppo pepper or
   1/2 tsp. crushed red pepper

Make Sausages: Put all sausage ingredients in large bowl. Thoroughly knead ingredients together with your hands, making sure herbs and spices are evenly distributed in meat.

For large sausages, divide meat into 1/4 cup portions (using a 1/4 cup lever-action scoop speeds up this task). For small sausages, divide meat into 1-2 Tbsp. portions. Shape each portion into oblong-shaped sausages. Brown sausages in frying pan, cooking them in batches, to make sure meat fries properly (if pan is crowded, sausages will steam rather than fry). Turn sausages regularly so they brown evenly on all sides.

As each batch is done, place sausages on paper towels to soak up excess oil.

Make Sauce: In large pot, sauté onions in olive oil, lightly seasoned with salt and freshly ground black pepper, until they soften and start to turn golden. Stir in remaining ingredients, and bring to a boil. Gently stir browned sausages into sauce, and bring to a boil. Cover pot, turn heat down to low, and simmer for 40-50 minutes, stirring occasionally and being careful not to break sausages. When sauce thickens, and flavors of sausages and sauce have blended, Soutzoukakia is done. Taste and add salt and freshly ground black pepper, as needed.

For main course, serve hot over rice or pasta, accompanied by olives, feta cheese, and plenty of crusty bread.

Leftovers: I plan for leftovers when I make Soutzoukakia. Its flavor improves with the passage of time and leftovers can be used in many ways. They're a welcome addition to an appetizer spread (mezedes) any time of year and, with melted cheese, make excellent open-faced sandwiches. Leftover Soutzoukakia over rice or pasta is a filling and enjoyable meal. Cold Soutzoukakia straight out of the refrigerator container is a wonderful, ready-made snack.

STUFFED LETTUCE OR SWISS CHARD WITH EGG-LEMON SAUCE
Dolmades Avgolemono

Makes 20 dolmades

One rainy day, I stopped by the Baskous house and found Maria making stuffed lettuce leaves. As I watched Maria roll leaves, she explained that when her children were small, they didn't like stuffed grape leaves. Maria's mother, Dena Baskurelou, made them stuffed lettuce leaves instead, which the kids loved. Maria worked quickly. The dolmades were soon done, and she gave me one to sample. The combined flavors of tart egg-lemon sauce, sweet lettuce, and herby filling were so amazingly good I made them for dinner the next day. It's unlikely I ever would have tried cooked lettuce if I'd not tasted it in Maria's kitchen that rainy afternoon. Maria says when she is being fancy, she wraps half the stuffing with lettuce and half with Swiss chard. You can also make these with cabbage, but Maria prefers the sweeter taste of lettuce and Swiss chard, as they bring out the filling's flavor and don't mask it as cabbage tends to do. You can make stuffed leaves any size, but I like making them relatively small so I taste meat and greens in every bite.

2 heads of romaine or iceberg lettuce, or equivalent amount of Swiss chard
1/3 cup olive oil
2 cups diced yellow onions, 1/4" dice
Salt
Freshly ground black pepper
1 cup water
1 pound ground beef or lamb
2 cups chopped fresh Italian parsley
1/4 cup minced fresh mint
1/4 cup minced fresh dill
1/2 tsp. Aleppo pepper or 1/4 tsp. crushed red pepper
1/2 cup chopped green onions
1/2 cup long-grain rice
1 3/4 cups chicken broth
1 3/4 cups water
1/2 cup fresh lemon juice
2–3 eggs, separated into whites and yolks
Lemon wedges for garnish

If using romaine lettuce, separate outer lettuce leaves, and reserve smaller inner leaves for lining pan. If using iceberg lettuce, separate lettuce leaves, being careful not to tear them; if you can't separate leaves without tearing them, blanch head whole. If using Swiss chard, remove lower stems. Blanch lettuce or Swiss chard in boiling salted water for 1–2 minutes, just until leaves are soft enough to roll. Drain greens in a colander.

Sauté onions, lightly seasoned with salt and freshly ground black pepper, in olive oil until they begin to soften and turn translucent. Stir in 1 cup of water, cook until water reduces by half, and remove pan from heat. In bowl, knead ground meat, parsley, mint, dill, Aleppo pepper, green onions, cooked onions and water, and rice. Season with salt and lots of freshly ground black pepper.

Spread out a blanched lettuce or chard leaf, with stem end facing away from you and inside of leaf facing up. If using romaine, press down on stem to split and flatten it (don't break all the way through stem, just split it on side facing up). If using iceberg lettuce that you blanched as a whole head, you need to tease leaves apart. Put 1/4 cup filling on end of each leaf, and fold lower end over filling. Fold in sides of leaf, and roll it up, ending with stem. Don't roll it too tight because rice expands as it cooks. Line pan with loose lettuce leaves, arrange stuffed leaves on top with loose edge of roll toward bottom of pan. Stack stuffed leaves, if necessary. Cover with additional loose lettuce leaves, and weigh stuffed leaves down with a plate. Add chicken stock and water, bring liquid to a boil, cover, reduce heat, simmer for 30 minutes, and remove from heat.

Drain liquid from stuffed leaves into a saucepan. Boil and reduce liquid until you have 1 cup left. Reduce heat to low. Beat two egg whites until soft peaks form, but they're not stiff. Whisk two egg yolks into whites, and whisk in lemon juice. Whisk a small amount of reduced cooking liquid into egg-lemon mix to temper eggs. Whisk tempered eggs into remaining cooking liquid. Cook slowly until sauce thickens, being careful not to let sauce boil or eggs will curdle. If sauce is too thin, whisk remaining egg and stir it quickly into sauce.

Arrange dolmades on a serving dish, pour egg-lemon sauce over them, garnish with lemon wedges and serve.

PAPRIKA PORK AND CABBAGE
Hirino me Paprika kai Lachano

Serves 4

Tina Karakatsanis Chowaniec says her father Apostolis, who lives in Filakto, Greece, "loves food and especially meat. His favorite dish is cabbage with pork." In this recipe from Tina's mother Ksanthi, cabbage is cooked until it's soft and infused with flavors of paprika, tomatoes, and meat juices. Slightly spicy paprika buoys up the mild taste of pork. Serve with feta cheese and boiled potatoes tossed with garlic, olive oil, and parsley.

4 pork chops (2 1/2 pounds), each cut into 2 pieces
Salt
Freshly ground black pepper
2 Tbsp. olive oil
3 cups sliced yellow onions, cut in half-moons
1 Tbsp. minced fresh garlic
2 Tbsp. sweet Hungarian paprika
1 cup water
1 8-ounce can tomato sauce
1 1/2 pounds cabbage (1/2–1 cabbage), cut into 2 inch chunks

Wash pork, dry it well, and season with salt and freshly ground black pepper on both sides. Heat olive oil in a large pan, and brown pork on both sides. Remove and set aside on a plate.

In same pan, sauté onions, lightly seasoned with salt and freshly ground pepper, until they soften and begin to turn golden. Stir in garlic and paprika, and mix well, being careful not to burn paprika. Quickly stir in water, scraping up any browned bits from bottom of pan. Add tomato sauce and bring to a boil. Stir in cabbage, cover, turn down heat, and simmer for 45 minutes, stirring occasionally, until pork is tender and cabbage is very soft and has melded with sauce. Serve immediately.

PORK WITH CELERY AND LEMON
Hirino me Selino kai Lemoni

Serves 4–6

Many Greek cookbooks have recipes for Pork with Celery and Egg-Lemon Sauce, but it's a tricky recipe to get right. Too often sauce overwhelms the pork, or goes in the opposite direction and vanishes into blandness. Other recipes taste good, but because the sauce is thick, gloppy, and pale, the finished dish looks terrible. I've made versions of this recipe more times than I care to count, and tinkered with the balance of flavors and textures. In this version, celery and lemon are just strong enough to balance the pork, and the eggless lemon sauce is bright and sharp. If you can find it, be sure to use leaf celery, which is usually available from Asian markets or farmer's markets (and sometimes called Chinese celery), because it has a concentrated herby flavor that is absent in supermarket celery. Serve with rice or pilaf.

2 pounds pork butt or shoulder, with bone
Salt
Freshly ground black pepper
1/4 cup olive oil
3 cups diced yellow onion, 1/2" dice
8 cups chopped leaf celery, 1/2" slices
1 Tbsp. minced fresh garlic
1/2 cup white wine
1/2 cup water
1/4 cup fresh lemon juice
Lemon wedges

Wash and dry pork well, and cut it into 1" cubes. Season cubes (and any bones) everywhere with salt and freshly ground black pepper. Heat olive oil in a large pot and brown pork and bones on all sides. Stir in onions and sauté until they soften and begin to turn golden. Mix in celery and garlic, and cook for an additional 2 minutes. Season with a little salt and lots of freshly ground black pepper. Stir in white wine and water, bring liquid to a boil, cover, turn down heat, and simmer for 45–60 minutes until pork is tender. Remove cover, bring liquid in pan to a boil, and bubble liquid until it's reduced by half. Mix in lemon juice. Taste and add salt or pepper, as needed. Serve immediately with lemon wedges.

PORK WITH CORIANDER SEEDS
Afelia Kyprou

Serves 8–12

Stathis Mataragas says when he cooks Afelia for guests, everyone loves it and can't believe how simple it is to make. Afelia is one of the best-known specialties of Cyprus, Stathis' homeland, where he says the method used to raise pigs creates extremely tender pork. Stathis marinates meat in red wine for one day, drains it, cooks it, and only sprinkles ground coriander over at the end. I made it Stathis' way and it was excellent, but in my constant search to accentuate flavors, I successfully experimented with adding coriander to the marinade, and braising pork in this liquid. The recipe below includes my modifications, and should be served with another of Stathis' recipes—Salata Kyprou (page 53) and potatoes or pilaf. Stathis says to use cuts of pork that are marbled with fat, as they have the best flavor and texture for Afelia. Lean pork is too tough and bland for this dish. Because Afelia must be marinated for a long time, be sure to plan ahead when you want to serve it.

4 1/2 pounds pork shoulder or butt roast
3 cups red wine
1 Tbsp. ground coriander
2 Tbsp. olive oil
Salt
Freshly ground black pepper
Whole coriander seeds, crushed

Wash and dry meat well. Cut pork into 2" chunks, and put in a large zip-lock bag. Mix wine and ground coriander. Pour spiced red wine into zip-lock bag; if wine doesn't cover pork, add more. Seal bag, and marinate pork in refrigerator for at least 18 hours, or up to three days.

When you're ready to cook, remove meat from marinade, and dry it very well. Reserve marinade. Season meat on all sides with salt and freshly ground black pepper. In a large pot, heat olive oil, and brown meat on all sides. Don't crowd meat in pan; instead, brown it in batches or it will steam rather than cook correctly. When meat is all browned, return it to pan along with reserved marinade. Bring liquid to a boil, turn heat down to low, cover, and simmer for 1 hour. Remove lid and cook for 30 minutes, or until meat is very tender and liquid almost gone. Sprinkle with crushed coriander and serve.

GRILLED PORK STEAK
Hirini Brizola

Serves 4

There isn't anything more Mediterranean than the heady smell of meat juices hitting a hot fire wafting through warm summer air. Local combinations of herbs, spices, and meats yield an array of variations on this simple theme, and every version is amazingly good. This is a Greek recipe, and is standard taverna fare, usually served on a plate piled high with fried potatoes. In Greece, meat is cut thinner than in this country and sometimes is pounded thin to tenderize it and shorten the cooking time, but it isn't necessary to do either. Be careful not to overcook pork steak or you'll transform this succulent delight into tough, tasteless cardboard. Brizola is best cooked just until meat is still slightly pink in the center. Serve with fried or roasted potatoes, a juicy tomato and onion salad, and slices of feta cheese.

4 pork steaks
4 cloves garlic
Salt
Freshly ground black pepper
4–8 tsp. dried oregano, crushed

Rinse steaks, and dry well. Using a garlic press, squeeze 1 clove of garlic over each steak and rub it all over pork. Season both sides with salt, freshly ground black pepper, and a generous amount of oregano.

Cook pork steaks over a medium hot fire, or in a grill pan on top of stove, turning regularly until meat is just done. Be careful not to overcook pork. Serve immediately.

Note: Marianna Apetroeai makes a Romanian version of this dish and seasons it with garlic, sweet paprika, salt, pepper, and a Croatian spice mix called Vegeta, which can be purchased at ethnic and gourmet markets. She buys pork steak in large quantities, seasons, and freezes it with the seasoning on, so the meat is marinated and ready to cook when she takes it out of the freezer.

ROAST PORK WITH SPINACH STUFFING AND ROAST POTATOES
Rollo Hirino me Patates

Serves 8

Lamb is closely associated with Greek cooking, but in many parts of Greece, pork is eaten just as frequently. Village cooks are remarkably creative with pork. They serve it grilled, fried, preserved, braised and, if you're very lucky, roasted and stuffed with cheese and vegetables. Once I attended a village festival in Greece during which a local restaurant served pan after pan of Pork Rollo with Spinach Stuffing. Tender pork was rolled around colorful vegetables and sliced to create an eye-catching and succulent meal. The taste of this special occasion dish lives on in my mind, and here I've recreated its memorable flavors. Garlicky spinach stuffing, rich with feta cheese, provides a moist counterpoint to roast meat. Be careful not to overcook the meat or it will dry out. While not traditional, brining pork loin, a relatively lean cut of meat, adds flavor and helps keep it moist. Roasted potatoes round out the meal.

2 1/2–4 1/2 pound boneless pork loin roast, roast with layer of fat on top
2 Tbsp. olive oil
Cotton kitchen string, cut in 8 pieces, each 18" long

Brine:
3/4 cup sugar
3/4 cup kosher salt
5 bay leaves, crumbled
2 Tbsp. dried thyme, crushed
1 Tbsp. black peppercorns, crushed
1 head garlic, separated into cloves and crushed
6-8 cups water

Stuffing:
2 pounds cleaned spinach leaves, or 2 10-ounce boxes frozen spinach
4 ounces crumbled feta cheese, about 2/3 cup
2 Tbsp. minced fresh garlic
1 egg
Salt
Freshly ground black pepper
2 tsp. dried thyme, crushed
8 ounce peeled carrots, about 8-9 small, cut into thin lengthwise quarters

Potatoes:
3 pounds Russet (baking) potatoes
1 tsp. dried thyme, crushed
2 cups chicken stock
2 cups white wine, divided

Butterfly Pork: Double-butterfly pork. (See Photos and Notes below). Open pork out flat between two sheets of plastic wrap and pound it to an even thickness with a meat pounder.

Make Brine: Dissolve salt and sugar in 2 cups hot water. Add bay leaves, thyme, peppercorns, garlic and 4–6 cups water, as needed, to cover pork. Immerse pork in brine, and refrigerate it for 1–2 hours.

Make Stuffing: Blanch fresh spinach for 30-60 seconds in boiling salted water (or thaw frozen spinach). Squeeze out as much water as possible from spinach using your hands or a clean dish towel. Thoroughly combine spinach with feta, garlic, and egg. Season to taste with salt and freshly ground black pepper. Feta cheese can be salty (and remember the meat has been brined), so be careful not to over-salt.

Stuff Roast: Preheat oven to 350°F. Remove pork from brine. Dry it well and remove any clinging brine ingredients. Place pork on plastic wrap with cut side facing up. Sprinkle crushed thyme and freshly ground black pepper over pork. Evenly lay out carrots on top of seasoned meat. Spread spinach filling evenly over carrots, leaving an inch border all the way around. Starting with a short end, and using plastic wrap to help lift meat, tightly roll meat up around stuffing. Tie roll tightly with kitchen twine at 1" intervals. Slash fat on top of roll, being careful not to cut string. Season outside of roll with freshly ground black pepper.

Cook Roast: Heat olive oil in heavy frying pan, brown roast well on all sides, paying particular attention to fatty side. While pork is browning, peel potatoes and cut into lengthwise wedges. Season potato wedges with salt, pepper, and thyme.

Place roast in large baking pan, fat side up, surrounded by potatoes. Pour chicken stock and 1 cup of wine around them. Place pan in oven and cook for 30–45 minutes, or until internal temperature of roast is 130-135°F. The meat cooks faster than you think because it's been cut thin before stuffing and because it's been browned. When it's done, remove pork to platter and let it rest, tented with aluminum foil, while you make sauce and finish potatoes. Finish cooking potatoes by browning them under broiler, turning as needed to prevent burning.

Drain off as much fat as possible from pan juices (a fat separator works well for this), and strain sauce. Boil pan juices and remaining wine until sauce is reduced and slightly thickened. Cut meat into slices, drizzle with sauce, and serve with roasted potatoes on the side.

Step #1: With a sharp knife held parallel to surface of roast, and starting one third of the way up from roast's bottom, slice horizontally through roast's long side, cutting from right to left. Don't cut completely through; stop 3/4" short of the edge. Open roast like a book, with the uncut long side acting as a hinge.

Step #2: Starting halfway up from bottom of roast's thicker portion, slice horizontally through roast's long side (parallel to surface of meat), cutting from right to left, once again stopping 3/4" short of edge to create another hinge.

Step #3: Unfold roast into large rectangle. Put between two layers of plastic wrap and pound meat lightly with meat pounder to smooth out "hinge" areas.

Step #4: Spread spinach filling evenly over carrots (in picture, stuffing is partially spread out), then roll it up and tie.

Note: Don't be afraid to butterfly pork loin; it's very easy to do. The purpose is to cut the meat into thirds, but to keep the thirds connected, so that you're left with one flat piece of uniformly thick meat.

PORK KEBABS WITH OREGANO
Souvlaki

Serves 4

In village tavernas across Greece, souvlaki is often made with pork and assertively seasoned with oregano. Cubes of meat are cut much smaller than what you usually get in American restaurants when you order kebabs. Smaller pieces of meat increases the amount of meat surface exposed to fire, improves browning, and enhances the smoky grilled flavor. Souvlaki needs to be made with fatty meat, or it will dry out and won't have as much flavor. If souvlaki is cooked right, meat is juicy on the inside and nicely browned on the outside. It tastes best when delivered by a friendly waiter to friends sitting at an outdoor table littered with bottles of red wine and ouzo. Ño matter where or how it's eaten, souvlaki is always a crowd-pleaser, so make sure there are multiple skewers for each person. Serve with an array of appetizers and salads, always including Tzatziki (page 20) as part of the spread. Since you have the fire going, brush slices of bread with olive oil, toast them on the fire, and eat hot, slightly smoky, grilled bread with souvlaki.

Ramzi Abuamsha grilling Souvlaki at the annual Greek Festival

2 pounds pork butt, shoulder, or boneless country ribs
Salt
Freshly ground black pepper
Olive oil
1/3 cup dried oregano, crushed

Cut meat into 3/4" squares, but don't trim off fat. Thread 4–5 pieces of meat on short bamboo skewers. Season all sides of meat with salt and freshly ground black pepper. Rub olive oil on skewered meat. Liberally sprinkle crushed oregano over meat, making sure that all sides are well-seasoned (this likely means putting on more oregano than you think reasonable).

Grill skewers over a medium fire, turning when one side is brown, or over a hot fire, turning frequently. Have a spray bottle of water handy to prevent flare-ups from melting pork fat, which burn meat and prevent it from cooking evenly. You can also cook skewers on top of stove in a hot grill pan where they take about 7–10 minutes. It's important not to overcook meat or it won't be juicy, but if it isn't adequately browned, you won't experience the true joy of perfectly grilled meat. The essence of souvlaki is the marriage of well-browned meat with oregano, the quintessential mountain herb.

SAUSAGE AND PEPPER STEW
Spetsofai

Serves 4

Spetsofai is a specialty of Pelion, a town in Northern Greece known for making sausages called "loukanika horiatiki" (village sausage). These sausages are not available in Alaska, but Tina Karakatsanis Chowaniec says you can make good Spetsofai using Italian sausages. Spetsofai is intended to be spicy, so I use the best quality hot Italian sausage available. Sweet, mild, Italian frying peppers are perfect in this recipe. If they aren't available, use ripe red bell peppers; the flavor of green bell peppers is too dominant for this recipe. Spetsofai is a hearty, rustic stew, the perfect meal for a cold winter evening.

1 1/2 pounds hot Italian sausage
1 1/2 pounds Italian frying or red bell peppers
Salt
Freshly ground black pepper
1/4 cup olive oil
3 cups diced yellow onion, 1/2" dice
1 14.5-ounce can diced tomatoes
1 14.5-ounce can full of water
3 Tbsp. dried oregano, crushed
Chopped fresh Italian parsley for garnish
Grated parmesan or kefalotyri cheese

Cut sausage into bite-sized pieces and brown them in a lightly oiled frying pan. Discard oil and reserve sausage.

Cut peppers in half lengthwise, discard stems and seeds, and cut into 1/2-inch strips. In a large pan, sauté peppers, lightly seasoned with salt and freshly ground black pepper, in olive oil just until they begin to brown. Add onions and sauté for 2 minutes. Stir in cooked sausage, tomatoes, water, oregano, and a little salt and freshly ground black pepper. Bring to a boil, cover, turn down heat, and simmer for 30 minutes, or until peppers are soft but not mushy. If sauce is too thin, remove cover, increase heat, and boil until sauce thickens, stirring frequently to prevent scorching. Taste, and add salt or pepper, as needed. Garnish with chopped parsley. Serve with thick slices of artisan-style bread and a bowl of grated cheese for sprinkling on top.

ALEXANDRIAN LIVER WITH SPICY GREEN PEPPERS
Kebdah Eskandaranie

Serves 2–4

"There is a very nice kind of food called Alexandrian liver," explained Nawal Bekheet. "Every restaurant in Alexandria (Egypt) has this, and everyone who goes to Alexandria has to order it right away." In Egypt, it's always made with lamb liver. In Alaska, where lamb liver isn't available, Nawal uses mild-tasting veal liver. She says the flavor of beef liver is too strong for this dish. As with all of Nawal's recipes, flavors here are well balanced and seasonings complement each other nicely. I've served this dish to liver skeptics, like the woman who first fretted about eating liver, and then about the number of jalapeños in the recipe. After she began eating Alexandrian Liver, the woman declared her doubts "wrong, wrong, wrong" and said the spicing was perfect and Alexandrian Liver "incredibly delicious." The liver has a rich, almost buttery flavor, which contrasts nicely with well-spiced vegetables. Serve hot with Rice and Pasta Pilaf (page 97).

1 pound veal liver, cut into 1/4" dice
1 1/2 Tbsp. olive oil
1 Tbsp. minced fresh garlic
1/3 cup minced green bell pepper
1/2 cup minced green jalapeños, or other hot peppers
Salt
Lots of freshly ground black pepper
1/4 tsp. ground nutmeg

Heat olive oil so it's hot, but not smoking. Add liver, stir well to coat it with oil, turn heat down to medium and stir in garlic. Cook until most, but not all, of liquid that comes out of liver evaporates (this only takes a few minutes). Add minced pepper and jalapeños. Season with salt, black pepper, and nutmeg, and cook for an additional five minutes to allow flavors to blend. Serve immediately.

* New recipe this edition

Stathis Mataragas fled the invasion of his Cyprus village with the clothes on his back and the memories of his mother's cooking in his head. He was 23 and an army veteran the day Turks launched a surprise invasion and permanently drove many Cypriots from their homes.

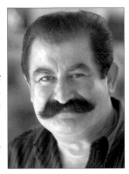

Although 30 years had passed when Stathis told me this story, the horrific events of July 1974 were seared deep in his memory and seemed as vivid as if they had just happened yesterday. Stathis was scheduled for a day off from his job and had asked his mother to let him sleep late. He was irritated to be awakened early in the morning by women chattering outside his window. When Stathis stuck his head out the window to grouse about the noise, Turkish war planes screamed down on the peaceful village. The planes raked the village streets with machine gun fire, killing his neighbors as Stathis watched in horror.

Stathis lived in Vasilia, a beautiful village on the north coast of Cyprus. The Mataragas family grew fruits and vegetables in fertile land around Vasilia. Everyone in the family worked. Starting when he was 10, Stathis helped out by loading the family's string of donkeys with whatever produce the family had picked the day before and taking them up to the mountain villages above Vasilia. Arriving in a village, Stathis would pass through the narrow stone streets hawking oranges, lemons, grapefruit, tomatoes, squash, or whatever was ready for harvest.

When Turks attacked Cyprus, Stathis left his village to help protect it. He joined an Army unit in the mountains and took part in a guerilla campaign against the invading Turks. After weeks of fighting in the mountains, Stathis was filthy and bedraggled. He decided to take a bold risk for a shower and a change of clothes. Using his childhood knowledge of donkey paths and hidden mountain trails, Stathis crept down to Vasilia.

Silence greeted him when he entered the abandoned village, which always before had teemed with the sounds and rhythms of life. Stealthily making his way through the empty streets, what Stathis saw shocked him deeply. The door to his house had been smashed from its hinges and hung akimbo like a bird's broken wing. Nothing remained of his family's belongings. Everything had been destroyed or looted, even the chickens. His neighbors' houses and belongings were in the same condition.

Despite the devastation, a garden hose behind his parents' house still ran with clear water. Stathis took his last bath in Vasilia standing outside under the hose, with only the sound of splashing water to break the ghostly silence. His gun rested against the wall within easy reach. Life as Stathis knew it was over forever.

A homeless uprooted refugee, Stathis began the immigrant's journey, searching for a new land to put down his roots. First, with Greek refugees from all the northern Cypriot towns, he made his way south to the remaining Greek part of Cyprus. From Cyprus he traveled across the Aegean to Athens, eventually to Canada, and finally, to Alaska. In the Mataragas family, women did the cooking, so Stathis had not cooked before he was driven from his village. As he made his way across the world, Stathis used memories of his mother's cooking, and his keen sense of taste, to recreate dishes of his childhood.

In Alaska, Stathis owns a successful restaurant, Anchorage's Pizza Plaza. As with many restaurants owned by Greek-Americans, the menu is mostly familiar Italian dishes. No matter how busy his restaurant is, Stathis makes sure there's always a table near the kitchen for expatriates to gather and speak the old language, watch satellite broadcasts of soccer matches from Greece, and eat one of the dishes he first enjoyed in the sunny peaceful days of Vasilia long past.

THREE BEAN, GREENS AND ZUCCHINI SALAD WITH SMOKED SALMON
Lachanika Salata me Kapnisto Solomo (Day 1)

Serves 4, with leftovers for Day 2 recipe

Many kinds of vegetables grew well in deep rich soils around the village of Vasilia, and Stathis Mataragas' mother used them to cook healthy and mouth-watering meals for her family. She made this salad with whatever green vegetables were in season and it's one of Stathis' favorite dishes. His mother always made enough for two meals, he explained. On the first day, she served it as a cooked salad with smoked fish (this recipe). On the second day, she cooked the vegetables again to make a tomato based stew (the following recipe). Stathis says he likes it better the second day, but the two versions are so different and so good, in my house we love them both and can't choose a favorite. In Cyprus, this dish is made with fresh fava beans (rarely available in Alaska), but edamame (green soy) beans taste similar to fava beans and make an ideal substitute. Stathis' use of smoked salmon is inspired and makes a dynamic flavor counterpoint to beans, green onion, and feta cheese.

1/2 pound fresh or frozen black-eyed peas
1/2 pound fresh, shelled, and skinned
   fava beans or 10 ounces frozen shelled
   edamame beans (green soybeans)
1/2 pound fresh or frozen green beans
1 bunch Swiss chard or other greens,
   including stems, roughly chopped
1/2 pound zucchini, cut into 1/2" slices
Salt

Freshly ground black pepper
Extra virgin olive oil
2 lemons
8 ounces lox or smoked salmon
8 green onions, cleaned
Feta cheese
Kalamata olives

If using fresh peas or beans, blanch them in boiling salted water for 1 minute, drain, rinse well, and return them to pot. Cover peas and beans with water, season with salt and freshly ground black pepper, and bring to a boil. When water boils, add Swiss chard and zucchini. Cover pot, reduce heat to low, and simmer until beans are tender. The lower the heat, the better the vegetables taste. Use stems of greens to test for doneness – when thick part is done, beans are too.

Use a ladle with holes to remove vegetables from cooking water, reserving part of water for the next day's dish. (I also save cooking water for soup stock.) Place vegetables in bowl, and dress with olive oil and freshly squeezed lemon juice to taste. Taste and add salt or pepper, as needed.

Serve, accompanied by a plate of smoked salmon, green onions, feta cheese, and olives.

THREE-BEAN, GREENS, ZUCCHINI AND TOMATO STEW
Lachanika me Domates (Day 2)

Serves 4

Nothing goes to waste in a village. "Leftovers" make some of the best ingredients because they've already developed complex flavors. Village women, like Stathis Mataragas' mother, creatively adapt ingredients at hand to serve their families satisfying rustic fare. In the Mataragas family this dish was made with planned leftovers (Day 1 recipe, above). Resting in the refrigerator overnight softens vegetables and harmonizes their flavors. Adding tomato sauce changes the character of the dish entirely. My husband said, "This is the best of beans. If you've ever looked with dismay at a bowl of mixed beans and dreamed of what it would taste like if the beans had real flavor and a sauce that brought them together, this is what you'd have." Stathis' family enjoyed this dish warmly seasoned with whole chilies and served with slices of feta cheese on the side.

2 cups diced yellow onions, 1/4" dice
1/4 cup olive oil
Salt
Freshly ground black pepper
1 tsp. minced fresh garlic
1/4 cup tomato paste
1 cup white wine
1 cup reserved vegetable cooking liquid
1–3 whole dried chilies
4 cups leftover vegetables from Day 1, liquid drained off

Sauté onions, lightly seasoned with salt and freshly ground black pepper, in olive oil until they soften and turn golden. Add garlic and tomato paste and mix in well. Stir in wine, cooking liquid, and dried chilies. Stir in leftover vegetables. Bring to a boil, then turn down heat and simmer for 30 minutes, or until sauce has thickened and flavors have melded. Taste, add salt or pepper, as needed, and serve immediately.

GREEN BEAN AND TOMATO STEW
Fasolakia

Serves 4–6

Fasolakia is familiar to patrons of old-style Greek restaurants where customers are invited into the kitchen to choose from the day's specials. My version is based on countless bowls of Fasolakia I've enjoyed in Greece, sitting under shade trees in outdoor restaurants, eating slowly to make it last, sipping wine, and watching the world go by. Earthy bean flavor, together with the sweetness of onion and the rich luxurious taste of tomatoes, make this an exceptional dish. Fasolakia is a wonderful meal on its own with a slice of feta cheese, or served alongside roasted chicken or meat. Be sure to have plenty of crusty bread on hand to sop up sauce, and round out the meal with a glass of full-bodied red wine.

2 pounds fresh green beans, or 20 ounces frozen and thawed
1 large yellow onion, sliced into 1/4" half-moons
2 Tbsp. minced fresh garlic
1/2 cup minced fresh Italian parsley
1/4 cup minced fresh mint
1/4 cup minced fresh dill
1 tsp. salt
Lots of freshly ground black pepper
1 14.5-ounce can crushed tomatoes
1/2 cup olive oil
1/2 cup water

Wash beans, break off ends, and break them in half. Mix all ingredients in a large pot. Bring to a boil over medium high heat. Cover pot, turn heat down to low, and simmer for 1 hour or until beans are very tender. Taste and add salt or pepper, as needed. Serve hot or at room temperature.

GREEN BEANS, ZUCCHINI AND POTATO STEW
Fasolakia me Kolokythakia kai Patates

Serves 4–6

Maria Baskous adds zucchini and potatoes to her Fasolakia recipe to produce a hearty and satisfying vegetable stew. Potatoes add a nice accent to vivid tomato sauce and, when you bite into them, they break apart without being mushy, the way well cooked boiled potatoes ought to do. I usually make this recipe with fresh green beans and it's fantastic, but Maria's recipe makes even frozen green beans taste amazingly good. Don't forget to serve with bread for mopping up sauce, slices of feta cheese, and marinated Kalamata olives.

1 pound fresh, or 10 ounces frozen and thawed, green beans
3/4 pound zucchini
3/4 pound potatoes, preferably Yukon Gold
1/3 cup olive oil
2 cups diced yellow onion, 1/2" dice
Salt
Freshly ground black pepper
1 14.5-ounce can diced tomatoes
1 14.5-ounce can crushed tomatoes
1 cup chopped fresh Italian parsley
2 Tbsp. dried mint, crushed
1 tsp. Aleppo pepper or 1/2 tsp. crushed red pepper
1 Tbsp. minced fresh garlic

If using fresh green beans, break off ends, and break them in half. Cut zucchini into 1" thick slices. Peel and cut potatoes into 1" chunks (if you're using young potatoes with tender skins, they don't need to be peeled).

Sauté onions, lightly seasoned with salt and freshly ground black pepper, in olive oil until they soften and begin to turn golden. Add tomatoes and bring to a boil. Add prepared beans, zucchini, potatoes, parsley, mint, Aleppo pepper, and garlic. Lightly season with salt and pepper. Return to a boil, cover, reduce heat, and simmer, stirring occasionally, until potatoes are tender (about 45 minutes). Taste, and add salt or pepper, as needed. Serve hot or at room temperature.

FRESH BEANS AND POTATOES IN GRAPE LEAVES
Fasolia kai Patates se Ambelofilla

Serves 4–6

Rosemary Barron's book, The Flavors of Greece, *captures the tastes of traditional Greek cooking. This adapted recipe uses frozen beans in place of the fresh fava beans recommended by Ms. Barron, and is one of my favorites. The unique flavor of cooked grape leaves permeates the olive oil and juices to form a remarkable sauce for potatoes and beans. It's good served hot or cold – hot it is a vegetable side dish and cold it makes a nice salad. This recipe is an easy way to incorporate the wonderful flavor of grape leaves in a meal without going to the trouble of stuffing and rolling them. Green Beans and Potatoes in Grape Leaves pairs well with roast lamb or grilled fish.*

3 cups peeled diced potatoes, 1/2" dice	1/4 cup fresh lemon juice
10 ounces frozen shelled edamame beans (green soybeans)	1/2 cup water
20 grape leaves, from a jar	Salt
1/2 cup olive oil	Freshly ground black pepper
	1/2 cup minced fresh Italian parsley
	Lemon wedges

Preheat oven to 350°F. Put potatoes in pot and cover with salted water. Bring water to a boil, cook potatoes for three minutes, and drain. Mix potatoes with frozen beans, olive oil, lemon juice, water, salt and freshly ground black pepper. Don't stint on salt, as potatoes really soak up seasoning. Line a deep baking dish with half the grape leaves. Pour in potato and bean mixture. Top with remaining grape leaves. Cover and bake for 40 minutes. Discard grape leaves, place potatoes, green beans and sauce in bowl, and stir in minced parsley. Serve with lemon wedges.

FAVA-STYLE BEANS WITH DILL AND ONIONS
Psefto Koukia

Serves 4 as a side dish

My husband's grandmother, Fotine Psiroukis Constantino, emigrated from Greece before the First World War, while the island of her birth was still under Turkish occupation. Fotine had a natural talent for nurturing plants and animals and people. Her wisdom has guided her grandson's vegetable gardening ever since, and inspires him to grow fresh fava beans. In Greece, fava beans are planted in winter and harvested in early spring. In Alaska, long green fava bean pods don't ripen until late July or early August. My husband has happy memories of summer afternoons at the kitchen table shelling and peeling the beans with Fotine. Fotine braised fresh favas with onions and dill, a dish that remains one of my husband's all-time favorites. Edamame beans have a flavor close enough to favas to work as a substitute in Alaska where fresh favas are a rarity.

1 large yellow onion
1/3 cup olive oil
Salt
Freshly ground black pepper
10 ounces frozen shelled edamame beans (green soybeans)
3/4 cup water
1/4 cup minced fresh dill
1/2 cup fresh lemon juice

Cut onion into thin, quarter-moon slices (cut onion in half vertically, slice very thinly, and cut thin slices in half). Sauté onions, lightly seasoned with salt and freshly ground black pepper, in olive oil. When onions are translucent, add beans, water, half the dill, and salt and pepper to taste. Cook over medium heat for 10 minutes, or until beans are softened. Add lemon juice and remaining dill, and cook for an additional 10 minutes, or until flavors have melded. Serve hot or at room temperature.

Note: If you're lucky enough to find fresh favas (or grow your own, since favas thrive in Alaska's climate), remove pod and peel each individual bean. Follow above recipe, but the beans take longer to cook, so you may need to add water to account for evaporation during the longer cooking time. When buying fresh favas, remember the pod accounts for most of the weight and buy one pound of favas in the pod per person.

FENNEL-SCENTED BLACK-EYED PEAS & WILD GREENS
Fasolia Mavromatika me Horta kai Maratho

Serves 8

Black-eyed peas paired with wild greens are a classic Greek combination. Served in a zesty broth, and seasoned with bulb fennel and fennel seed, black-eyed peas and greens make a great soup for fighting off winter cold. For soup, use the larger amount of liquid called for in the recipe. In Greece, however, black-eyed peas are made with the smaller amount of water and served with most of it cooked off; this version is also delicious. If you like spicy fare, use the larger amounts of Aleppo and black peppers in the recipe; for less highly seasoned food, use the smaller amounts or leave out Aleppo pepper entirely. If using spinach, Swiss chard, or other tender greens, add 15 minutes before the end of the cooking time rather than when you add water.

2 cups (1 pound) black-eyed peas
3 cups diced yellow onion, 1/4" dice
3 Tbsp. olive oil
1 cup diced carrots, 1/4" dice
1 cup diced celery, leaves included, 1/4" dice
1 cup diced leeks, white and light green parts only, 1/4" dice
1 cup diced fennel bulb, 1/4" dice
2 Tbsp. minced garlic
1-2 tsp. Aleppo pepper or 1/2-1 tsp. crushed red pepper (optional)
2 tsp. fennel, crushed
1-2 tsp. black pepper
1 tsp. fine sea salt or 2 tsp. kosher salt
3 Tbsp. tomato paste
6-10 cups water
3 bay leaves

1 pound cleaned mixed greens (wild greens, kale, Swiss chard, spinach, escarole), tough stems removed and greens cut into 1/4" strips

Spread out black-eyed peas on a tray and inspect carefully, removing any pebbles, debris, or damaged peas. Put peas in a large pot, and add enough water to cover them by 2 inches. Bring water to a boil, and cook peas for 5 minutes. Turn off heat and let peas soak in hot water while you dice vegetables.

When vegetables are ready, drain and rinse peas. Rinse out and dry pot and return it to burner.

Sauté onions in olive oil, lightly seasoned with salt and freshly ground black pepper, until they soften and start to turn golden. Add carrots, celery, leeks, fennel, garlic, Aleppo pepper, crushed fennel, black pepper, and salt, and sauté for two minutes. Stir in tomato paste until it's evenly distributed in vegetables. Stir in water, bay leaves, and greens (unless using spinach, Swiss chard, or other tender greens). Bring water to a boil, turn down heat, and simmer for 45 minutes (add spinach, Swiss chard, or other tender greens after simmering for 30 minutes), or until black-eyed peas are done and flavors have blended. Taste and add salt or freshly ground black pepper, as needed.

Serve with grated Parmesan cheese on the side for sprinkling over soup, or with slices of feta cheese; Roasted Kalamata Olives and crusty bread are good accompaniments.

PEAS BAKED WITH TOMATOES AND DILL
Arakas sto Fourno

Serves 4

By popular demand, John Maroulis makes large quantities of his baked peas for many special occasions at Holy Transfiguration. It's inevitably one of the first dishes to disappear from the table. It goes particularly well with roast Easter lamb, and may be served by itself as an eccentric entrée. The distinct flavors of dill and tomatoes make even frozen peas taste astonishingly good.

1 pound fresh or frozen peas	1 14.5-ounce can diced tomatoes
8 green onions, chopped	Salt
1 leek, white and pale green parts, chopped	Freshly ground black pepper
2 Tbsp. olive oil	1/3 cup minced fresh dill

Preheat oven to 350°F.

If peas are fresh, cook them for 5 minutes in boiling salted water. Thaw frozen peas, but don't cook them. Sauté onion and leek in olive oil just until they begin to soften. Stir in tomatoes, salt, and freshly ground black pepper and bring to a boil. Turn off heat, stir dill and peas into sauce, and put in baking dish. Bake, covered with foil, for 35–40 minutes. Taste, and add salt or freshly ground black pepper, as needed. Serve hot or at room temperature.

FRIED ZUCCHINI WITH FETA
Kolokythakia Tiganita me Feta

Serves 2–4

Fried zucchini is good plain or with garlic sauce, but I like it best with a little feta on top, broiled until cheese is brown and bubbly. This recipe may be made with any size zucchini, but is a particularly good way to use larger zucchini (3" or more in diameter) that crowd Alaskan larders in August. I can easily make a meal of this, so double or triple the recipe if there are zucchini lovers at the table.

1 1/2 pounds zucchini
2 Tbsp. salt
4 cups water

1 cup crumbled feta cheese
Oil for frying

Cut zucchini into 3/8" rounds, if you're using larger zucchini, or into lengthwise 3/8" slices if you have small or medium sized zucchini. Mix 2 Tbsp. salt and water in bowl, add zucchini, weight it down with a plate or pan lid, and leave in salted water for 30 minutes. If there isn't enough liquid to submerge zucchini, mix up additional salt and water in same proportions. After it has been in salt water for 30 minutes, drain and rinse zucchini, and dry it well.

Heat 1/4" of olive oil in a frying pan until hot, but not smoking. Fry zucchini in batches, being careful not to crowd it in pan, until both sides are golden brown. As each batch is cooked, place zucchini slices on paper towels to drain.

Preheat broiler. Place a layer of fried zucchini in a rimmed baking pan, and cover each piece with crumbled feta. Broil zucchini until feta melts and is golden brown on top, about 3 minutes. Serve hot or at room temperature.

MINT MARINATED ZUCCHINI
Kolokythakia me Thiosmo

Serves 2–4

Because it needs to marinate for at least two hours, and is best served at room temperature, Mint Marinated Zucchini can be made well in advance. This makes it just the thing for a meal eaten outdoors on hot summer days, when you don't want to be rushing around making food at the last minute. Mint Marinated Zucchini, with its heady flavors of garlic and mint, is a refreshing side dish for grilled fish or chicken.

Zucchini:
1 1/2 pounds zucchini
2 Tbsp. salt
4 cups water
Oil for frying

Marinade:
2 Tbsp. finely minced fresh mint
2 Tbsp. finely minced fresh garlic
1/4 cup lemon juice or red wine vinegar
1/2 tsp. salt

Cut zucchini into 3/8" rounds, if you're using larger zucchini, or into lengthwise 3/8" slices if you have small or medium sized zucchini. Mix 2 Tbsp. salt and water in bowl, add zucchini, weight it down with a plate or pan lid, and leave in salted water for 30 minutes. If there isn't enough liquid to submerge zucchini, mix up additional salt and water in same proportions. After it has been in salt water for 30 minutes, drain and rinse zucchini, and dry it well.

Mix marinade ingredients. Heat 1/4" olive oil in a frying pan until hot, but not smoking. Fry zucchini in batches until both sides are golden brown. Place each batch of cooked zucchini on fresh paper towels to drain. When all zucchini is cooked, toss it in a glass or stainless steel bowl with marinade, and let sit for at least two hours, turning zucchini occasionally to make sure marinade is evenly distributed. Serve at room temperature.

GREEK STUFFED ZUCCHINI
Kolokythakia Gemista

Serves 4

Zucchini stuffed with meat filling is a common dish in Greece. One day I had one too many small pieces of leftover cheese in the refrigerator, I decided to experiment by including cheese in my stuffed zucchini recipe. The addition of cheese is unconventional, but I like the rich, savory taste it contributes—kasseri is melted and runny, while kefalotyri adds depth to the flavor. The recipe can be made successfully without the cheese, but if you opt not to add cheese, cook meat sauce with one stick of cinnamon. Serve with olives, hot cherry peppers, and bread for a very filling meal.

4 medium-small zucchini
1 cup diced yellow onion (1/8" dice)
1/4 cup olive oil
Salt
Freshly ground black pepper
1 pound ground beef or lamb
1 Tbsp. minced fresh garlic
1/4 cup minced fresh mint
1/2 cup minced fresh Italian parsley

1/2 cup tomato paste
1 cup red wine
4 tsp. dried oregano, crushed
2 cups coarsely shredded kasseri
  or fontina cheese
1 cup finely shredded kefalotyri
  or parmesan cheese
2 cups water

Preheat oven to 400° F.

Cut ends off each zucchini, and cut zucchini in half lengthwise. With a small spoon, scoop out inside of each zucchini half, being careful not to break through skin of zucchini. Lightly salt zucchini shells. Chop zucchini flesh you removed from centers.

Sauté onion, lightly seasoned with salt and freshly ground black pepper, in olive oil until it starts to turn golden. Add chopped zucchini insides, and sauté for 2 minutes. Add ground meat, mix well with zucchini, and cook until meat begins to brown. Stir in garlic, mint, parsley, and a little salt and freshly ground black pepper, and cook until meat is browned. Add 1/4 cup tomato paste, wine, and oregano, and cook until wine is reduced and sauce is thick. Remove from heat and let cool.

Wipe inside of zucchini shells with paper towels to remove any accumulated moisture. Mix half of each cheese into cooled meat sauce, and spoon this filling into zucchini shells.

Mix water and remaining 1/4 cup of tomato paste in a glass or stainless steel 9" x 13" baking pan. Set filled zucchini boats in baking pan with water and tomato paste. Place in 400° F oven and bake 15–20 minutes, or until zucchini shells are tender.

Mix remaining cheeses. Remove zucchini from oven, top with combined cheeses, and return to oven for 3–5 minutes, or until cheese is thoroughly melted. Place on plates, pour over tomato sauce from baking pan, and serve.

PALESTINIAN STUFFED ZUCCHINI
Kousa Mahshe

Serves 4

Salwa Abuamsha's Kousa Mahshe recipe highlights the flavor of zucchini, rather than stuffing. She usually cooks her stuffed zucchini in the same pot as stuffed grape leaves, and places lamb bones on the pan's bottom to add flavor. I opted for the equally traditional technique of braising stuffed zucchini in tomato sauce. Hollowing out the center of small plump zucchinis turned out to be easy with an apple corer. Stuffing the centers of whole squash infuses filling with fresh zucchini flavors. Serve with a fresh salad, bread and Kalamata olives.

8 zucchini, short fat ones,
   6–7 inches long
1/2 pound ground lamb or beef
3/4 cup long-grain rice
1 tsp. allspice
1/4 tsp. ground nutmeg
1/2 tsp. salt
Lots of freshly ground black pepper

Sauce:
1/3 cup olive oil
4 cups diced yellow onions (1/2" dice)
Salt
Freshly ground black pepper
2 14.5-ounce cans crushed tomatoes
1 Tbsp. minced fresh garlic
2 Tbsp. minced fresh mint
1/4 cup minced fresh Italian parsley

Cut stem end off each zucchini. Using an apple corer, hollow out zucchini from an opening in the stem end, being careful not to break through skin and to keep the opening as small as possible. Mix ground meat, rice, and seasonings, and loosely stuff zucchini with this mixture. Don't fill zucchini all the way, because filling needs room to expand as the rice cooks.

Sauté onions, lightly seasoned with salt and freshly ground black pepper, in olive oil. Mix in crushed tomatoes and minced garlic, and bring to a boil. Place stuffed zucchini in cooking liquid in a single layer and return to a boil. Cover, turn down heat, and simmer until zucchini are just tender, about 45 minutes. Stir in mint and parsley, and cook for 2–3 minutes. Taste and add herbs, salt, or freshly ground black pepper, as needed. Serve with sauce poured over whole stuffed zucchini.

Note: If you can't find short fat zucchini, buy a large one, cut it in half, and hollow out each half as described above.

ZUCCHINI FLOWERS STUFFED WITH CHEESE
Kolokythoanthi Gemisti me Tyri

Serves 4 as an appetizer, or 2–3 as a main course

When zucchini plants start to flower, I go to the Farmer's Market early in the day to buy squash blossoms before they're sold out, and continue to buy them every week until they're no longer available. Every year I'm surprised by how good they are—the taste of young zucchini and cheese is an exceptional combination. The stuffing changes every time I make the recipe, a tribute to my quest for the ultimate stuffed squash blossoms. These are two of my favorite fillings—ricotta and feta replicates mild fresh cheese used in Greece for this dish, while the goat cheese version appeals to those who like stronger tastes. Each filling recipe makes enough to stuff 12 squash blossoms. If the blossoms are too tattered to hold stuffing, or you want a lighter dish with only the unique delicate flavor of zucchini flowers, dip clean, dry blossoms in a light tempura batter, and fry, for a quick and easy treat.

Filling #1:
2/3 cup fresh ricotta, preferably whole-milk
2/3 cup crumbled feta cheese
1 Tbsp. very finely minced fresh mint
2 cloves garlic, mashed
Freshly ground black pepper

Filling #2:
8 ounces goat cheese
1/3 cup finely grated kefalotyri or parmesan cheese
8 anchovy fillets
1 egg
3 cloves garlic, pressed
3 Tbsp. finely minced dill
Freshly ground black pepper

12 squash blossoms, with or without baby squash attached
2 eggs
3/4 cup all-purpose flour
Salt
Freshly ground black pepper
Olive oil for frying

Filling #1: Mix cheeses. Mix mint, garlic, and freshly ground black pepper into cheeses.

Filling #2: Mix cheeses. Finely chop anchovy fillets. Mix anchovies, egg, garlic, dill, and freshly ground black pepper into cheeses.

Gently clean and dry outside of zucchini flowers, and check to make sure there aren't any insects or other garden hitchhikers inside. Stand one zucchini flower up in a small jar or vase (I leave stem attached, but remove stamens). Gently spread flower opening so it's wide enough to accept large tip of a pastry bag or cut-off corner of a sturdy plastic bag. Pipe filling into zucchini flowers. Flowers can be made ahead to this point and refrigerated until ready to cook.

Beat eggs in a shallow bowl until yolks and whites are well combined. Put flour on a large plate and season with salt and freshly ground black pepper. Heat 1/8" of olive oil in frying pan until hot. Dip stuffed zucchini flowers in beaten eggs, then in seasoned flour, and fry in oil until flowers are nicely browned on both sides. Because fried zucchini blossoms taste better hot, I cook them in two frying pans so they're all done at the same time.

STUFFED EGGPLANT WITH TOMATO SAUCE
Doosma

Serves 4

Sonia Sarkissian grew up in Syria, where her parents found refuge after fleeing the massacre of Armenians living in Turkey. Her father, Arten, was seven when he escaped Turkey on foot. He lost his parents during the long march. When he reached Syria, Arten was taken in by a rich Muslim man who used Armenian laborers in his business. One day the rich man's son intentionally burned Arten with boiling hot garbanzo beans, for which the boy's father roundly scolded him. Years later, Arten ran into the rich man's son and invited him to eat at the Sarkissian family table. When he sat down to eat, the son said the invitation fulfilled a prediction his father had made during that memorable scolding—someday the Armenian workers would have their own lives and families and the son would find himself eating at their tables, so the son should always treat them the workers with respect.

Sonia learned to make Doosma from her mother, and this recipe comes from her family's table. Seasoned ground meat sandwiched between slices of eggplant, and dressed with a light tomato sauce, is as attractive as it is appetizing. Serve eggplant in its cooking pot, so your guests can see its beauty, savor the aromas as it's dished, and better appreciate its wonderful flavor.

1 pound ground lamb or beef`
3/4 cup finely minced yellow onion
1/4 cup minced fresh Italian parsley`
1 Tbsp. minced fresh garlic
1/2 tsp. crushed red pepper
1 Tbsp. allspice
1/2 tsp. salt

1 1/2 pounds eggplant
2 Tbsp. salt
4 cups water
1–2 large tomatoes
1–2 green peppers
2 Tbsp. tomato paste
2 cups water

Knead ground meat, onion, parsley, garlic, crushed red pepper, allspice, and salt together with your hands.

Cut vertical strips of skin off eggplant, cutting from top to bottom, so you're left with alternating stripes of purple skin and white flesh. Cut eggplant crosswise into 3/4" thick slices. Mix 2 Tbsp. salt and water in bowl, add eggplant, weight it down with a small plate or pan lid, and leave eggplant submerged in salted water for 30 minutes. If there isn't enough liquid to submerge eggplant, mix additional salt and water in the same proportions. After 30 minutes, drain and rinse eggplant, and dry it well.

Cut a small slice off top and bottom of one tomato, and cut rest of tomato into thick slices. Cut top and bottom off one pepper, cut a slit in the side, flatten out pepper, and cut it into squares approximately the same size as tomato slices. (One tomato and one pepper are often enough for this recipe; prepare second tomato and pepper only as needed.) Mince tops and bottoms of tomatoes and peppers and knead them into meat mixture. Reserve pepper squares and tomato slices.

Spread meat mixture thinly on eggplant slice, top with piece of pepper, and then with an eggplant slice spread with meat. Top with tomato slice, then eggplant slice spread with meat, and then a piece of pepper. Continue adding eggplant slices spread with meat and topped with alternating slices of peppers and tomatoes. Before your stack of slices becomes too high, grasp it firmly, turn it on its side so eggplant slices are vertical, and curve them around inside circumference of cooking pot. Repeat until pot is full or your ingredients are gone.

Whisk tomato paste into water, lightly season with salt and freshly ground black pepper, and pour this sauce over meat and vertical slices of eggplant. Bring to a boil, cover, reduce heat, and simmer for 45 minutes or until eggplant is done. From time to time, spoon liquid over vegetables as they cook. If sauce is too thin at end of cooking time, remove cover, and boil until sauce has thickened. Taste and add salt or pepper, as needed. Serve immediately.

BAKED EGGPLANT AND GARBANZO BEANS
Melitzanes kai Revithia

Serves 6

One year when we were living in Greece, I made this dish frequently. After living in Bethel, Alaska without fresh produce for five years, I couldn't stop myself from buying too many of the gorgeous eggplants and juicy ripe tomatoes that abound in Greek markets, but then had to keep coming up with new ways to cook them. My husband said I was on a mission to prove to him that meatless food can be flavorful and satisfying. (I succeeded). This thick vegetable stew is easy and loaded with savory flavor. It tastes better if you allow eggplant to char slightly when you sauté it. For a crowd, double or triple the recipe, and serve Melitzanes kai Revithia with feta cheese and a crisp green salad.

1 1/2 pounds eggplant
2/3 cup olive oil
Salt
Freshly ground black pepper
6 cups diced yellow onion, 1/2" dice
1/2 cup minced fresh Italian parsley
1/4 cup minced fresh dill

1 Tbsp. minced fresh garlic
1 tsp. Aleppo pepper, or 1/2 tsp.
    crushed red pepper
2 15-ounce cans garbanzo beans
    (chickpeas), rinsed and drained
2 14.5-ounce cans diced tomatoes
1 cup chicken stock (or water)

Preheat oven to 400°F.

Cut unpeeled eggplant into cubes. Sauté eggplant, lightly seasoned with salt and freshly ground black pepper, in 1/3 cup olive oil, letting it char a little as it cooks, for 5–8 minutes or until eggplant cubes have just softened. Spread eggplant in bottom of oiled 9" x 13" baking pan.

Sauté onion, lightly seasoned with salt and freshly ground black pepper, in remaining 1/3 cup olive oil until it just starts to turn brown. Spread onions over eggplant. Sprinkle parsley, dill, garlic, Aleppo pepper, and a little salt and pepper over onions. Spread garbanzos evenly over vegetables, and pour diced tomatoes (and their juices) over top. Heat chicken stock or water in pan in which you cooked vegetables, scraping up any brown bits on bottom of pan, and evenly pour over tomatoes. Bake uncovered for 45 minutes. Serve hot or at room temperature.

BAKED EGGPLANT AND POTATOES WITH MEAT SAUCE AND BÉCHAMEL
Moussaka

GREEK FESTIVAL RECIPE

Serves 8 to 12

Moussaka is one of the most popular dishes served at the annual Greek Festival in Anchorage and always goes quickly. Over the years, the recipe has evolved and changed, depending on who has the primary responsibility for making it. Since spices are always added to taste and without measuring, and since some cooks prefer more cinnamon or oregano or allspice than others, seasoning preferences of the cook inevitably shape Moussaka's final flavor. Béchamel topping is another source of debate: some prefer it thick and others, like Spiro Bellas, the cook who made Festival Moussaka for many years, prefer a lighter béchamel. Spiro also adds Panko (packaged Japanese bread crumbs) to the meat sauce to absorb the juices, thus adding deeper flavor. The hottest debate is about the role of potatoes. Spiro insists potatoes should be boiled to reduce the amount of oil and because boiled potatoes better absorb the sauce's flavors. Other local cooks are adamant potatoes must be deep fried, and say boiled potatoes are too bland for Moussaka. In this recipe, which is mostly Spiro's, I've compromised by quickly baking potatoes, which intensifies their flavor but still leaves their surface soft enough to absorb Moussaka's rich juices.

Meat Sauce:
2 pounds ground beef or lamb
3 1/2–4 cups diced yellow onion,
   1/4" dice
2 Tbsp. minced fresh garlic
1 5-ounce can tomato paste
1 1/2 cups red wine
1 tsp. salt
1 Tbsp. freshly ground black pepper
1 tsp. allspice
2 cinnamon sticks
1/4 cup minced fresh Italian parsley
1/2 cup Panko or dried bread crumbs

Vegetables:
2–3 large eggplants (3 pounds)
Olive oil
Salt
Freshly ground black pepper
2 large baking potatoes

Béchamel:
1/2 cup butter
1/2 cup all-purpose flour
5 cups whole milk
4 egg yolks
1/2 tsp. ground nutmeg
Salt
1 tsp. freshly ground white pepper
1 cup freshly grated kefalotyri or
   parmesan cheese

Brown meat, lightly seasoned with salt and freshly ground black pepper, in a large pot. Add onions and continue browning. When onions have softened and begun to turn golden, add garlic and cook for 1 minute. Stir in tomato paste, wine, salt, pepper, cinnamon sticks, and allspice, and cook for one hour, until sauce is thick and rich. Stir in minced parsley and Panko or bread crumbs. Taste and add salt, pepper, or cinnamon, as needed.

While sauce is cooking, preheat oven to 450°F. Slice eggplant lengthwise 1/2" thick. Brush both sides of each eggplant slice with olive oil, and season lightly with salt and freshly ground black pepper. Bake eggplant slices for 15 to 20 minutes, turning them over after 10 minutes, or until slices are golden brown.

Peel and slice potatoes lengthwise 3/8" thick. Brush both sides of each potato slice with olive oil, and season lightly with salt and freshly ground black pepper. Bake potato slices for 10 to 12 minutes in a preheated 450°F oven until they're just tender. Potatoes should not be cooked all the way through.

Warm milk over low heat or in microwave. Melt butter in a large saucepan, mix in flour and cook for two minutes, stirring constantly. Slowly stir in warm milk and cook, stirring, until sauce is thick and smooth. Add nutmeg, salt and white pepper to taste. Quickly whisk one cup of hot milk sauce into egg yolks, and stir this mixture back into sauce. Cook over very low heat for two minutes, stirring constantly, and being careful not to let sauce get hotter than a low simmer. Remove sauce from heat and whisk in 1/2 cup grated cheese. Taste and add salt, pepper, or nutmeg, as needed.

Preheat oven to 350°F.

To assemble Moussaka, lightly brush sides and bottom of a 9" x 13" pan with olive oil. Place a layer of potatoes on bottom of pan. Spread half the meat sauce evenly over potatoes, and sprinkle 1/4 cup grated cheese over meat sauce. Layer half the eggplant over cheese. Cover with remaining meat sauce, and sprinkle with 1/4 cup cheese. Cover with remaining eggplant. Pour as much béchamel as possible over eggplant. Bake for 50 to 60 minutes, or until béchamel is puffed and golden brown. Let cool for 15 minutes, cut into large squares, and serve.

BAKED EGGPLANT WITH MEAT SAUCE AND YOGURT TOPPING
Moussaka me Yaourti

Serves 8–12

Like Imam Baildi, Moussaka is made in every country that used to be part of the Ottoman Empire, and there are as many ways to cook it as there are cooks. This is the version I prefer. Unlike the Festival recipe, this Moussaka is made without potatoes, the meat sauce is spicier, and instead of béchamel, this is finished with a lighter yogurt topping. To ensure the topping is the right consistency, yogurt is placed in a paper-towel lined colander and strained for 2 hours to remove some of the whey. Without potatoes to compete against, the eggplant flavor stands out. Components of this and Festival Moussaka recipe are interchangeable – this version can be made with Festival meat sauce, and the Festival version can be made with yogurt topping. Serve with Festival "Greek" Salad, or with Horiatiki Salata.

Meat Sauce:
1/4 cup olive oil
2 cups diced yellow onions, 1/4" dice
2 stalks celery, cut in 1/4" dice
Salt
Freshly ground black pepper
1 pound ground lamb or beef
1 14.5-ounce can crushed tomatoes
1 1/2 Tbsp. minced fresh garlic
1/3 cup finely minced parsley, stems included
5 whole cloves
1 cinnamon stick
1 tsp. Aleppo pepper or 1/2 tsp. crushed red pepper
3 bay leaves
1 cup red wine

3 large globe eggplants (about 3 pounds)
Olive oil
3/4 cup freshly grated kefalotyri or parmesan cheese for layering with eggplant

Topping:
2 cups whole-milk yogurt, strained for 2 hours
2/3 cup heavy cream
6 eggs
2/3 cup freshly grated kefalotyri or parmesan cheese
Salt
Freshly ground black pepper
Freshly grated nutmeg

Sauté onions and celery, lightly seasoned with salt and freshly ground black pepper, in olive oil until they start to turn golden. Add ground lamb and brown, adding a little salt and pepper. Wrap cloves tightly in a piece of cheesecloth, and tie it into a closed packet with string. When lamb has browned, add tomatoes, garlic, parsley, bag of cloves, cinnamon stick, Aleppo pepper, bay leaves, and red wine, and bring to a boil. Turn heat down to low, and slowly simmer for about 45 minutes, or until sauce has thickened and flavors have blended. Taste and add salt or pepper, as needed. Remove bag of cloves, cinnamon stick, and bay leaves. Sauce can be made ahead, or the recipe made in larger quantities with leftovers frozen for later use.

While sauce is cooking, preheat oven to 450°F. Slice eggplant lengthwise 1/2" thick. Brush both sides of each eggplant slice with olive oil, and season lightly with salt and freshly ground black pepper. Bake eggplant slices for 15–20 minutes, turning them over after 10 minutes, or until slices are golden brown. Let cool.

Reduce oven temperature to 400°F. To assemble Moussaka, lightly brush sides and bottom of a 9" x 13" pan with olive oil. Place half the eggplant in a layer on bottom of pan. Sprinkle with 1/4 cup grated cheese. Spread meat sauce over eggplant. Sprinkle with 1/4 cup grated cheese. Layer remaining eggplant on top of meat sauce, and sprinkle with 1/4 cup grated cheese.

Whisk together topping ingredients, taste, add salt, pepper, or nutmeg, as needed, and pour over eggplant. Bake for 40 minutes, or until topping is firm and golden brown. Let cool for 10 minutes, cut into large squares, and serve.

BAKED EGGPLANT WITH TOMATOES AND ONION
Imam Baildi

Serves 4

When Maria Baskous was 13, her brother went to Athens to study for his university tests and live with their Uncle Aristotle. Maria's family sent her along to cook and clean for her brother and uncle. Maria had helped her mother in the kitchen, but had never actually cooked a meal on her own and wasn't sure where to start. A neighbor lady took Maria under her wing, and taught her how to make Imam Baildi (often known simply as Imam), a dish popular in every country where Ottoman Turks once ruled. The name of the dish means "the priest fainted," referring to either the imam's reaction to the incredible rich flavors of the dish, or the high cost of olive oil used to prepare it. When finished, Imam's layers of flavor mingle on your palate: concentrated eggplant, rich sweet onions and fresh parsley, and finally, perfectly cooked tomatoes. Imam goes well with pasta or as a side dish with roast lamb.

8 small Japanese eggplants	1 cup minced fresh Italian parsley
1 cup olive oil	Salt
2 large yellow onions	Freshly ground black pepper
2 Tbsp. minced fresh garlic	1 14.5-ounce can crushed tomatoes

Preheat oven to 350° F.

Prepare Eggplant: Cut a deep, narrow, V-shaped wedge lengthwise out of each eggplant, reserving flesh from cut-away wedges for stuffing (don't cut all the way through eggplant). Salt cut part of eggplant, and set aside. After 30 minutes, wipe out inside of each eggplant with a paper towel.

Heat olive oil, and cook half the eggplants over high heat until they begin to soften, turning eggplants in oil so they cook evenly on all sides. Repeat with remaining eggplant, adding olive oil to pan as necessary. Each batch takes about 5 minutes to cook. Place cooked eggplants, cut side up, in baking pan large enough to hold them in a single layer.

Make Stuffing: Skin and chop reserved eggplant wedges. Cut onions into thin, quarter-moon slices (cut onion in half vertically, slice very thinly, and cut thin slices in half). Using pan in which you cooked eggplant, sauté onions and reserved eggplant flesh, lightly seasoned with salt and freshly ground black pepper, in olive oil. Cook until vegetables turn golden. Add garlic, and cook an additional minute. Using a slotted spoon, remove vegetables from oil and place in bowl, reserving cooking oil. Mix in parsley, taste, and add salt or pepper, as needed.

Assemble/Cook: Fill cut-out wedge in cooked eggplants with stuffing. Spoon crushed tomatoes over stuffed eggplants, and drizzle with olive oil in which onions were cooked. Bake for 30–40 minutes until eggplants are tender. The length of cooking time depends on the size of eggplants. Serve two eggplants per person, pouring any juices remaining in pan over eggplant as you serve.

FRIED EGGPLANT AND PEPPERS IN TOMATO SAUCE
Melitzanes Kai Piperies Tiganites me Saltsa

Serves 4

When Tina Karakatsanis Chowaniec visits her mother, Ksanthi, in the small village of Filakto in Northern Greece, the first thing she asks Ksanthi to cook is Fried Eggplant and Peppers in Tomato Sauce. It's quintessential Greek food: vegetable-based, hearty, savory, and complex. The stewing technique, the flavor combinations, the textures, how well it goes with feta cheese, and the need for eating it with bread and olives, all identify its Greek origins. Tina says the dish tastes better made with Japanese eggplants, as they have less water and better texture than the big fat ones. Eggplant flavors richen and deepen if you char eggplant slightly when it's sautéed. Tina likes this dish best made with lots of tomato sauce, so there are plenty of good juices to soak up with her bread. If your tastes follow Tina's, double sauce ingredients listed below.

6 Japanese eggplants or 1 very large
   globe eggplant
2 Tbsp. salt
4 cups water
6 green Italian frying, Hungarian,
   or banana peppers
Olive oil for frying

Sauce:
1 14.5-ounce can crushed tomatoes
1/4 cup olive oil
Salt
Freshly ground black pepper
1 Tbsp. dried oregano, crushed
2 tsp. sugar (optional)

Cut Japanese eggplants lengthwise in half or in 1/2" thick slices, or large eggplant crosswise in 1/2" rounds. Mix 2 Tbsp. salt and water in bowl, add eggplant, weight it down with a small plate or pan lid, and leave eggplant submerged in salted water for 30 minutes. If there isn't enough liquid to submerge eggplant, mix up additional salt and water in same proportions. After 30 minutes, drain and rinse eggplant, and dry it well.

Cut peppers in half and discard seeds and stems. Salt peppers and fry them in olive oil, until they have softened and browned, but are not charred. Set aside.

In same pan, sauté eggplant until it's well-browned on both sides, adding olive oil as needed. Don't crowd pan; you most likely will need to fry eggplant in batches. Place fried eggplant on paper towels to soak up any excess oil, and set aside.

In a clean pan, heat 1/4 cup olive oil. Sauté crushed tomatoes, seasoned with salt, freshly ground black pepper, and oregano to taste, in olive oil for 5–10 minutes or until water in tomatoes has evaporated. Taste, and if tomatoes aren't sweet or well-flavored, add optional sugar. Gently stir fried vegetables into tomato sauce, cover and let simmer over low heat for 10 minutes or until flavors have merged. Taste, and add salt, pepper, or crushed oregano, as needed. Serve hot or at room temperature.

TOMATOES AND EGGS
Kokkina Avga

Serves 2

For a hearty, simple, winter dinner, Andy and Carol Gialopsos make eggs in red sauce. Andy says it's important to cook the sauce down long enough that it isn't watery and is a good base for eggs, but not so long that you lose the bright tomato flavor. Olive oil makes this dish very filling and adds wonderful flavor. Carol uses fresh tomatoes, but except at the height of summer, in Alaska canned tomatoes generally have better flavor than "fresh.". Serve with fresh bread, feta cheese and olives.

1/4 cup olive oil
1 cup diced yellow onion (1/8" dice)
1 14.5-ounce can diced tomatoes
Salt
Freshly ground black pepper
1/4 – 1/2 tsp. cayenne pepper
4 eggs

Sauté onions, lightly seasoned with salt and freshly ground black pepper, in olive oil. When onions are golden, add tomatoes, salt, pepper, and cayenne to taste (be careful, cayenne is spicy). Cook over medium high heat until it boils, then turn heat down to medium low. Cook for 30 minutes, or until sauce thickens, mashing tomatoes as they cook to break them into pieces. Taste and add salt, pepper, or cayenne, as needed.

Turn heat down to very low. Make four indentations in sauce, and crack one egg into each indentation. Grind black pepper over eggs, cover pan, and let cook until egg whites just solidify, and yolks are still liquid. Serve immediately, with sauce spooned over eggs.

TOMATO SAUCE WITH CELERY & MINT
Saltsa me Selino kai Diosmo

Serves 4

Tomato Sauce with Celery and Mint is for days when you want a quick meal, with lots of flavor, that doesn't take much effort. From start to finish, this full-flavored sauce is finished in about 30 minutes. Serve over pasta with fresh goat cheese, if you eat dairy; the sauce is particularly good over cheese or spinach stuffed ravioli or tortelloni. Watercress and curly endive salad, lightly dressed with vinegar and olive oil, goes well with pasta and this sauce. Leaf celery (aka cutting celery or Chinese celery) is grown for its leaves, and is used as an herb in Europe and China. In Alaska and most of the United States, the only place to buy it is in Asian and farmers' markets. Leaf celery has a stronger, more herby and assertive flavor than the stalk celery and is generally not eaten raw. It gives more flavor to soups and stews than does stalk celery, and I prefer using it for these purposes. Leaf celery is more perishable than stalk celery. To store it, rinse off any dirt and wrap it in paper towels before putting it in plastic bags in the refrigerator. At up to 2 feet long, it takes up lots of space. In Greece, rural kitchen gardens often contain one or two leaf celery plants. Villagers don't harvest celery all at once, as a single plant, as is done in the US with stalk celery. Individual stalks are cut as needed (the "cut and come again" harvesting technique), while the plant continues to thrive and grow more stalks. Tomato Sauce with Celery and Mint is made with leaf celery, the only variety available most places in Greece. The sauce may also be made with ordinary stalk celery, although the celery flavor will be less distinct if ordinary celery is used.

2 cups diced onions, 1/4" dice
3/4 cup finely sliced stalks from leaf celery
3 Tbsp. olive oil
Salt
Freshly ground black pepper
1 tsp. Aleppo pepper or 1/2 tsp. crushed red pepper
1 14.5-ounce can crushed tomatoes
3/4 cup dry white wine
3/4 cup finely shredded leaves from leaf celery
2 Tbsp. minced mint
1 Tbsp. minced garlic
1 tsp. sugar (optional)

Sauté onions and celery stalks, lightly seasoned with salt and freshly ground black pepper, in olive oil until onion starts to turn golden. Stir in Aleppo pepper and cook for one minute. Stir in crushed tomatoes and wine and bring to a boil. Cook rapidly for five minutes, stirring constantly. Turn down heat to medium, stir in celery, mint, and garlic and simmer for 10 minutes. Taste and add optional sugar if sauce is too acidic. Simmer for 5 minutes or until sauce is the thickness you desire. Taste and add salt and freshly ground black pepper, if needed.

ROASTED MIXED VEGETABLES
Briami

Serves 4–8

Briami is a medley of roasted vegetables that can be served as a main course or as a side dish in a more elaborate meal. Roasting vegetables in a hot oven concentrates and develops subtle vegetable flavors that can be lost when the same vegetables are boiled, stewed, or fried. Roasting also imparts its own slightly smoky flavor that each vegetable expresses in its own distinctive way. This classic of the Greek vegetarian table can be made with almost any fresh vegetables: carrots, cauliflower, bell peppers, mushrooms, turnips, or whatever is fresh in the garden or crowding the refrigerator. The recipe presented below is a mixture of vegetables available in high summer and is Maria Baskous' favorite combination. Roasted vegetables maintain their integrity and individual tastes, with dill and parsley pulling the various flavors together in the completed dish. Depending on the region of Greece and the vegetables used, Briami is also known as Tourlou. I like it because it tastes great, is very easy to prepare, and uses up beautiful vegetables that entice me each week at the local Farmers' Market.

1/2 pound Japanese eggplant,
   cut into chunks
1/2 pound zucchini, cut into chunks
1/2 pound okra, fresh or frozen
   whole
1/2 pound potato, peeled and
   cut into chunks
1/2 pound yellow onion, peeled
   and cut into chunks

1 14.5-ounce can diced tomatoes
1 Tbsp. minced fresh garlic
1 cup chopped fresh Italian parsley
1 cup chopped fresh dill
1 cup olive oil
1 tsp. crushed red pepper
Salt
Freshly ground black pepper

Preheat oven to 400°F.

Mix all ingredients, except half the garlic, in a large baking pan so vegetables are well coated with oil and seasoning. Bake uncovered for 45 minutes or until potatoes are done, and the other vegetables are tender and slightly browned. When vegetables are done, mix in remaining minced garlic, taste, and add salt, pepper, or fresh minced garlic, as needed. Serve hot or at room temperature with feta cheese, and bread for dipping in oil that is infused with delicate vegetable flavors.

SPICY FRIED OKRA
Bamies Tiganites

Greeks love okra. It's a common ingredient in their summer meals. Before I ate okra in Greece, I thought it was soft, slimy, and unappetizing. Greek cooks taught me this doesn't have to be true. Okra is best when small, about the size of your little finger. Cook okra until it softens, but still retains its shape. Fried Spicy Okra makes a good meze (appetizer) to serve with ouzo and cheese on a warm summer evening. It can also be served as a side dish with grilled fish or chicken. The spicy seasoning mix brings out the delicate flavor of okra. Even though it's fried, if oil is at the right temperature when okra is added, it emerges light and tasty. The easiest way to season okra evenly is to put it in a brown paper bag while hot, add the appropriate amount of seasoning, and shake the bag. Leftover seasoning mix can be used in place of salt and pepper in almost any dish. When desperate for a fast hot appetizer, I've made this dish with still-frozen okra, cut into chunks and fried while frozen. The taste and texture are not as good as when okra is pre-treated in the oven, but speed and convenience can definitely make up for a little loss of flavor. If you're using fresh okra, treat it the same as thawed frozen okra.

Okra:
10 ounces fresh or thawed frozen okra
2 Tbsp. red wine vinegar
Salt

Seasoning:
2 Tbsp. salt
2 tsp. freshly ground black pepper
1/2 tsp. cayenne

Oil for deep frying

Preheat oven to 300°F.

Place fresh or thawed frozen okra on a rimmed baking sheet, and sprinkle with red wine vinegar and a little salt. Gently mix okra, vinegar, and salt, and spread it in a single layer on baking sheet. Bake okra for 20 minutes. The recipe can be made ahead up to this point.

Cut off okra stems. If you fortunate enough to have tiny fresh okra, avoid cutting into the flesh when you remove stems as doing so liberates okra sap. If your okra is bigger, cut into halves or thirds. Mix seasoning ingredients.

Heat frying oil to 360°F. Add okra to oil in small batches, to ensure oil maintains a constant temperature and okra cooks evenly. Fry until okra is golden brown, about 1–2 minutes. Drain okra on paper towels. Sprinkle with seasoning mix to taste, and serve hot.

ARTICHOKES WITH DILL
Anginares Polita

Serves 4–6

Helene Georgas Dennison's mother was from Constantinople (Istanbul), the center of Greek culture and religion for over a thousand years. The word "Polita" ("the city") in the name of this recipe reflects its origins in that city. Helene's mother cooked artichokes regularly, as does Helene, who discovered that frozen artichokes work well in braised recipes such as this one. The first time I tried Helene's recipe, I had extra chopped parsley sitting on the cutting board from another dish, so I threw it in. Although not included in Helene's original recipe, parsley was a successful addition. The interplay between parsley and dill allows more of the subtle artichoke flavors to come through. Adding dill in two stages contributes to the complexity of flavors; dill added early gives a deep rounded flavor, while that added at the end imparts fresh distinctive dill high notes. This dish is a symphony of spring tastes, and makes a good vegetarian main dish when served with rice.

2 cup diced yellow onion, 1/8" dice
2 Tbsp. minced fresh garlic
1/2 cup olive oil
Salt
Freshly ground black pepper
24 ounces frozen artichoke hearts

1/2 cup fresh lemon juice
2 cups water
1 cup minced fresh dill
1/2 cup minced fresh Italian parsley
Lemon wedges

Sauté onion, lightly seasoned with salt and freshly ground black pepper, over medium heat until onion starts to turn golden. Stir in garlic and cook for 1 minute. Stir in artichoke hearts, lemon juice, water, 1/2 cup dill, and salt and pepper to taste, and bring to a boil. Reduce heat to medium so liquid is bubbling slowly, and cook uncovered for 20–30 minutes until liquid has thickened. Add remaining 1/2 cup dill and parsley, and cook for 5 minutes. Serve with fresh lemon wedges.

SAUTÉED NETTLES
Orzicka

Serves 4

Marianna Apetroeai says nettles are a welcome spring treat in Romania. Nettles grow prolifically in Alaska, so we can share this delicacy. Cooked nettles have a distinctive, fresh "greens" flavor that combines especially well with onion and garlic. I've also made this dish many times with spinach and kale to good effect. When you luck into a patch of nettles, pick only fresh young leaves and be sure to wear gloves because they sting like, well, nettles. Have faith that once they're blanched in boiling water, nettles lose their sting and taste delicious.

1 cup thinly sliced yellow onions, cut in quarters
1/2 cup olive oil
Salt
Freshly ground black pepper
1 Tbsp. minced fresh garlic
1/2 tsp. Aleppo pepper or 1/4 tsp. crushed red pepper (optional)
1 cup blanched drained nettles, water squeezed out, packed in cup

Sauté onions, lightly seasoned with salt and freshly ground black pepper, in olive oil until they begin to turn golden. Add garlic and Aleppo pepper and sauté for an additional minute. Add nettles, additional salt and pepper, and sauté over medium heat until nettles are hot and flavors have blended, about 5–10 minutes, depending on how well you like your greens cooked. Taste, add salt or pepper, as needed, and serve.

BAKED GARLIC SPINACH WITH CHEESE
Spanaki me Skordo kai Tyri

Serves 6

I lived for one beautiful year in a seaside village on a northern Aegean island. Nearby, Yiannis sold organic vegetables from his market garden. Since my refrigerator was tiny, I "shopped" almost every day by strolling with Yiannis through his rows of growing vegetables, selecting the ripest, most perfect vegetables for that day's meal. The freshness and quality of Yiannis' offerings more than made up for the limited choice. In winter, the garden produced only celery, carrots, beets, cauliflower, cabbage, and leeks. In spring, we gorged on fresh artichokes, fava beans, peas, spinach, and lettuce. The first tomatoes, cucumbers, green beans, and summer squash were ready before the first of June, followed by eggplant, peppers, okra, and melons that continued to produce through early fall. This is a dish I made frequently that spring, when it sometimes seemed I had more fresh spinach than I could possibly use. Except for spinach, the ingredients are pantry staples. Even when you don't have spinach fresh from Yiannis' garden, this dish is a fast and easy treat. The recipe uses an entire head of garlic, but the garlic is cooked long enough so its flavor is sweet and mellow, blends well with other ingredients, and doesn't dominate the dish. In the village, I often made this as the main course of an evening supper. In Alaska, I make it as a side dish with roast chicken and roasted potatoes.

1 1/2 pounds cleaned fresh spinach
1 1/2 cups minced yellow onions
1 head fresh garlic, minced
1/4 cup olive oil
Salt

Freshly ground black pepper
1 tsp. Aleppo pepper or 1/2 tsp.
  crushed red pepper (optional)
1 cup grated kefalotyri, kasseri,
  or any other cheese

Preheat oven to 350° F.

Sauté onion and garlic, lightly seasoned with salt and freshly ground black pepper, in olive oil over medium heat until onions are translucent. Don't brown onions and garlic. Stir in Aleppo pepper.

If you're using baby spinach leaves, add them in handfuls to pot. If you're using larger spinach, tear it into pieces before cooking. Cook spinach just until it wilts, 30-90 seconds. When spinach is all wilted, take off heat and mix in 3/4 cup grated cheese. Taste and add salt or pepper, as needed.

Place spinach in oiled pie pan, sprinkle with remaining 1/4 cup cheese, and bake for 20 minutes, or until top is lightly browned. Let cool at least 15 minutes before serving.

SWISS CHARD AND EGGS
Ijjet Siliq

Serves 4

Between cooking, eating, reading cookbooks, traveling to see how other people raise and prepare food, and talking about food wherever I go, I'm constantly learning new recipes and techniques. Swiss Chard and Eggs came out of a conversation with Marie Markossian about what we each had for dinner the night before. I'd eaten sautéed Swiss chard was part of my meal. Marie asked if I'd ever combined sautéed Swiss chard with eggs. I hadn't, but her description of the recipe, with its beautiful layers of green and yellow, was so vivid I went home and made it immediately. It was delicious. The recipe is for a large omelet that can be divided into quarters to serve 4, or into smaller pieces as an appetizer. To make it for 1 or 2 people, scale down the recipe proportionally, and cook it in a smaller frying pan. Spinach may be substituted for Swiss chard.

1 pound Swiss chard, leaves only	Salt
(2 pounds with stems)	Freshly ground black pepper
2 cups diced yellow onions, 1/4" dice	1 Tbsp. minced fresh garlic
1/4 cup olive oil	6–8 eggs

Wash and roughly chop Swiss chard leaves. In large frying pan, sauté onions, lightly seasoned with salt and freshly ground black pepper, in olive oil over medium heat until they start to turn golden. Add garlic and sauté for an additional minute. Stir in Swiss chard and cook, stirring every minute or two, until Swiss chard is tender (you may need to add Swiss chard in batches if it won't all fit in pan at one time).

Whisk 6 or 8 eggs together until they're thoroughly mixed, with the number of eggs depending on how hungry the eaters are. Spread cooked Swiss chard evenly over bottom of frying pan. Pour eggs over Swiss chard, and after 1 minute, turn heat down to medium low and cover pan. After a few minutes, take off cover. Using a spatula, loosen cooked edge of egg all around pan, lifting edge and tilting pan so any runny, uncooked egg runs under cooked edge. This helps make sure eggs cook evenly, and results in an egg "rim" around finished omelet. Re-cover pan and cook until eggs are set. This may take awhile, but eggs taste better when cooked over low heat.

When eggs are set to your liking, loosen edges of omelet, invert a platter over frying pan, and flip pan so omelet comes out with egg side down and green Swiss chard side up. Cut into quarters, or wedges, and serve immediately.

SWISS CHARD AND ONIONS BRAISED IN OLIVE OIL
Siliq bi-Zayt

Serves 4

Swiss chard thrives in Alaska's cool climate, and can be harvested throughout the summer in home gardens, or purchased in giant bunches at the Farmers' Market. It has a well-rounded earthy flavor that many people prefer to spinach. Slow cooked onions add sweetness to chard's natural sugars in this Lebanese dish, and fresh green onions added at the end liven it up. Freshly squeezed lemon juice is essential to the success of the dish, but needs to be added at the very last minute. Swiss chard prepared this way goes well with roasted or grilled meat or poultry, but when it's very fresh, I can make a light meal of braised Swiss chard, feta cheese, and olives.

2 pounds Swiss chard, leaves only
  (4 pounds with stems)
4 cups diced yellow onions, 1/4" dice
1/2 cup olive oil
Salt

Freshly ground black pepper
2 Tbsp. minced fresh garlic
1/2 cup chopped green onions
1/4 cup fresh lemon juice
1 lemon, cut into wedges

Wash and roughly chop Swiss chard leaves. In large pot, sauté onions, lightly seasoned with salt and freshly ground black pepper, in olive oil over medium heat until they start to turn golden. Add garlic and sauté for 1 minute. Stir in Swiss chard, cover, and let cook over low heat until chard is very tender, but not falling apart. The dish may be made ahead to this point, and gently reheated just before serving. Place cooked chard and onions on a serving dish, leaving most of the liquid in pot. Sprinkle with lemon juice and chopped green onions. Arrange lemon wedges around edge of dish, and serve.

PAPRIKA POTATOES
Patates 'Bloum'

Serves 4

After the First World War, tensions between Greece and Turkey escalated and a catastrophic but brief war caused the deaths of thousands. To end the violence, the Great Powers forced Greece and Turkey to exchange populations. Ethnic Greek Christians living in Turkey were moved to Greece, and ethnic Turkish Muslims in Greece were shipped to Turkey. For forcibly uprooted people on both sides, most of whose families had lived in their adopted countries for generations, tragedy and confusion reigned. Tina Karakatsanis Chowaniec's grandfather, Christos, was a boy when he set out to walk from his old home in Turkey to Greece. Alas, Christos made a wrong turn and ended up in Bulgaria. He finally ran into a family friend, who turned Christos around and pointed him toward his family in Northern Greece. In Filakto, the village near the Greek-Turkish border where Christos settled, paprika and red peppers flourish and are often used in cooking. Potatoes "Bloum" are a favorite of his granddaughter Tina. I asked her what "bloum" meant in Greek, since it was a new word to me. She laughed and said it was just the name her family used for this dish because you put everything in the pot and "bloum" it's done. Although this recipe is for potatoes, Tina uses the same seasonings for stewed green beans, or pots of mixed greens and potatoes. She says paprika burns easily, so you must be ready to add tomato sauce as soon as you add paprika to the pan. The resulting dish has a well-flavored sauce for potatoes, with the not-very-spicy, but still peppery, flavor of paprika and cooked garlic. These potatoes make a substantial side dish to serve with roast lamb, pork, or beef, or a light vegetarian main course with cheese, olives, and bread.

2 cups diced yellow onion, 1/2" dice
1/2 cup olive oil
Salt
Freshly ground black pepper
1/4 cup sweet Hungarian paprika
1 14.5-ounce can tomato sauce

2 cups water
2 1/2 pounds red, white, or yellow
  potatoes, peeled and cut into wedges
16 whole cloves garlic, peeled
2 Tbsp. dried oregano, crushed

In pot large enough to hold potatoes, sauté onions, lightly seasoned with salt and freshly ground black pepper, in olive oil until they soften and start to turn golden. Stir in paprika and quickly add tomato sauce, so paprika doesn't burn. Add water, potatoes wedges, garlic, oregano, garlic, salt, and pepper. Bring liquid to boil, cover, turn down heat, and simmer until potatoes are done. Remove cover and boil until sauce has slightly thickened. Taste and add salt, pepper, or oregano, as needed. Serve immediately.

ROASTED LEMON POTATOES
Patates sto Fourno me Lemoni

Serves 4

In 1978, John Maroulis went to New York for six months to help his brothers. While there, he learned a trick for improving the taste of roasted potatoes from local diner cooks. Before roasting, John soaks potatoes for an hour or two in lemon and salt brine. John said brining removes excess starches from potatoes and improves their flavor. I agree. Brining potatoes before cooking yields potatoes with better texture and a rounder, more complete flavor than unsoaked potatoes. The result is a dish rich with potato flavor and a hint of lemon, an ideal accompaniment for meat or chicken dishes. Although oregano may be roasted with potatoes, I prefer adding it at the end.

2 pounds Russet (baking) potatoes
2 Tbsp. salt
1 lemon
1/2 cup olive oil
1/4 cup fresh lemon juice
Salt
Freshly ground black pepper
1-2 Tbsp. dried oregano, crushed

Fill large bowl with cold water. Mix in 2 Tbsp. salt, juice of 1 to 2 lemons, and squeezed lemon rinds. Peel potatoes, cut lengthwise into quarters or sixths (depending on size of potatoes), and add to salted water. Let potatoes soak for 1-2 hours.

Preheat oven to 425°F.

Remove potatoes from water, and dry well. Place in baking pan large enough to hold potatoes in single layer. Whisk together olive oil and lemon juice, adding salt and freshly ground pepper to taste, and pour over potatoes. Stir to thoroughly coat potatoes with oil. Make sure one flat side of each potato wedge touches bottom of pan. Cover pan with aluminum foil, and bake for 20 minutes. Remove foil and bake for 20 minutes, until underside of potato slices is nicely browned. Turn potatoes over, and cook for 20 minutes, uncovered, to brown other side. If top of potatoes isn't browned when potatoes can be pierced easily with a fork, place under broiler for 1-2 minutes. Remove potatoes from oven, sprinkle with crushed dried oregano, and toss well. Taste; add salt, freshly ground black pepper, or oregano, as needed; and toss again. Serve.

ROASTED CRACKED POTATOES AND HERBS
Psites Patates me Throumba

Serves 4

When I asked Andy Gialopsos about his favorite childhood foods in Corfu, Greece, he smiled and told me about his mother's oven-roasted potatoes. She cracked potatoes open with a smooth stone and seasoned them with "throumba," an herb that grows wild along Corfu's rocky coast. To this day, Andy's wife, Carol, keeps a special rock in her kitchen that she uses only for cracking potatoes. Throumba is Satureia thymbra (also known as goat's-thyme), a relative of summer savory and thyme. You can approximate throumba's flavor by combining the two herbs.

12 small white, red, or yellow potatoes
2 tsp. dried thyme, crushed
1 Tbsp. minced fresh summer savory
Salt
Freshly ground black pepper
1/2 cup olive oil
1/2 cup water

Preheat oven to 400° F.

Wash potatoes and cut out any bad spots, but don't peel. Dry potatoes well. Place on flat surface and crack open (but don't break apart) by whacking each potato with heavy meat pounder or clean rock. Put cracked potatoes in baking pan large enough to hold them without crowding, and sprinkle with dried thyme, fresh summer savory, salt, and freshly ground black pepper. Toss potatoes in seasonings, and make sure some of seasoning goes into cracks. Pour olive oil over potatoes, mix well, and pour water into baking pan.

Cover baking pan tightly with aluminum foil, and bake potatoes 45–60 minutes, turning halfway through baking time. The length of cooking time depends on potatoes' size. When potatoes are tender, removefrom oven and serve. If you'd like to brown potatoes before serving, place under broiler for 1-2 minutes.

FRIED POTATOES
Patates Tiganites

Potatoes are native to South America. When Conquistadores first brought potatoes back to Europe in the 16th century, Greece was an Ottoman backwater. Andy Gialopsos tells the story, perhaps apocryphal, of how Greeks were introduced to potatoes in the 19th century. Yiannis Kapodistrias was the first president of Greece and, like Andy, a native of Corfu. Kapodistrias brought a shipment of potatoes to Greece to provide a cheap source of food. Greek farmers are a conservative and suspicious lot, and showed no interest in planting this strange-looking, untried vegetable. Kapodistrias responded by steeply raising the price of potatoes and placing them under guard, leading the populace to think they were being denied a precious commodity. Kapodistrias ordered the guards to look the other way if anyone tried to steal potatoes. Many were stolen and planted, and potatoes soon spread throughout Greece. Today, it sometimes seems as if fried potatoes are the national dish of Greece. They're included with almost every meal in village restaurants, and are increasingly tucked inside pita bread surrounding gyros and souvlaki. I learned to make Greek-style fried potatoes by watching Froso Kriaris, who waits until her family is seated at the table before she starts frying batch after batch. This means the cook stands at the stove for the first part of the meal, but also lets everyone else enjoy the delicious, but fleeting, flavor of hot fried potatoes.

Russet (baking) potatoes
Salt
Olive oil for frying
Dried oregano, crushed (optional)

Peel potatoes and cut into the shape of French fries. Place potatoes in bowl of cold salted water until you're ready to cook. Drain potatoes, dry very well, and salt lightly on all sides. Pour olive oil into deep frying pan to depth of about 1/2". Heat oil until it's hot, but not smoking. Add potatoes to hot oil in one layer. Don't crowd too many potatoes in the pan at one time, or the oil's temperature will drop quickly, and the potatoes won't cook evenly. Cook until potatoes are golden brown, turning halfway through cooking time. Depending on the size of the cut potatoes, they take 3–6 minutes to cook. Drain potatoes on paper towels, taste, and salt, as needed. If using, sprinkle with oregano and serve.

SPICY FRIED CAULIFLOWER
Arnabeet Makli

Kamal Bebawy loved Spicy Fried Cauliflower, according to his wife Nawal. She made it for him often, always accompanied by a fresh green salad and sometimes by stuffed eggplant. I've modified Nawal's original recipe by "oven-frying," rather than deep-fat frying cauliflower. Oven-frying (roasting with oil) preserves the crispness and essence of fresh cauliflower, while retaining the flavor balance of Nawal's version. Cumin, red pepper, parsley and garlic raise cauliflower to flavor heights undreamed of by those who only know cauliflower boiled or steamed in plain water. Spicy Fried Cauliflower also makes a fantastic addition to an appetizer spread. As for how many people this serves, it's hard to judge since I often make a meal of the entire recipe. Just decide how many cauliflower florets you want to cook, and adjust the other ingredients proportionally. Be forewarned – this disappears quickly!

1 pound cauliflower florets
1/2 tsp. freshly ground cumin
1/2 tsp. Aleppo pepper, or 1/4 tsp. crushed red pepper
1/2 tsp. salt
Freshly ground black pepper
1/3 cup olive oil
1 tsp. finely minced fresh garlic
1/3 cup minced fresh Italian parsley

Preheat oven to 500° F. Wash and dry cauliflower and break or cut it into florets. Place cauliflower florets in baking pan large enough to hold them in a single layer. Cauliflower should not be jammed together in pan or it steams rather than cooks properly. Sprinkle with cumin, Aleppo pepper, salt, and freshly ground black pepper. Toss florets well to ensure spices reach into cauliflower's cracks and crevices. Drizzle with olive oil, and stir well to coat florets evenly. Roast for 10–15 minutes, or until cauliflower begins to brown. The length of cooking time depends on the floret's size and how soft you like cauliflower. When done to your liking, remove from oven and toss with garlic and parsley. Serve immediately.

Note: To make Nawal's original recipe, add 2 eggs and 2 Tbsp. all-purpose flour to the ingredients list. Blanch cauliflower florets in boiling salted water for 1–2 minutes, then drain and dry it. Make a batter with all ingredients except cauliflower. Dip florets in batter and deep fat fry at 350°F until cauliflower is golden brown.

CAULIFLOWER STEW
Kounoupidi Stifado

Serves 4 as main course

Maria Kakouratou Reilly's family left the port city of Patras, Greece for Germany when she was 6 years old. The post-war German economy was booming and immigrants were pouring in from all over Europe looking for work. Despite living in Germany, Maria's family spoke and cooked Greek at home, and returned to Patras each summer. As eldest daughter, Maria helped her mother cook dinner and learned to make the foods of her homeland. One dish Maria remembers her mother making is a stew of cauliflower cooked in a piquant tomato sauce. Some people cook cauliflower before adding it to Stifado. Maria's mother added cauliflower raw, to preserve its fresh taste and texture, and to prevent its flavors from being overwhelmed by tomato sauce. Cooking pearl onions separately is my innovation, and helps the onion retain a separate sweet flavor. I also added rosemary, a traditional seasoning for beef Stifado, and Aleppo pepper, whose spiciness rounds out the sauce. The result is a hearty alternative to beef stew. Be sure to serve Cauliflower Stew with plenty of feta cheese and Kalamata olives.

1 cauliflower, 2 1/2 pounds
1 1/4 pounds yellow onions, sliced
1/4 cup olive oil, plus 3 Tbsp., divided
2 Tbsp. minced fresh garlic
1 Tbsp. minced rosemary (optional)
1/2 tsp. salt
1/2 tsp. freshly ground black pepper
1 tsp. Aleppo pepper or 1/2 tsp. crushed red pepper (optional)
1 28-ounce can crushed tomatoes
1 1/2 cups water
5 bay leaves
2 Tbsp. red wine vinegar
10 ounces fresh pearl onions
Salt
Freshly ground black pepper
1/4 cup minced fresh Italian parsley

Remove leaves from cauliflower, and cut out stem and core. Wash cauliflower and break it into large florets. In pot large enough to hold cauliflower, sauté onions, lightly seasoned with salt and freshly ground black pepper, in 1/4 cup olive oil. When onions soften and begin to turn golden, add cauliflower, garlic, rosemary, salt, pepper, Aleppo pepper, tomatoes, water, and bay leaves to pot. Bring liquid to a boil, reduce heat, and simmer. After cauliflower has cooked for 15 minutes, add red wine vinegar. Continue simmering for 5-15 minutes or until cauliflower begins to soften. This dish is best when cauliflower is slightly underdone and retains a slight crunch.

As cauliflower cooks, peel pearl onions and cut X in root end to help hold onion layers together. An easy way to peel onions is to drop them in boiling water for one minute. Remove onions from water and slip off peels. Sauté peeled pearl onions, lightly seasoned with salt and freshly ground black pepper, in 3 Tbsp. olive oil until onions are well browned on all sides and cooked through.

Five minutes before cauliflower is done, stir in browned pearl onions and minced parsley. When cauliflower is done, taste and add salt or pepper, as needed. Remove bay leaves and serve immediately.

Herb vendor in the Athens Central Market

· DESSERTS ·

* New recipe this edition

Greeks rarely eat sweets the way Americans do—as dessert, the post-script to a big meal. For Greeks, sweets like cakes and pastries are meals in themselves eaten in the morning for breakfast, in mid-morning when guests come calling, or in the afternoon with coffee.

Bougatsa, one of Maria Baskous' favorites, is a perfect example: moderately sweetened custard baked in light crisp filo layers and served sprinkled with powdered sugar and cinnamon. Maria bakes creamy Bougatsa in the morning and serves it warm in a kitchen filled with the aromas of baked filo pastry and creamy custard.

Maria grew up around sweets. Her mother, Dena Baskurelou, owned a café in their village of Kastori, near the ancient site of Sparta, and baked bread and pastries for her customers. Dena taught many young women in Kastori the tricks of working with filo dough. For baklava, Dena insisted that five alternating layers of filo and filling are the minimum to produce a quality result. Ten layers are better.

Dena refused to use an electric oven, choosing instead to take her pastries to one of the village's two wood-fueled public ovens made with special heat-retentive tiles. "Anything you bake in those ovens comes out so tasty," Maria said. No self-respecting village cook used an electric oven for special family occasions or for festival baking, she said, because for special occasions, the food must always be "the best."

As Maria worked in her mother's café, she passively absorbed Dena's cooking and baking wisdom. As a teenager, however, Maria announced to her mother she didn't plan on having a kitchen in her future home because "it was easier to just eat out." Dena only smiled, knowing that a daughter of hers would grow to love cooking for her family, her church, and her community. Dena was right.

Among the sweets regularly served at Dena's café were Ravani, a semolina and syrup cake, Walnut Cake, Galactobourcko, Kourambiedes, and, of course, Baklava. Today, Maria excels at making them all.

HONEY-NUT PASTRIES
Baklava
GREEK FESTIVAL RECIPE

If asked to name a Greek pastry, Baklava immediately springs to mind. Wildly popular in Greece, Baklava is prized throughout the Balkans and Middle East (the territory that once made up the Ottoman Empire). It can be made with walnuts, almonds, pistachios, hazelnuts, or sesame seeds, but the essential recipe of syrup-drenched layers of buttery filo and nuts never changes. Dena Baskurelou taught her daughter, Maria that a small amount of crushed crackers or bread crumbs added to nuts gives Baklava better volume, and makes it look more attractive, without changing the flavor. For the same reason, Dena slightly crumpled filo sheets used between layers of nuts. Baklava is very sweet and rich, so is best cut into very small diamonds.

Filling:
3/4 pound walnuts
1/4 cup crushed graham crackers
1/4 cup sugar
1 Tbsp. cinnamon
1/2 tsp. cloves

Syrup:
2 cups water
2 cups sugar
Peel from one lemon (in large pieces)
1 cinnamon stick

Pastry:
1–2 pounds filo (18" x 14")
1 pound butter
Whole cloves

Filling: Chop half the walnuts very finely, and the remaining half in medium-sized pieces. Mix all filling ingredients.

Preheat oven to 350° F.

Clarify butter as described on page 13 in Cook's Notes.

Pastry: Butter 9" x 13" baking pan with clarified butter. Remove filo from box, unroll it, and cover any you're not actively using with plastic wrap so it doesn't dry out. Lay one sheet of filo in buttered pan, letting it overhang sides, and brush lightly with melted butter. Be sure to butter edges of filo that overhang pan. Continue layering and buttering sheets of filo, making sure pan is evenly covered and has plenty of overhanging filo, until you've used up 8 sheets of filo.

Sprinkle one fifth of filling over filo, layer with two sheets of buttered and crumpled filo, sprinkle with one fifth of filling, layer with two sheets of buttered and crumpled filo, and continue alternating filling and filo until all filling is gone. Turn overhanging edges of bottom crust over last layer of filling.

Layer with eight sheets of buttered filo. Cut off any overhang, or tuck overhanging edges down into pan. Re-butter top layer, making sure butter extends all the way to edges. With sharp paring knife, cut top few layers of filo into diamonds and place a whole clove in center of each piece; don't cut through to filling. (The recipe can be made ahead to this point and frozen.)

Bake for 40 minutes. Turn heat down to 325° F, and bake for 10–20 minutes, or until filo is golden brown. (Frozen Baklava takes longer to bake.) When Baklava is done, remove it from oven, and let cool all the way through.

Syrup: When Baklava is cool, make syrup. Mix sugar, water, honey, lemon peel, and cinnamon stick in saucepan, bring to a boil, turn down heat, and simmer for 10 minutes or until syrup is slightly thickened. Remove lemon peel and cinnamon stick, and pour hot syrup evenly over cooled pastry. Allow syrup to cool and be fully absorbed before cutting pastry into small diamond-shaped pieces. Advise guests unfamiliar with baklava to remove clove before eating.

CUSTARD IN FILO WITH LEMON SYRUP
Galactoboureko
GREEK FESTIVAL RECIPE

Galactoboureko is a popular pastry at Holy Transfiguration's annual Festival. It's always one of the first to sell out, and volunteers have spent many late nights during the Festival baking extra pans of Galactoboureko. I prefer this dessert when it's baked in individual rolls because the filo is crunchier, but it's so easy to make in a large pan—and so good—that I seldom bother with the fiddly work of making individual rolls when I make Galactoboureko at home.

Custard:
5 eggs
1 1/4 cups sugar
2 tsp. vanilla
1 Tbsp. finely grated lemon rind
5 cups whole milk
3/4 cup semolina flour
2 Tbsp. butter

Pastry:
1 pound filo (18" x 14")
1/2–1 pound butter
Syrup:
2 cups sugar
1 cup water
Peel from one lemon (in large pieces)
1 cinnamon stick

Custard: Beat eggs and sugar in bowl until they're very thick and creamy. Add vanilla and lemon rind and mix well. In large saucepan, whisk semolina flour into milk and bring almost to a boil. Quickly stir cup of hot milk mixture into blended egg and sugar, and stir this into remainder of hot milk. Cook for 3–5 minutes, stirring constantly and being careful not to let mixture boil, until custard has consistency of thick pudding. Stir in butter and let cool.

Preheat oven to 350° F.

Clarify butter as described on page 13 in Cook's Notes.

Pastry: Butter 9" x 13" baking pan with clarified butter. Remove filo from box, unroll it, and cover any you're not actively using with plastic wrap so it doesn't dry out. Lay one sheet of filo in buttered pan, letting it overhang sides, and brush it lightly with melted butter. Be sure to butter edges of filo that overhang the pan. Continue layering and buttering sheets of filo, making sure pan is evenly covered and has plenty of overhanging filo, until you've used up half the filo.

Pour filling over filo and spread it out evenly. Turn overhanging edges of botton crust over filling. Layer remaining filo over filling, brushing each sheet lightly with butter. When all filo is used, cut off any overhang or tuck overhanging edges down into pan. Re-butter top layer, making sure butter extends all the way to edges. With sharp paring knife, cut top few layers of filo into diamonds or squares; don't cut through to filling. (The recipe can be made ahead to this point and frozen.)

Bake for 35–45 minutes, or until filo is golden brown and custard is set. (Frozen pastry takes longer to bake.) When pastry is done, remove it from oven, and let cool all the way through.

Syrup: When pastry is cool, make syrup. Mix sugar, water, lemon peel, and cinnamon stick in a saucepan, bring to a boil, turn down heat, and simmer for 10 minutes or until syrup is slightly thickened. Remove lemon peel and cinnamon stick, and pour hot syrup evenly over cooled pastry. Cut into pieces and serve.

Note: This recipe can also be made in individual rolls. To do so, cut each sheet of filo crosswise into three pieces (this is easiest to do by cutting the entire roll of filo into thirds), butter and stack two of the pieces, put small amount of cooled custard filling at short end of filo stack, fold in sides to enclose filling, and roll it up. Butter outside of roll. Repeat until all filling is used. Bake as set out above, let rolls cool, and pour hot syrup over cold rolls.

SWEET CUSTARD IN FILO
Bougatsa

Bougatsa is my absolute favorite Greek pastry, without exception. Since it isn't syruped, it isn't overwhelmingly sweet. Cinnamon sprinkled on top brings out custard's best, particularly when it's served slightly warm. In Athens, little bakeries sell pieces of Bougatsa to lines of locals and tourists wanting good breakfasts on the run or mid-morning snacks. Whether for breakfast or dessert, Bougatsa is enchanting.

Custard:
4 eggs
1 cup sugar
1/2 cup semolina flour
2 tsp. vanilla
4 cups whole milk
1/4 cup butter

Pastry:
1/2 pound filo (18" x 14")
1/2 pound butter

Topping:
1/3 cup powdered sugar
1 tsp. cinnamon

Custard: Beat eggs, sugar, and vanilla in bowl until they're very thick and creamy. In large saucepan, whisk semolina flour into milk and bring almost to a boil. Quickly stir a cup of hot milk mixture into egg and sugar mixture to temper it, and stir this into remainder of hot milk. Cook for 3–5 minutes, stirring constantly and being careful not to let mixture boil, until custard has consistency of thick pudding. Stir in butter and let cool.

Preheat oven to 350°F.

Clarify butter as described on page 13 in Cook's Notes.

Pastry: Butter 9" x 13" baking pan with clarified butter. Remove filo from a 1-pound box, unroll it, place half on counter, and cover with plastic wrap so it doesn't dry out. Wrap remaining filo tightly and refrigerate it for another use.

Lay one sheet of filo in buttered pan, letting it overhang sides, and brush it lightly with melted butter. Be sure to butter edges of filo that overhang pan. Continue layering and buttering sheets of filo in pan, making sure pan is evenly covered and has plenty of overhanging filo, until you've used up half the filo sheets.

Pour filling over filo and spread it out evenly. Turn overhanging edges of bottom crust over filling. Layer remaining filo sheets over filling, brushing each sheet lightly with butter. When all filo is used, cut off any overhang or tuck overhanging edges down into pan. Re-butter top layer, making sure butter extends all the way to edges. With sharp knife, cut top few layers of filo into large squares; don't cut through to filling. (The recipe can be made ahead to this point and frozen.)

Bake for 35–45 minutes, or until filo is golden brown and custard is set. (If Bougatsa is frozen when it goes in oven, it takes longer to bake.) When filo is done, remove it from oven and allow to cool until custard is set enough to cut into pieces. Sprinkle Bougatsa with powdered sugar and cinnamon, and serve while still warm.

APRICOT-ALMOND SQUARES
Pasta Flora

George Chrimat has been chef-owner of restaurants in Greece, San Francisco, and Anchorage, where he now owns Villa Nova restaurant. For the annual Greek Festival, George pitches in to bake trays of Pasta Flora, a popular Greek pastry, spread with high quality fruit preserves, and covered with attractive pastry latticework. The pastry is light and fragile, so must be handled carefully, Avoid rolling it out in a too-warm room. This recipe makes enough for a 13" x 17" rimmed baking sheet. You can also cut the recipe in half and make it in a 9" x 13" baking pan.

Pastry:
1 cup butter, cold
3 1/2–4 cups all-purpose flour
1/4 cup sugar
1 Tbsp. baking powder
1/8 tsp. salt
3 egg yolks

1/4 cup brandy, plus more as needed
1 1/2 tsp. pure almond extract

Filling:
4 cups apricot preserves
1/4 cup brandy

Blanched almonds for garnish

Cut butter into 3/4" pieces. Mix flour, sugar, baking powder, and salt. Cut butter into flour and sugar until it has the consistency of cornmeal. This is easiest to do in a food processor, but be careful not to over-process.

Mix egg yolks, 1/4 cup brandy, and almond extract. Slowly stir this mixture into butter and flour until mixture comes together and is no longer sticky. Add more brandy if necessary to bring dough together. Don't over-mix or pastry will be tough. Dump dough onto counter, shape into rectangle, wrap in plastic wrap, and refrigerate for 2 hours or overnight.

Preheat oven to 350° F.

If dough has been in refrigerator overnight, let sit at room temperature for at least 1/2 hour before attempting to roll it out. Cut off 1/4 of dough and reserve it for lattice crust. Flour pastry cloth, and roll out remaining dough until it's 15" x 19". Place dough on 13" x 17" baking sheet, and press dough into pan's corners and edges. Prick dough all over with fork.

Mix apricot preserves and 1/4 cup brandy. Spread evenly over pastry.

Roll out reserved dough and cut it into 3/4" strips. Lay strips diagonally across filling, first in one direction and then the other, to form diamond lattice. Place whole blanched almond or several slivered almonds in center of each diamond. Crimp lattice strips and bottom crust together and form decorative edges with fork or your fingers.

Bake 40–45 minutes, turning baking sheet halfway through baking time, until pastry is golden brown and preserves are bubbling. Remove from oven, and use small fork to move any almonds that have slid out of position back to center of each diamond. Cool, cut in squares, and serve.

BUTTER COOKIES WITH ALMONDS
Kourambiedes
GREEK FESTIVAL RECIPE

For Christmas, weddings, and religious feasts, grandmothers, sisters, aunts, and friends gather in Greek kitchens to make mountains of Kourambiedes, shortbread cookies that are so rich they melt in your mouth. It's hard to eat Kourambiedes without showering yourself with telltale powdered sugar. To make them easier to eat in public, I always serve Kourambiedes in muffin papers. Even so, I'm careful to brush off my mouth and chin when I've finished the last bite. The Festival recipe for Kourambiedes uses the smaller amount of almonds shown below, while I prefer mine with the larger amount. Either way, Kourambiedes are delicious. For the Greek Festival, Kourambiedes are spritzed with rose water right when they come out of the oven. At home, I prefer to bake them with a whole clove stuck in each cookie's center, especially at Christmas. The clove symbolizes the three wise mens' gifts to the Christ child.

1–2 cups slivered almonds	1 tsp. baking powder
1 1/2 pounds unsalted butter	5–6 cups all-purpose flour
2 egg yolks	Whole cloves (optional)
1 tsp. almond extract	Rose water (optional)
1 cup powdered sugar	Powdered sugar

Preheat oven to 350° F.

Place blanched almonds on baking sheet, and roast for 5–10 minutes until almonds are lightly toasted. Chop almonds, and set aside to cool.

In bowl of electric mixer, beat butter until it's very light and creamy. Add egg yolks and almond extract, and continue beating until eggs are well incorporated and color lightens to pale yellow. Add powdered sugar, and beat until mixture is smooth. Using paddle attachment for mixer or wooden spoon, mix in baking powder, 3 cups of flour, and chopped almonds. Beat in remaining flour by hand, a little at a time, using only enough flour so dough holds together, but isn't hard and dry. Refrigerate dough for 1 hour or until you're ready to bake. (Dough can be made ahead to this point and frozen.) Bring to room temperature before shaping.

Shape 1 Tbsp. pieces of dough into rounded and slightly flattened circles that are slightly thicker in the center than around the edges. A tablespoon-sized scoop with a thumb-release makes this task go quickly. If using cloves, stick one in the center of each cookie. Place cookies 1 inch apart on baking sheet, and bake for 20–25 minutes, or until cookies just start to turn golden. Be careful not to brown cookies.

While cookies are baking, sift powdered sugar into a rimmed baking sheet to completely cover the sheet's bottom. When cookies are done, remove them from oven and spritz lightly with rosewater, if using (a tiny, unused, perfume atomizer works well for spritzing). Remove cookies from baking sheet and, while they're still warm, place them on sifted powdered sugar. Sift additional powdered sugar over cookies to completely cover them. Lift each cookie from pan of powdered sugar, giving it a shake so any extra sugar falls back in pan. Put cookie back down on powdered sugar to ensure bottom is evenly covered. After cookies have cooled completely, place them in muffin papers. If a cookie isn't evenly covered with powdered sugar, sprinkle it with a little more sugar. Store in tightly covered, air-tight container.

Assortment of sweets from the Festival's Kafenion

GREEK EASTER COOKIES
Koulourakia

GREEK FESTIVAL RECIPE

Makes 5 1/2 dozen

Koulourakia are to Greek Easter as Christmas cookies are to America's December holiday. Greeks traditionally celebrate Easter by delivering plates of Koulourakia to family, friends, and neighbors. Since families are large and neighborhoods friendly, everyone ends up with plenty of Koulourakia to eat with morning coffee and share with guests. One year, I was given so many different kinds of Koulourakia that we had an informal tasting to compare which version was the best. All were different—some were flavored with lemon, others with orange, brandy, or ouzo. Some were made with white flour, others used more rustic semolina flour. Leavenings differed, as did the amount of sugar. After careful consideration, and very rigorous sampling, we decided we liked them all. Fortunately, Koulourakia freeze well, so many were saved for a later day. The Festival recipe given here is for a light vanilla cookie that is perfect for dunking in coffee.

1 cup butter
5 eggs (reserve one egg yolk)
2 tsp. vanilla
1 3/4 cups powdered sugar

3–3 1/2 cups all-purpose flour
2 tsp. baking powder
1/2 tsp. baking soda
1/2-1 cup sesame seeds

Preheat oven to 350° F.

In bowl of electric mixer, beat butter until it's very light and creamy. Add eggs one at a time (four whole eggs and one egg white) and continue to beat until eggs are well-incorporated and color lightens to pale yellow. Add vanilla and powdered sugar, and beat until mixture is smooth.

Mix flour, baking powder, and baking soda. Using paddle attachment for mixer, or wooden spoon, mix in 2 cups of flour. Add remaining flour by hand, a little at a time, using only enough flour so dough is soft, but not sticky. Refrigerate dough for 1 hour or until you're ready to bake. (Dough can be made ahead to this point and frozen.) Bring to room temperature before shaping.

Separate dough into 1 Tbsp. pieces, either using a tablespoon-sized scoop with a thumb-release or by shaping dough into long rolls and cutting off 1 Tbsp. pieces. Roll the pieces of dough into 7-inch cylinders and shape into twists, coils, wreaths, snakes, or whatever shape catches your fancy.

Whisk reserved egg yolk with a little water and brush lightly over each cookie. Sprinkle cookies with sesame seeds. Bake for 15–20 minutes or until cookies are golden brown. Remove cookies from baking sheet, let cool, and store in tightly covered container.

GREEK BISCOTTI
Paximadakia

GREEK FESTIVAL RECIPE

Greeks love dry bread (paximadia) and dry cookies (paximadakia), and eat them for snacks with coffee any time of day. Paximadakia are familiar to Americans as biscotti, the Italian name for this sweet. The Festival recipe for Paximadakia calls for 1 cup of almonds, but I prefer them loaded with nuts, so use the larger amount. Although they're tasty eaten on their own, many people swear Paximadakia are best when dunked in either coffee or wine. This recipe is from Maria Baskous' aunt, Christina Patsatzis, who hails from Pardali, Sparta and now lives in Montreal.

1 cup sugar	3–3 1/2 cups all-purpose flour
1 cup vegetable oil	2 tsp. baking powder
4 eggs	1–2 cups blanched slivered almonds
1 tsp. almond extract	

Preheat oven to 350° F. Place blanched almonds on baking sheet, and roast for 5–10 minutes until almonds are lightly toasted. Set aside to cool.

Mix sugar and oil until well-blended. Add eggs, one at a time, beating well after each addition. Continue to beat for 5 minutes. Mix flour and baking powder, and slowly stir flour and almonds into eggs until dough is very soft, but not sticky.

Flour your hands and shape dough into 3" x 12" logs. Place logs on baking sheet and bake for 20–30 minutes, or until logs are cracked and golden. Remove from oven and cool for 5 minutes. Reduce oven temperature to 300° F.

Cut each loaf into 3/4" diagonal slices; this is easiest to do on a cutting board using a serrated knife. Arrange slices on baking sheets, flat side down. Bake for 15–25 minutes, turning slices over after 10 minutes, or until slices are golden-brown and dry in centers. Remove cookies from baking sheet, and let cool completely.

Once Paximadakia are cool, they're ready to eat. For the Greek Festival, the cookies are some-times made fancier and sweeter by dipping one end of each finished cookie in melted semi-sweet or milk chocolate and then in toasted sliced almonds. Allow chocolate to harden before serving. If cookies are stored in a tightly covered, air-tight container, they keep for weeks.

HONEY SPICE COOKIES
Melomakarouna
GREEK FESTIVAL RECIPE

Packed with spices, nuts, honey, and tantalizing hints of orange, Melomakarouna epitomize Christmas in Greece. Because these cookies appear somewhat plain beside other Greek Festival sweets, newcomers sometimes pass right over Melomakarouna. Once they're enticed to try one, they're usually hooked. Festival veterans tell us these rich spicy flavorful gems are one reason they return to the Festival's "Kafenion" year after year. This recipe came from Karen McQueen's mother, Calliope, who now lives in Texas.

Cookies:
1 cup butter
3/4 cup sugar
1 cup olive oil
3 egg yolks
1/2 cup orange juice
2 Tbsp. finely grated orange peel (zest)
5 1/2–6 1/2 cups all-purpose flour
2 tsp. baking power
1 tsp. baking soda
2 tsp. cinnamon
2 tsp. ground nutmeg
2 cups finely chopped walnuts

Syrup:
2 cups sugar
1 1/2 cups water
1 cup honey
1 cinnamon stick

Topping:
1/3 cup finely chopped walnuts
1 Tbsp. sugar
1 1/2 tsp. cinnamon

Preheat oven to 350° F.

Cookies: Cream butter and sugar until light and very airy. Slowly beat in olive oil, and then egg yolks. Add orange juice and orange zest and beat until all is smooth. Mix flour, baking powder, baking soda, cinnamon, nutmeg, and walnuts. Stir dry ingredients into liquid ingredients to form a smooth, but not sticky, dough. (Dough may be made ahead and frozen.) Bring to room temperature before shaping.

Shape 1 Tbsp. pieces of dough into oval shapes. Curl your fingers as you're shaping dough, using your fingertips to indent bottom of cookie and give it a slightly cupped shape. Place cookies on baking sheet with indented side down. Poke top of each cookie 3 or 4 times with fork; the fork holes will later help cookies absorb syrup. Bake for 15–20 minutes, or until cookies are light brown. Remove cookies from baking sheet, and let cool completely. Mix topping ingredients.

Syrup: Mix sugar and water in saucepan, bring to a boil, turn down heat, and simmer for 10 minutes or until syrup is slightly thickened. Stir in honey and cook for five minutes, then turn heat down to low and keep syrup warm for dipping cookies.

Dipping: Dip cold cookies in hot syrup, using fork to turn cookies over several times to make sure they're well-coated with syrup, but not saturated. Handle cookies carefully so they don't break. Remove from syrup and sprinkle each cookie with small amount of topping. Place on rack to cool. When cookies have cooled completely, store in tightly covered container.

WALNUT CAKE
Karithopita
GREEK FESTIVAL RECIPE

Even though the Greek Festival's Karithopita recipe calls for 40 eggs and 10 pounds of flour, it needs to be doubled or tripled, and made several times, to fulfill the Festival demand for this rich cake. Here, the Festival recipe has been scaled back for home use, but its wonderful taste remains the same. The cake is best if some walnuts are finely chopped, and others left in slightly larger pieces. Because Karithopita is moist and tender, it lasts a long time if carefully wrapped.

Syrup:
2 cups sugar
1 cups water
Peel from one lemon (in large pieces)
1 cinnamon stick

Cake:
1/4 cup vegetable oil
1/4 cup butter
1 1/4 cups sugar

4 eggs, separated into yolks and whites
1 cup milk
1/2 cup honey
1/4 cup fresh lemon juice
1 Tbsp. finely grated lemon peel (zest)
2 cups all-purpose flour
2 tsp. baking powder
1 tsp. baking soda
2 tsp. cinnamon
1 1/2 cups chopped walnuts

Preheat oven to 350° F. Butter a 9" x 13" baking pan and set aside.

Syrup: Mix sugar, water, lemon peel, and cinnamon stick in saucepan, bring to a boil, turn down heat, and simmer for 10 minutes or until syrup is slightly thickened. Set syrup aside to cool. Remove lemon peel and cinnamon stick when you're ready to pour syrup over cake.

Cake: Cream vegetable oil, butter and sugar until they're light and airy. Add egg yolks, milk, honey, lemon juice, and grated lemon peel (zest), and beat until all is smooth. Mix flour, baking powder, baking soda, cinnamon, and walnuts, and stir into liquid ingredients. Beat egg whites until they're stiff, but not dry, and fold into batter.

Pour batter into buttered pan, and bake for 25–30 minutes until top springs back and toothpick stuck into center of cake comes out clean. Don't overcook. Remove cake from oven, and evenly pour cold syrup over hot cake. Let cool and serve.

LEMON-RAISIN YOGURT CAKE WITH CRUNCHY ALMOND TOPPING
Giaourtopita me Stafida Glyko tou Koutaliou

Serves 10

Dotted with sweet tender raisins, Lemon-Raisin Yogurt Cake is moist, flavorful, not too sweet, and finished with a crunchy, lemon-glazed, roasted almond topping. The cake must be glazed while hot, so make the glaze while the cake is baking.

Syruped Raisins:
1/2 cup sugar
1/4 cup water
4" piece lemon peel
2 Tbsp. lemon juice
1 cup raisins, preferably golden

Cake:
1/2 cup butter (1 stick) room temperature
1 cup sugar
1 cup plain yogurt
3 eggs, room temperature
1 Tbsp. finely grated lemon peel
3 Tbsp. lemon juice
1 tsp. pure vanilla extract
2 1/2 cups flour
1/2 tsp. baking soda
1 tsp. baking powder
1/4 tsp. salt
1 cup coarsely chopped unblanched almonds

Lemon Glaze:
1/2 cup sugar
1/4 cup water
1 Tbsp. lemon juice
1/2 tsp. finely grated lemon peel or 1/4 tsp. lemon extract

Make Syruped Raisins: Boil sugar and water with lemon peel until it reaches 235° – 240°F on candy thermometer, or until syrup forms soft ball when dropped into bowl of cold water. Stir in lemon juice and raisins and cook for 5 minutes. Remove from burner and let cool until ready to use (may be made ahead).

Make Cake: Preheat oven to 350°F. Butter and flour 10-inch springform pan.

Using electric mixer and whisk attachment, beat butter and sugar together until smooth and creamy, scraping down sides of bowl as needed. Add yogurt, and beat until smooth. Add eggs, one at a time, beating well between additions; don't forget to scrape down sides of bowl. Add lemon zest, lemon juice, and vanilla extract and beat well.

Change to mixer's flat paddle attachment and mix in syruped raisins. If mixer doesn't have paddle attachment, mix raisins in with wooden spoon. In separate bowl, whisk together flour, baking soda, baking powder, and salt. Using either paddle attachment or wooden spoon, stir dry ingredients into batter just until they're incorporated.

Pour batter into prepared springform pan. Sprinkle chopped almonds evenly over batter, and press them down lightly until they're half-submerged in batter.

Bake cake for 35–40 minutes until top is golden brown, cake is set in center, and toothpick inserted into cake's center comes out clean. Place cake on wire rack to cool, and immediately brush top of cake with lemon glaze, using all of glaze. Cool cake for 10 minutes, and remove sides of springform pan. Let cake cool for at least 2 hours before cutting.

Make Lemon Glaze: While cake is baking, make lemon glaze. To make in microwave, mix water and sugar together and microwave on high for 2 minutes. Remove from microwave and stir. The glaze is done when it begins to thicken slightly. If it's not done after 2 minutes, return to microwave in 30 second increments, stirring after each 30 seconds. When glaze thickens slightly, stir in lemon juice and lemon zest (or extract), and set aside until cake is out of oven. To make on top of stove, boil sugar and water until mixture thickens slightly, stir in lemon juice and lemon zest, and set aside until cake is done.

SEMOLINA CAKE
Ravani
GREEK FESTIVAL RECIPE

Serves 12–16

Ravani is a simple vanilla cake popular throughout Greece, and at the annual Greek Festival in Anchorage. Semolina flour improves the cake's texture and helps it soak up syrup without becoming soggy. It's an easy cake to make, and to love.

Syrup:
2 cups sugar
2 cups water
Peel from one lemon (in large pieces)

Cake:
1 cup butter
1 cup sugar
5 eggs, separated into yolks and whites
2 tsp. vanilla extract
2 cups semolina flour
1 1/2 cups all-purpose flour
2 tsp. baking powder
1 tsp. baking soda

Preheat oven to 350° F. Butter a 9" x 13" baking pan and set it aside.

Syrup: Mix sugar, water, and lemon peel in saucepan, bring to a boil, turn down heat, and simmer for 10 minutes or until syrup is slightly thickened. Set syrup aside to cool. Remove lemon peel when you're ready to pour syrup over cake.

Cake: Cream butter and sugar until they're light and airy. Add egg yolks and vanilla, and beat until all is smooth. Mix flours, baking powder, and baking soda, and stir into liquid ingredients. Beat egg whites until stiff, but not dry, and fold into batter.

Pour batter into buttered pan, and bake for 25–30 minutes until top springs back and toothpick stuck into center of cake comes out clean. Don't overcook. Remove cake from oven, and evenly pour cold syrup over hot cake. Let cool and serve.

COCONUT CAKE
Karyda Ravani

Serves 12–16

Maria Baskous learned to make coconut cake from her aunt Maria Patsatzis, who lives in Alevrou, Sparta, Greece. It's a reliable cake that Maria makes when she has a crowd to feed, and is a particular favorite of her kids and their friends.

Syrup:
2 cups sugar
2 cups water
2 Tbsp. fresh lemon juice
1/4 cup cognac

Cake:
1 cup butter
1 cup sugar
8 eggs, separated into yolks and whites
1 tsp. vanilla
1/2 cup cognac
2 cups all-purpose flour
1 Tbsp. baking powder
2 cups sweetened, shredded coconut

Preheat oven to 350° F. Butter a 9" x 13" baking pan and set it aside.

Syrup: Mix sugar, water, lemon juice, and cognac in a saucepan, bring to a boil, turn down heat, and simmer for 10 minutes or until syrup is slightly thickened. Set syrup aside to cool.

Cake: Cream butter and sugar until they're light and airy. Add egg yolks, vanilla, and cognac, and beat until all is smooth. Mix flour, baking powder, and 1 1/2 cups coconut, and stir into liquid ingredients. Beat egg whites until stiff, but not dry, and fold into batter.

Pour batter into buttered pan, and bake for 25–30 minutes until top springs back and toothpick stuck into center of cake comes out clean. Don't overcook. Remove cake from oven, and evenly pour cold syrup over hot cake. Sprinkle remaining 1/2 cup coconut over cake, let cool, and serve.

NANA'S NEW YEAR'S CAKE
Vasilopita

Serves 12–16

In Antonia Fowler's family, it isn't New Year's unless there is a Vasilopita on the table. Although many Vasilopita recipes are for sweet bread, this unusual recipe from Antonia's grandmother "Nana" makes a light spice cake, rich with dates and nuts. Antonia's family follows Greek tradition of baking a foil-wrapped coin (in Antonia's family a large silver dollar) into New Year's cake. After the cake is blessed, Antonia's father cuts one piece for the house, and divides the rest among family members, distributing pieces of cake from oldest to youngest. The person finding the coin will have luck throughout the New Year. If the coin is found in the house piece, everyone at the table shares in the coming good fortune. Even without a coin, Nana's Vasilopita is a moist and flavorful cake to enjoy any time of year.

1/2 cup butter, room temperature
1 cup sugar
4 eggs separated into yolks and whites
1 tsp. vanilla
2 1/2 cups all-purpose flour
1/2 tsp. salt
2 tsp. baking powder
1 tsp. ground cinnamon
1/2 tsp. ground nutmeg
1/4 tsp. ground cloves
1/4 tsp. ground allspice
1 cup chopped dates
1 cup chopped walnuts
1 1/2 cups milk
Powdered sugar, sifted, for topping

Preheat oven to 350° F. Butter 9" x 13" baking pan and set aside.

Cream butter and sugar until light and airy. Add egg yolks and vanilla, and beat until all is smooth. Sift together flour, salt, baking powder, cinnamon, nutmeg, cloves, and allspice. Stir dates into flour. Add milk and flour mixture to butter mixture in thirds, mixing thoroughly after each addition, first adding 1/3 of milk and then 1/3 of flour and repeating until all ingredients are incorporated. Stir walnuts into batter. Beat egg whites until stiff, but not dry, and fold into batter.

Pour batter into buttered pan, and bake for 25–30 minutes until top springs back and toothpick stuck into center of cake comes out clean. Don't overcook. When cake is cool, sprinkle with lots of sifted powdered sugar, and serve.

Note: If using prepackaged chopped dates with slightly more than 1 cup in the package, use entire package.

MOROCCAN PANCAKES WITH HONEY
Beghrir

Serves 6–8

House guests in Morocco are often welcomed with Beghrir, a sweet treat similar to pancakes. When Helene Georgas Dennison returns to Morocco to visit family and friends, she looks forward to eating Beghrir. Using Helene's description of her treasured treat, I experimented until I came up with this recipe, which she judged to be exactly right. Helene eats Beghrir warm and served with butter and honey, and says it can easily be made ahead and reheated without loss of flavor. The recipe describes how to reheat pancakes in the oven, but Helene said she reheats them for a few seconds in the microwave. Beghrir is leavened with yeast, so be sure to allow time for it to rise.

3 cups lukewarm water	1/2 cup all-purpose flour
4 tsp. yeast	1 tsp. salt
2 tsp. sugar	Butter for frying
1 cup milk	1/2 cup butter for dipping
2 eggs	Honey for serving
2 cups semolina flour	

Put lukewarm water in bowl, stir in yeast and sugar, and let sit for 10 minutes or until yeast starts to froth. Add milk, eggs, flours, and salt and beat for 10 minutes until batter is very smooth (easiest done in a standing mixer). Cover mixing bowl with plastic wrap, place in a warm location, and allow batter to rise for 1–2 hours, or until it's very frothy and bubbly.

Melt small amount of butter in medium hot frying pan, and ladle 1/3 cup batter into pan, spreading it out to form 7" circle. Cook on one side until many little bubbles rise to surface and batter on top is no longer wet. Don't cook second side. Remove pancake from pan, and place, cooked side down, on clean cloth. Repeat process until all batter is used. Once pancakes are thoroughly cooled, they can be stacked on top of each other.

When all pancakes are cooked and cooled, melt 1/2 cup butter in pan. Quickly dip uncooked side of one pancake in butter and place it on plate. Top with second pancake that hasn't been buttered, uncooked side down. Continue stacking pancakes, one buttered followed by one dry, until all are in a stack. (The recipe can be made ahead to this point.)

To serve, preheat oven to 300° F. Warm honey in microwave or by placing jar in pan of boiling water. Put pancakes on baking sheet, uncooked side up. Cover with foil and place in oven to reheat for 10 minutes. Serve hot with warm honey.

RICE PUDDING
Rizogalo

Serves 6

Maria Kakouratou Reilly's mother cooked rice pudding regularly because it was easy to make and her children loved it. Rizogalo remains one of Maria's favorite desserts, and she still makes it following the steps she learned from her mother. Rice in good Rizogalo should be very creamy. The Kakouratou family recipe accomplishes this by cooking rice first in water and then slowly in milk. Maria's mother beats an egg white before adding it to Rizogalo to lighten the pudding's texture. On a warm, summer afternoon or evening there isn't anything better for cooling off than a cold bowl of Rizogalo.

1/2 cup short-grain rice
1 cup water
1 Tbsp. butter
4 cups whole milk, plus 2 Tbsp., divided
1/4 cup sugar
1 egg, separated into white and yolk
1 tsp. vanilla
Ground cinnamon

In pot large enough to hold all the ingredients, mix rice, water, and butter, bring to a boil, cover, turn heat down as low as possible, and cook for 15 minutes. Stir in 2 cups milk, bring almost to a boil, turn down heat, and simmer for 15 minutes. Stir in 2 cups milk and sugar. Simmer until liquid is thickness of heavy cream.

Whisk together egg yolk, vanilla, and 2 Tbsp. milk, and quickly whisk this mixture into rice. Remove pot from heat. Beat egg white until it's stiff, but not dry, and fold into pudding. Pour Rizogalo into individual serving bowls, or one large bowl, and refrigerate. Serve cold, sprinkled with plenty of ground cinnamon.

· BIBLIOGRAPHY ·

Baboian, Rose, *Armenian-American Cook Book*, Lexington, Massachusetts, self-published, 1964

Barron, Rosemary, *Flavors of Greece*, New York, William Morrow and Company, 1991

Bennani-Smires, Latifa, *Moroccan Cooking*, Casablanca, Morocco, Al Madariss, 1979

Bezjian, Alice, *The Complete Armenian Cookbook*, New Jersey, Rosekeer Press, 1983

Cook's Illustrated, Brookline, Massachusetts, 1993-2004

Corriher, Shirley O., *Cookwise*, New York, William Morrow, 1997

Der Haroutunian, Arto, *Middle Eastern Cookery*, London, Century Publishing, 1982

Der Haroutunian, Arto, *North African Cookery*, London, Century Publishing, 1985

Freeman, Meera, *A Season in Morocco: A Culinary Journey*, Melbourne, Australia, 2004

G.A.P.A. Women, *A Festival of Recipes: A Collection of Recipes from the Annunciation Greek Orthodox Church*, Dayton, Ohio, 2001

Graham, Frances Kelso, *Plant Lore of an Alaskan Island*, Anchorage, Alaska, Alaska Northwest Publishing Company, 1985

Harris, Andy, *Modern Greek: 170 Contemporary Recipes from the Mediterranean*, San Francisco, California, Chronicle Books, 2002

Hillman, Howard, *Kitchen Science* (Rev. Ed.), Boston, Massachusetts, Houghton Mifflin, 1989

Holy Transfiguration Greek Orthodox Church Ladies Philoptochos Society, *Greek Festival Cookbook 1995*, Anchorage, Alaska, Pilkington Press, 1995

Holy Transfiguration Greek Orthodox Church Ladies Philoptochos Society, *Greek Festival Cookbook 1996*, Anchorage, Alaska, Pilkington Press, 1996

Hulten, Eric, *Flora of Alaska and Neighboring Territories*, Stanford, California, Stanford University Press, 1968

Karaoglan, Aida, *Food for the Vegetarian: Traditional Lebanese Recipes*, New York, Interlink Books, 1988

Klepper, Nicolae, *Taste of Romania*, New York, Hippocrene, 1997

Kochilas, Diane, *Meze*, New York, HarperCollins, 2003

Kochilas, Diane, *The Food and Wine of Greece*, New York, St. Martin's Press, 1990

Kochilas, Diane, *The Glorious Foods of Greece*, New York, HarperCollins, 2001

Kochilas, Diane, *The Greek Vegetarian*, New York, St. Martin's Press, 1996

Kremezi, Aglaia, *The Foods of Greece*, New York, Stewart, Tabori & Chang, 1993

Kremezi, Aglaia, *The Foods of the Greek Islands*, New York, Houghton Mifflin, 2000

Lambraki, Myrsini and Engin Akin, *Ellada Sto Idio Trapezi Tourkia*, Athens, Greece, Ellinika Grammata, 2002

Lambraki, Myrsini, *Ta Horta*, Athens, Greece, Troxalia, 1997

Ksoula Chalkousi, *Mirodies kai Gevseis tis Polis*, Athens, Greece, Tsoukatou, 2002

McGee, Harold, *On Food and Cooking*, New York, Charles Scribner's Sons, 1984

McGee, Harold, *The Curious Cook*, San Francisco, California, North Point Press, 1990

Moudiotis, George, *Traditional Greek Cooking*, Reading, UK, Garnet Publishing Limited, 1998

Mowery, Pat, *From Mykonos to Moose*, unpublished manuscript

Niebuhr, Alta Dodds, *Herbs of Greece*, Athens, Greece, J. Makris, 1970

Panagos, Stratis P., *Voreianatoliaka tis Gevsis*, Athens, Greece, Indiktos, 2002

Philoptochos Society of Nativity of Christ Greek Orthodox Church, *Greek Cookery Marin*, Novato, California, self-published, 1981

Politistikos Syllogos Gynaikon tou Dimou Messapion 'Ekfrasi,' *Aroma kai Gevseis Tis Messapias*, Psaxna, Greece, self-published, 2003

Psilakis, Maria and Nikos, *Cretan Cooking*, Heraklion, Crete, Karmanor

Roden, Claudia, *The New Book of Middle Eastern Food*, New York, Alfred A. Knopf, 2000

Rousounelou, Dimitri, *Mykoniatiki Mageiriki*, Athens, Greece, Indiktos, 2001

Salloum, Habeeb, *Classic Vegetarian Cooking from the Middle East and North Africa*, New York, Interlink Books, 2000

Schofield, Janice J., *Discovering Wild Plants*, Anchorage, Alaska Northwest Books, 1989

Skoura, Sophia, *The Greek Cook Book*, New York, Crown Publishers, 1967

Spieler, Marlena, *"How I Learned to Love Eggplant,"* San Francisco Chronicle, July 21, 2004

St. Gregory's Armenian Apostolic Church, *Adventures in Armenian Cooking*, Indian Orchard, Massachusetts, 1973 (www.cilicia.com/armo-cookbook.html)

Tofallis, Candida, *Let's Eat Greek at Home*, Berkshire, United Kingdom, Foulsham, 1992

Uvezian, Sonia, *The Cuisine of Armenia*, New York, Harper & Row, 1974

Vayiakou, Ourania, *Sintages Limniakis Kouzinas*, Athens, Greece, Lyxnos E.P.E., 2000

Venardou, Filena, *Kouzina tis Kimolos*, Athens, Greece, 2001

Weiss-Armush, Anne Marie, *Arabian Cuisine*, Beirut, Lebanon, Dar An-Nafaes, 1984

Women of St. Paul's Greek Orthodox Church, *The Art of Greek Cookery*, New York, Doubleday & Company, 1961

www.gourmed.gr

· INDEX ·

Recipe names in italics are ethnic names

Printed by Everbest Printing Co. Ltd. in Guangzhou, China
through Alaska Print Brokers, Anchorage, Alaska.